THE
RISE OF THE
BRITISH RUBBER INDUSTRY
DURING THE NINETEENTH CENTURY

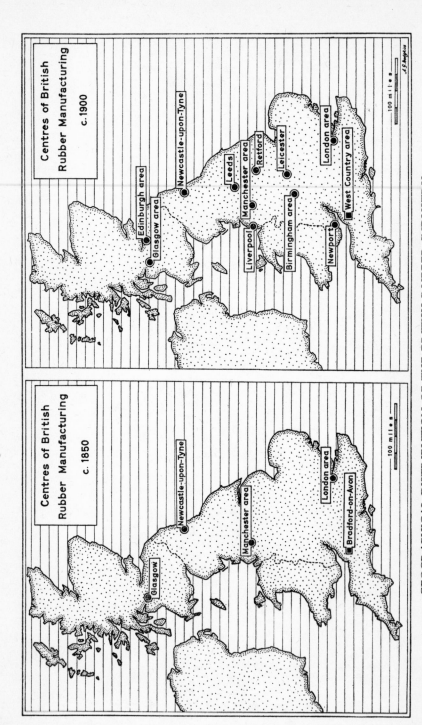

GEOGRAPHICAL DISTRIBUTION OF THE BRITISH RUBBER INDUSTRY

THE RISE OF

THE

BRITISH RUBBER

INDUSTRY

DURING THE NINETEENTH CENTURY

by

William Woodruff

Head of the Department of Economic History
in the University of Melbourne

LIVERPOOL UNIVERSITY PRESS
1958

Published by

LIVERPOOL UNIVERSITY PRESS

123 Grove Street · Liverpool 7

First published 1958

Printed in Great Britain by C. Tinling and Company
Liverpool, London and Prescot

To
MY WIFE

PREFACE

THE purpose of this volume is to tell the story of the origins and rise of the rubber industry in the West Country during the second half of the nineteenth century. While there is much in these pages that concerns the origins and development of rubber manufacture as a whole the history of the British rubber industry still remains to be written.

To assist me I have had at my disposal the hitherto unpublished papers and documents of the Moulton Company founded at Bradford-on-Avon in 1848. Incomplete though some of these records are they provide an invaluable guide to the history of the house of Moulton as well as to the origins of the rubber industry in Great Britain. In addition, I have made use of the records of the Macintosh Company, dealing with the rise and concentration of the industry in the North Western region of England since 1824, The North British Rubber Company of Edinburgh, founded by a group of American industrialists in 1856, and the Avon India Rubber Company, whose origins can be traced to the disused mill at Limpley Stoke, Wiltshire, where rubber working was begun in 1875. While these records provide invaluable source material on the origins of this industry, and have enabled me to support my narrative with original documents, their deficiencies have also made parts of my treatment less systematic than I would wish them to be. This is particularly true of the factors governing investment policy and profit trends.

As for the handling of this material, I became convinced shortly after I had begun my work that an adequate description of the vital (and at times dramatic) role played by Stephen Moulton in laying the foundations of this industry in the West Country could not be given without relating it to the experiences of other early rubber pioneers. The comprehensive nature of the Moulton papers demanded this course. Doubtless it will be argued that I might have done better to have narrowed my field and given more prominence to Moulton himself. I did not do so because I thought my time would be better spent in emphasising the historical at the expense of the biographical aspects of this work. There is much in these pages that concerns the life of Stephen Moulton, but (with the exception of what is to be found in Chapter IX) the only biographical material included is that which is relevant to the main historical theme. As it is unlikely that this book will reach the hands of many readers outside the small group of specialists to which I belong it is hardly necessary for me to explain why I chose to study what is, after all, a small branch of the industry. In an age when a premium is placed on bigness it will do none of us any harm to be reminded that all vast enterprises have small origins, and that it is in the history of relatively small undertakings, such as the Moulton Company, that the general pattern of industrial development during the nineteenth century can best be discerned.

It remains to thank those who have helped me in so many ways; indeed, the merits of this book arise in large part out of the unselfish assistance of others. Above all I am indebted to George Spencer, Moulton & Company of Bradford-on-Avon for their generous and far-sighted co-operation. Without their help this project could never have been started. The talks I had with Dr. S. S. Pickles —doyen of the British rubber industry—have added immeasurably to the value of this book, and from Mr. A. E. Moulton (great-grandson of Stephen Moulton) I received many valuable suggestions, and complete freedom to consult the family papers. The Company and its officers, especially Mr. J. M. Chrystal and Miss M. C. Bridge-land, have earned my sincere gratitude.

I am glad to say that these happy relations have existed with the Birleys (Macintosh & Co.), and the North British Company as well; and the same is true of the other houses such as the Avon Company of Melksham. In recent years, I have troubled many people in the British rubber industry—not the least the staff of the Research Association of British Rubber Manufacturers at Shawbury—but I have always been met with good will and a desire to help.

As for sources outside the industry, it is impossible to name all those who have answered my questions and volunteered inform-ation, but I must make an exception of certain individuals. I gratefully acknowledge assistance given by Miss Barbara Birley, Miss Anne Brugh, Mr. S. Weiner, Mr. E. T. Steer of the Board of Trade, Mr. R. C. Jarvis of H.M. Customs and Excise, the Somerset Herald of Arms, Mr. H. G. Ivatt of the Railway Executive, Mr. S. E. Clark of the Docks & Inland Waterways Executive, Mr. R. T. Rimington of Stationers' Hall, Councillor H. Eastwood (General Secretary of the United Rubber Workers of Great Britain), Mr. J. E. Nicholson of the Liverpool Chamber of Commerce, Mr. F. D. Arney of the Port of Bristol Authority, Mr. W. T. Barkus of the Westminster Bank, Mr. T. Wills of Bradford-on-Avon, Mr. D. J. B. Copp of the British Association for the Advancement of Science, and Messrs. C. and W. Fletcher of the house of Hecht, Levis & Kahn, rubber importers. Valuable help was also given me by the staff of

Nottingham University Library and Mr. K. Watson of the Nottingham City Library. Assistance with the use of botanical terms was provided by Dr. G. N. Jones, Curator of the Herbarium, University of Illinois.

It is a particular pleasure to acknowledge obligations incurred in the United States. Dr. Kathleen Dunlop of Illinois and Dr. Nancy Norton of Harvard could not have been more generous in sharing the result of their researches on the Dunlop and Naugatuck Rubber Companies; and to Mr. Walter H. Norton (Vice-President of the United States Rubber Company), who went to great trouble to make my American visit successful, I owe an especial debt. For the American trade statistics contained in Chapter III, I have to thank Mr. Donn N. Bent of the American Bureau of Foreign and Domestic Commerce.

I have also to acknowledge the kind permission of the editors of the *Harvard Bulletin of Business History, Oxford Economic Papers,* and the *Scottish Journal of Political Economy,* to reprint parts of my articles published by them. The same is true of the article accepted by the editor of the Victoria County History of Wiltshire to be published shortly.

Among those who have read and criticised this manuscript I should like to mention especially Dr. J. D. Chambers, who not only directed my steps towards the Moulton collection, but also provided me with a constant source of advice and encouragement; the late Sir Henry Clay; the late Sir Hubert Henderson; Professor A. H. Cole; Professor W. H. B. Court; Professor H. Heaton; Mr. A. B. Rodger and Miss G. L. Wallace, all of whom have helped me on my way.

For the drawings of the charts and maps I am indebted to Mr. N. H. Cuthbert. The diagrams of "Mechanical Applications of India-rubber" were kindly provided by Mr. N. Pearson.

I wish also to thank the Houblon-Norman and the Fulbright Committees for financial assistance.

This volume forms part of a larger study for which I am pleased to record I was awarded an *official* Doctorate of Philosophy on my departure from Nottingham University in 1953.

Lastly, I gratefully acknowledge the work of Miss M. Short and Mrs. B. Shoho, who helped me to prepare my work for publication. Its dedication to my wife is a small acknowledgement of the great debt this work owes to her.

W.W.

October, 1957

CONTENTS

ILLUSTRATIONS

With the exception of those which are otherwise acknowledged these illustrations are reproduced by kind permission of G. Spencer, Moulton & Co. Ltd., Bradford-on-Avon

TABLES IN TEXT

Only principal tables are shown here

FIGURES IN TEXT

APPENDICES

B

Chapter I

THE EARLY YEARS

INDIA-RUBBER,[1] or caoutchouc (the milk-like fluid of many tropical and semi-tropical plants) has been known to Europe since the discovery of the New World, yet the story whereby it became the basis of one of the most critical and strategic industries of modern times extends only to the past century. Possessed of unique physical properties, there can be few materials that have wrought so many changes in the progress of the arts and the sciences. Despite the strides made in the production of synthetic rubber at the present day this industry has created a new and vital inter-dependence between the most advanced industrial nations of the West with the equatorial regions of the East.

The first European to describe the elastic gum was Pietro Martyre d'Anghiera, chaplain to the court of Ferdinand and Isabella, who in his *De Orbo Novo,* published in 1530, describes an Aztec game played with balls " made of the juice of a certain herbe . . . [which] being stricken upon the ground but softly " rebounded "incredibly into the ayer." Other early references are contained in the work of Antonio de Herrera y Tordesillas[2], historian to Philip II, who told how Columbus on his second voyage to the New World in 1493-1496 saw balls " made of the gum of a tree " being used by the Indians of Haiti. The first mention of rubber being used for purposes other than sport was made by F. Juan de Torquemada in 1615[3]. He related how the Indians, having gathered the milk from incisions made in the various trees, brushed it onto their cloaks, and obtained crude footwear and bottles by coating earthen moulds and allowing them to dry. He also made reference to the use of a medicinal oil obtained from rubber by distillation.

---

[1] The term " India-rubber " or " Indian-rubber " came to be used because of its origins with the natives of South America, and its properties as an eraser. Joseph Priestley wrote in the Preface to his *Introduction to the Theory and Practice of Perspective* (1770) : " Since this work was printed off, I have seen a substance excellently adapted to the purpose of wiping from paper the marks of a black-lead pencil . . ."

[2] Antonio de Herrera : *The General History of the vast Continent and Islands of America.* Translated by Captain John Stevens (London, 1725), I, 166.

[3] *De la Monarquia Indiana* (Madrid, 1615), II, 663.

The first scientific account of india-rubber was given in the eighteenth century by two Frenchmen: Charles de la Condamine and François Fresneau. De la Condamine was a member of a French geographical expedition sent out to South America in 1735, to measure an arc of the meridian, and is best known for his report to the French Academy in 1736 in which he described caoutchouc as the condensed juice of the hevea tree.[1] The result of Fresneau's more comprehensive researches were presented to the Academy as a mémoire by de la Condamine in 1751.[2] It is to these two men that the honour falls of having placed before European minds the first serious account of rubber production and the primitive native system of manufacture.

Similarly, it is in the work of two other Frenchmen, François David Herrissent, a physician, and Pierre Joseph Macquer[3], a chemist, that the first attempts were made to employ caoutchouc in Europe. Their efforts, as those of other Europeans,[4] to discover a cheap and effective solvent for the crude mass of rubber brought from South America—usually in the shape of cakes and balls—were not entirely successful. The Frenchmen, however, can be credited with introducing the use of turpentine and pure ether as solvents, and by this means—ineffective and costly as they were in comparison with later developments—some of the earliest rubber surgical instruments were made. But the greatest progress in the easy manipulation of rubber came at the beginning of the nine-

---

[1] This report was sent to the Académie des Sciences in Paris in 1736 by de la Condamine and his companion Benquer. An abstract of it appears in the *Mémoires de l'Académie Royale des Sciences* (1751), 319. It was the English scientist Michael Faraday who first determined in 1836 the chemical composition of rubber. See William C. Geer, *The Reign of Rubber* (New York, 1922), 103.

[2] Considerable dispute has arisen as to the relative contribution of these men to the early scientific knowledge of the india-rubber plant. See the *Revue generale du Caoutchouc*, October 1936, No. 125, 28, and the *Revue de Botanique Appliquée et d'Agriculture tropicale*, XVI, 1936, 525 et seq. A recent appraisement of Fresneau's contribution is made by F. de Chasseloup Laubat : *François Fresneau, Père du Caoutchouc*. (Paris, 1942).

[3] E. Chapel, *Le Caoutchouc et la Gutta-Percha* (Paris 1892), 18. On the work of other eighteenth-century Frenchmen in this field such as Grossart, Berniard and Fourcroy, *ibid.* 23 et seq.

[4] Two important European works published in the eighteenth century were : Aernoud Juliaans, *Dissertatio Chemica Inauguralis de Resina Elastica Cajennensis,* (Utrecht, 1780) ; Franz Carl Achard, *Chemische-Physische Schriften,* (Berlin, 1780.)

LYNCH. LITH

HANHART, IMT

THOMAS HANCOCK

Reproduced from *Hancock on India Rubber Manufacture* (1857)

teenth century from the experiments of a Scottish chemist, Charles Macintosh,[1] (1766-1843), and an English inventor, Thomas Hancock,[2] (1786-1865).

When Macintosh and Hancock began their experiments at the beginning of the nineteenth century the process of india-rubber manufacture was crude and unsatisfactory. The solvents used to prepare the gum, normally turpentine or camphene, were expensive and imperfect, and the dissolved rubber was applied without the aid of machinery in almost as primitive a manner as by the natives themselves.

Macintosh's contribution was the discovery—re-discovery it really was[3]—about 1820 of the use of coal tar oil as a cheap and effective solvent. Having contracted with the Glasgow Gas Works in 1819 to receive their by-products of tar and ammonia, which he required for his experiments with vegetable dyes, the thought occurred to him to use the tar oil as a solvent for rubber. The experiment proving a success Macintosh placed the solution between two fabrics and avoided the sticky or brittle surface of the earlier garments. Manufacture of these double-texture waterproofed cloaks[4]—henceforth to be known incorrectly in the English language as "mackintoshes"—began in the Glasgow area in the

---

[1] See *Biographical Memoir* by his son, George Macintosh (1847). Privately printed.

[2] The story of his life's work is told in his *Personal Narrative of the Origin and Progress of Caoutchouc or India-Rubber Manufacture in England*, published in London, 1857. The opinion expressed by an authoritative American writer, P. W. Barker, *Charles Goodyear* (Boston, Mass., privately printed, 1940), 95, that " Hancock never visited any foreign country with the purpose of spreading the knowledge of rubber manufacture ; therefore no claim as a rubber pioneer or missionary may be made in his behalf . . ." is fundamentally inaccurate, as reference to E. Chapel's work shows ; also Hancock, *ibid.* 63-4, and the American *India Rubber World*, New York (hereafter referred to as *IRW*), 1 October 1939, 67.

[3] *Proceedings of the Royal Society of London,* Abstract of Papers, Vol. V, 486-8. *Chemistry & Industry,* 28 June, 1952, 606. *Glasgow Annals of Philosophy,* August 1818, Vol. XII, 112. Also L. Eck, *Gummi Zeitung,* 47, 1315 (1933); 53, 1015, 1032 (1939); 54, 385-6 (1940).

[4] The first English patent for " making waterproof all kinds of leather, cloth &c.," by the application of a solution of rubber, was obtained by Samuel Peal in 1791. (Patent No. 1801). In 1627 John Wolfen had been granted English letters patent of invention " to use or exercise, practize or putt in use, a newe invencion for making and preparing of certaine stuffs and skynns to hould out the wett and rayne", though this could hardly refer to india-rubber.

early 'twenties and was later removed to Manchester.[1] The discovery not only meant a stimulus to the young industry, but also useful employment for coal tar—a troublesome by-product of coal gas manufacture.

It would be difficult to exaggerate the contribution made by the man who was to become his colleague and partner: Thomas Hancock. He has many claims to the title "Father of the India-Rubber Industry"—and his experiments in rubber working were of the greatest importance in laying the foundations of the modern rubber industry. Convinced that "something must eventually be done with so singular a substance", he first attempted to dissolve the rubber with turpentine, but his hand-coated fabrics were unsatisfactory in surface and smell. Unsuccessful in this he then turned to the production of elastic thread. Strips of rubber were cut from the imported lumps and applied in their crude state to clothing and footwear. On 29 April 1820 he obtained an English patent (No. 4451) for this purpose. In the same year, in an effort to find use for his waste cuttings he introduced the use of his famous masticator or "pickle", (so-called to avoid imitation), which became the model for the much larger rubber masticators that followed. Constructed with a hollow wooden cylinder armed with teeth in which a hand-driven spiked roller was turned, this tiny machine, originally taking a charge of 2 oz. of rubber, fulfilled his greatest hopes. Instead of the "pickle" tearing the rubber to shreds, as he thought it might do, the heat welded together the scraps of rubber into a homogeneous dough which could be applied in further manufacture. On the success of this device the inventor wrote:[2]

> I had now at command the means of reducing all kinds of rubber, whatever size or form . . . without . . . the use of any solvent, or having recourse to any chemical process, the effect being produced solely by a mechanical action on the rubber itself . . .

---

[1] George Macintosh, op.cit. 82 : " Mr. Macintosh obtained a patent for this process . . . and established a manufactory of water-proof articles, which was, in the first instance, carried on at Glasgow . . ." The New Statistical Account for Stirlingshire, dated 1845, makes no mention of a water-proofing factory. In the Glasgow Post Office Directory during the 1820's and the 1830's there are entries for Charles Macintosh & Co., who had tar works in Hill Street, Glasgow, and George Macintosh & Co., who had cudbear works in Duke Street.

[2] Hancock, op. cit., 12-13. Also S. C. Stillwagon, " The Development of Basic Rubber Processing Machinery ", IRW, 1 October 1939, 50 et seq.

This was only the first of many important successes for Thomas Hancock. Between 1820-47 he took out sixteen patents dealing with most aspects of rubber working.

The efforts of these two men—Macintosh making his approach to the problem as a chemist, Hancock as a mechanical engineer[1]— had resolved the initial problem facing the rubber industry: the manipulation of the raw material. By the 'thirties there had been a consolidation of the Hancock-Macintosh forces with certain textile interests in the Manchester area. This combination, trading under the name of Chas. Macintosh & Co.,[2] represented the most important group of British textile and chemical interests engaged in rubber manufacture. It was under the shadow of these two industries that the new manufacture grew. There could be no rapid extension of the use of india-rubber, however, until one further obstacle had been overcome. Manufactured rubber was affected by changing degrees of temperature: softening with the heat and hardening with

[1] Hancock, op. cit. 2 : " I had spent my earlier days in mechanical pursuits, and was well acquainted with the materials generally employed therein, and also with the use of tools, so far as to enable me to make with my own hands almost any kind of machinery required to carry out my views ; but of chemical knowledge I had almost none. I premise this because . . . although the substance I was contemplating apparently required to be treated chemically, I owe my success principally to the practical knowledge and the degree of skill I had acquired in mechanical manipulation, which proved eventually to be the best preparation I could have had . . . "

[2] On the origin of this firm the following undated note found with the Birley MSS. is of some interest. After describing Macintosh's early experiments with coal tar oil the note continues : " Wishing to extend his business he [Macintosh] looked out for someone to join him with capital, and was introduced to Mr. Hugh Hornby Birley and his brother Mr. Joseph Birley. They were cotton spinners and manufacturers in Manchester, and owned the premises on the east side of Cambridge Street, from the river to the further end of the block of buildings known as the ' New Mill ', all of which were then employed in spinning and weaving. These three gentlemen, Mr. Macintosh and Messrs. Hugh and Joseph Birley, together with a Mr. R. W. Barton, formed the firm of Chas. Macintosh & Co., in 1824, and, for the purpose of carrying on the waterproof business, erected on the west side of Cambridge Street the building now known as the ' Old Mill.' They built it so that, should the waterproof business prove a failure, it might be added to and converted into a cotton mill. The new business did not turn out a failure, and the building remains with an unfinished side to this day." It appears to have been the belief of the Birley family, passed on from one generation to the next, that Macintosh could not get financial support for his patent in Scotland. By the end of the 'sixties both " Old " and the " New " mills were engaged in rubber manufacture ; a state of affairs occasioned in part by the growing difficulties of cotton supply during the American Civil War.

the cold. The solution of this problem was bound up with the progress of the American industry.

In the United States the story of the growth of the rubber manufacturing industry is part of the unequalled commercial and industrial expansion that ensued after 1819 and culminated in the general crisis of 1837. Until the 1830's rubber was largely a curiosity, the estimated net imports into the United States in 1830 being 160 long tons. Attempts had been made at an earlier date to imitate the crude native-manufactured shoes imported from South America,[1] but with the quickening of the economy in the 'thirties, there followed a period of activity that the industry was not to experience again for another decade. Numerous factories came into operation along the waterfalls of the Eastern seaboard, and, stimulated by the gold discoveries of 1848, efforts were made to extend the use of rubber to clothing and machinery.

As details of British developments were probably unknown to the Americans their earliest attempts to reduce the rubber to a plastic state by the aid of machinery followed along other lines. Instead of the rubber being mixed inside a chamber, as with Hancock's "pickle", the method chosen was to compress it between wooden or iron cylinders.

The earliest American patent for rubber machinery was that secured by John J. Howe on the 10 April 1820, for a grinding or mixing mill, consisting of two heavy iron rolls. In 1836 there followed the much more important patent (No. 16 dated 31 August), of Edwin Marcus Chaffee—one of the original members of America's first india-rubber company formed at Roxbury, Massachusetts in 1833—for a mill and a spreading machine. Chaffee's invention, foreshadowed in Howe's patent, and owing a good deal to the earlier efforts of the rubber pioneers Nathaniel and Martin Hayward, who operated a small manufactory at Woburn, Massachusetts, represented the culmination of a series of experiments extending over many years.[2] His two-roll mill, one roll being 6 ft. long and 27 inches in diameter, the other of the same length but only 18

---

[1] The first American patent for a rubber varnish for footwear was secured by Jacob F. Hummel of Philadelphia in 1813. Other early American patents for waterproofing were those of A. Dana (1821) ; Arnold Buffum (1822) ; Patrick G. Nagle (1825) ; and J. T. Howe (1829).

[2] Early rubber technology owes much to the existing practices of other industries. Cylindering or calendering was already known in the finishing processes of textile manufacture, and the rubber mill or grinder might well have evolved from the " pug mill " used by builders for the kneading of clay.

inches in diameter, compressed the rubber, and aided the compounding process. In this respect it followed the pattern of earlier inventions. Unlike them, however, Chaffee's rolls were steam-heated to about 200°F and allowed for the grinding and mixing of the rubber either without the addition of solvents or with their limited use. The calender or coating machine, included in this patent, set the pattern for spreading machines until the present day. Built in 1837 at a cost of $30,000 and weighing 30 tons, its great size earned for it the title of the " Monster". With four 6 ft. long steam-heated rolls, built on top of each other, of varying diameter, it was the biggest machine built for the rubber industry. After the rubber had been ground and mixed in the mill it was fed, together with the cloth to be proofed, into this machine. The revolving cylinders were of such tremendous power as to be able to force into the fabric a thin film of rubber. Apart from the economies in labour costs, and the speeding up of the whole process of manufacture, the spreader, which before vulcanisation could be regarded as the final machine employed in the manufacturing process, meant in certain instances the almost total elimination of the use of solvents. While business conditions and inadequate power resources delayed the general adoption of Chaffee's inventions, they remained the pattern of rubber machinery in Europe as well as in America for at least another generation.

In 1855, thirty-five years after John Howe had taken out the first American patent for rubber machinery, Charles Goodyear, American rubber pioneer, wrote:[1]

> It is now generally agreed by manufacturers in this business that the machinery, or at least the principle of it, is perfect . . . the best reason for believing that this machinery does not admit of further improvement in principle, is that no complaint is made of it. It is of the simplest kind, doing the work with great rapidity . . .

As far as the mechanical treatment of the raw material was concerned the manufacturing process was perfected quickly. Simple as these machines were (to cut, wash, soften, grind and spread the crude rubber) they met the needs of the industry in such a manner that few changes were called for in later years. At the outset, it was not chemical knowledge that was paramount in the development of the industry but the ability to devise a suitable method of rubber manipulation.

[1] Goodyear, *Gum Elastic* (Newhaven, 1855), I, 152.

Ability to devise suitable machinery, however, either on the part of the Americans or the British, did not change the nature of rubber. The American industry in particular received a fillip from the progress made in rubber technology but this did not stave off a recession when the inherent fault of the early manufactured rubber became apparent; it softened in the heat and hardened in the cold (particularly in the more extreme climate of the United States), it was tacky, odorous, and perished easily. By the autumn of 1837 the American rubber boom was followed by a collapse and most of the undertakings were abandoned. These were the circumstances that preceded the coming of a far-reaching invention: the discovery of the vulcanisation process by Charles Goodyear in 1839.[1]

It is impossible in a few words to do justice to the American inventor Charles Goodyear. Son of a hardware dealer, he was born at New Haven, Connecticut, in 1800. Becoming interested in the manufacture of rubber in 1832, his experiments—unaided at the outset by any chemical knowledge—continued until his death in 1860. His efforts to solve the fatal defect of rubber, whose consistency changed with the temperature, are described by the inventor in his book *Gum Elastic*. In June 1837 he took out a patent (U.S. Patent No. 240) for an " acid gas process " whereby the rubber was treated in a solution of dilute nitric acid, but his goods decomposed in the summer heat, and the manufactory established at Woburn, Massachusetts, failed. It was Nathaniel Hayward,[2] a foreman at the Woburn plant, who first suggested to him the use of sulphur as a compounding ingredient to "cure" rubber, and for which Hayward obtained a patent (U.S. Patent

---

[1] It is appreciated that there are competing claims for this honour. Of those made for the German (F. W. Ludersdorff) the Swedish (Peter Jonas Bergius), and Dutch (Jan van Guens) inventors see the following articles : F. Fritz, *Gummi Zeitung*, XLIV, 33 (1929) ; L. Eck, *Gummi Zeitung*, LI, 1185 (1937) ; W. Esch, *Gummi Zeitung*, LII, 12 (1938). It would appear from the evidence that the claims made by the Germans on behalf of Ludersdorff (whose work, *Auflösen und Wiederherstellen des Federharzes, gennant : Gummielastikum ; zur Darstellung luft und wasser-dichter Gegenstande* u.s.w., published in Berlin in June 1832, supposedly contained the first published reference to the use of sulphur with rubber) are disputable. An earlier reference to the use of sulphur was made by Erhard Friedrich Leuchs in *Archiv für die Gesamte Naturlehre*, XXI, 107-8 (1831).

[2] See Hayward's account of his *Experiments with India-Rubber which resulted in Discovering the Invaluable Compound of that Article with Sulphur*. (Norwich, Conn., Bulletin Job Office, 1865).

No. 1090) which he later sold to Goodyear. Goodyear's own momentous discovery of "improved" rubber was made at the beginning of 1839 with his compound of rubber, lead and sulphur. In 1864, Hayward stated before the courts how "Charles Goodyear himself soon after told me he had made the discovery by putting a piece of rubber cloth on a hot cylinder stove . . .", how the specimen . . . "soon began to change color, grow darker, and finally turned to a slate color, when it underwent no further change, and was no longer affected by heat or cold, and all this without injuring the fibre of the cloth. This was at that time called heated or fireproof gum, but afterwards vulcanised rubber."[1] The years that followed in the life of Charles Goodyear constitute a chapter in the long history of rubber that would surpass the powers of the best story-teller. Imprisoned for debt in America and Europe, awarded the highest distinctions by the British and the French for his work, dogged with ill-health, harried and impoverished, the inventor died in a New York hotel on Sunday, 1 July 1860. Few men have given so much and received so little. Yet he had written in his book: "I am not disposed to repine, and say that I have planted and others have gathered the fruits . . . Man has just cause for regret only when he sows and no one reaps."

Of greater moment here: what was the nature of Goodyear's discovery? It would be foolhardy for the historian to attempt to give a precise answer to this question when the chemists and physicists are not as yet agreed on a common definition of vulcanisation. "Essentially, it is the result of the chemical and physical action of sulphur upon rubber."[2] For the purpose of this work it is the consequences of vulcanisation rather than the process that are of paramount importance. The vital fact is that Goodyear's

[1] Sworn affidavit of Nathaniel Hayward at Colchester, Connecticut, on 28 December 1864 ; " in The Matter of the Application for the Extension of Charles Goodyear's Vulcanizing Patent of 15 June 1844". Circuit Court of the United States, District of Connecticut.

[2] I am indebted to Dr. Sam S. Pickles for this precise definition. As this is not a technical work the author does not intend to discuss the chemical and physical reaction of rubber to vulcanisation—particularly as there is so little known about the nature of this change. For those interested in the technical aspect a paper by C. O. Weber in the *Journal of the Society of the Chemical Industry*, January 1894, is most helpful in endeavouring to explain this apparently inexplicable subject. A more up-to-date account—though more difficult for the layman to follow—is contained in the *American Chemical Society's Year Book* for 1939 : " What is Vulcanization ? ", by A. Babcock. Also, E. G. Holt : " Vulcanization of Rubber. Its Discovery and Practical application ", *IRW*, 1 July 1937, 35 *et seq.*

act in combining rubber with sulphur and lead at a high temperature imparted to this substance a durable quality which it had not hitherto possessed:[1]

> . . . the effect of this process is not simply the improvement of a substance; but it amounts, in fact, to the production of a *new material*. The durability imparted to gum-elastic by the heating or vulcanising process, not only improves it for its own peculiar and legitimate uses, but also renders it a fit substitute for a variety of other substances where its use had not before been contemplated . . .

Goodyear's discovery of " elastic metal " meant that rubber could be used for purposes where hitherto it had been totally unsuited. Until now the backbone of the rubber industry had been the proofing of fabric and the making of overshoes. While the use of rubber in the unvulcanised state was by no means insignificant, Goodyear's discovery made possible the rise of the mechanical trade (the use of rubber with machinery), the bicycle and the motor-car tyre.

With this invention the desired " change "— the desideratum of all those who had worked with rubber—was accomplished, but it was a different matter to convince the American business community and the general public that such was the case. With the recent bankruptcy of the industry in mind they would have nothing to do with it. Goodyear was shortly to return to jail for debt ; and William Rider, who believed in the genius of this man, failed in business in 1841. To restore the confidence of the American public in rubber manufacture was too great a task, even for Charles Goodyear. Heavily in debt and without the necessary capital to carry forward his experiments his only alternative was to place the invention before other minds; with this purpose he set his face towards Europe, and in August 1842, Stephen Moulton, empowered to dispose of the inventor's secret for £50,000 sailed to England carrying with him the first samples of the " improved rubber ".

Stephen Moulton, founder of one of the earliest branches of the rubber industry in Great Britain and a principal actor in the unfolding drama of rubber, was born at Whorlton, County Durham, on 7 July 1794. He was the youngest of three children of Stephen Moulton, law stationer, whose permanent home was in the

---

[1] C. Goodyear, *op. cit.* I, 132-3.

CHARLES GOODYEAR
First portrait on hard rubber panel by G. P. A. Healey, Paris, 1855

STEPHEN MOULTON, Esq., J.P.
1794–1880
Founder of the manufacture at Kingston Mills, Bradford-on-Avon, in 1848

Parish of St. Dunstan's in the West, London.   Of Moulton's birth, ancestry and early life there is almost no information.   In 1827 he married Elizabeth Hales at St. George's Church, Hanover Square, and in 1839 (having previously emigrated to America) he appears in the New York City street directory as: " Stephen Moulton of 48 Greenwich, Broker." It was in this capacity that he became the friend and associate of a small group of American rubber pioneers which included, amongst others, Charles Goodyear, Nathaniel Hayward, and the brothers, William, John and Emory Rider. It is not surprising that Goodyear should have chosen Moulton to negotiate the sale of his vulcanisation formula in England.   Moulton was accustomed to business dealings.   He was familiar with the English scene and he had insufficient technical knowledge to deprive Goodyear of his discovery.   Yet, with all these qualifications, Moulton's mission was a failure and Goodyear's hopes of raising capital in England were never realised.

On this phase of the story, which is based on the notes made by Stephen Moulton at the time, it will suffice to state that the British rubber group (approached by Moulton to buy the secret of the samples he carried), suggested that the inventor, whose identity was not revealed, should patent his improvement so that they could form a judgment of its merit, or that he should come over to England and treat with them himself.   Meanwhile, the samples had passed into the hands of the Englishman, Thomas Hancock. The latter, along with the best brains of European science, had worked for this " change " in rubber for almost twenty years without success; but: " Finding now that this object appeared to have been somehow or other effected, and therefore demonstrated to be practicable . . . I set to work in earnest, resolved, if possible, not to be outdone by any . . . The little bits . . . certainly showed me for the first time that the desirable change in the condition of rubber of not stiffening by cold had been attained . . . "[1]   For more than a year he worked unceasingly, and on November 21st 1843, eight weeks before Charles Goodyear belatedly applied for his English patent on 30 January 1844,[2] Hancock entered his

[1] Hancock, op. cit. 93-5.

[2] Goodyear, op. cit. I, 86-7.   English Patent No. 10027, 30 Jan. 1844. United States Patent No. 3633, 15 June 1844.   Whereas Hancock considered that sulphur alone combined with the rubber and subjected to a certain degree of heat was sufficient for vulcanisation to take place, Goodyear included salts of lead, which accelerated the change and made it possible at lower temperatures.

specification for an improvement in the manufacture of rubber.[1]
As far as the English market was concerned Goodyear was forestalled.

Goodyear's belief that the British would not be able to guess the
secret of the samples carried by Moulton was shared by others.
There is extant an affidavit filed in May 1852 in which a whole
galaxy of eminent English chemists swear that :

> . . . The specimens or samples of goods alleged to have been
> exhibited or sent from the United States of America . . .
> conveyed no information whatsoever as to the manufacture
> of the same or as to the mode or process whereby the same
> had been or could be procured and that such mode of producing
> the change could not be anticipated by any *a priori* reasoning
> even with a knowledge of the presence of sulphur and of the
> composition of such samples . . .[2]

Despite this evidence Goodyear remained convinced to the end that
the source of Hancock's patent for vulcanisation was the samples of
" improved rubber " which he had sent with Moulton in 1842.
Moulton himself shared that view.[3] Alexander Parkes, English
inventor of the cold process of vulcanisation in 1846 (whereby in
certain processes heat could be dispensed with and replaced by a

[1] Great Britain, Patent Office, Abridgement of Specifications, Class 16,
Relating to the Preparation of India-Rubber and Gutta-Percha (1791-1866),
17-18 Patent No. 9952.

[2] Arthur Aiken, F.L.S., Lecturer in Chemistry in Guy's Hospital, William
Thos. Brande, Royal Mint, late Professor of Chemistry in the Royal
Institution, John Thos. Cooper, Consulting and Analytical Chemist, and
Thos. Graham, Professor in Chemistry, University College, London.
Affidavit Sworn 3rd, Filed 5th May 1852. (Moulton MSS.)

[3] See Moulton's affidavit filed 20 April 1852, in the case in Chancery,
Hancock v. Moulton. And in the margin of the copy affidavit filed by
Wm. Brockedon on 5 May 1852, against the words : " Say that I never heard
and do not now know or believe that the said plaintiff Thomas Hancock ever
analysed the said samples . . . or procured the same or any portion of the same
to be analysed by any person or persons . . . " Stephen Moulton has written :
" Why ! Hancock employed Cooper and others to analyse these samples and
Cooper swears he did." A decade later Moulton's opinion remained unchanged : " after 25 years experience, no real improvement (beyond what
practice and a knowledge of the business in all its parts would give), has been
invented since the art of curing by means of the combined action of heat and
sulphur upon Rubber was discovered by the late Mr. Chas. Goodyear of
New York." SM to Tongue & Birkbeck, 8 November 1861.

solely chemical process),[1] made this note in his original copy of
Hancock's *Personal Narrative* :

> I think it is a sad thing for Mr. Thomas Hancock to try to
> claim the discovery of vulcanization from the fact of the
> vulcanized rubber being first brought by Goodyear from
> America and pieces given to Brockedon "Hancock's co-
> partner" and others. These were seen, examined and experi-
> mented on by several and it was found to be free sulphur in a
> heated and in a molten state that produced the permanent
> elasticity of Rubber. The above facts related to me both by
> Brockedon and Thomas Hancock. It is quite true that Mr.
> Thomas Hancock obtained the first Patent in England.[2]

A study of many original and unpublished documents, specifically
the unpublished letters written by Charles Goodyear and William
Rider to Stephen Moulton, leads to the conclusion that it is a dis-
service to the greatness of Hancock's reputation, which is assured
regardless of the origins of vulcanisation, and an injustice to Charles
Goodyear to claim for Hancock the "undoubted right to be
recognized as the discoverer of vulcanization".[3]

The Goodyear letters make it abundantly clear that the American
never shifted from his opinion that the English inventor had deprived
him of the fruits of his labours. What hurt him most was Hancock's
ungenerous attitude. The first pieces of vulcanised rubber that
Hancock ever saw came from Goodyear's hands. He had an ample
opportunity to judge the quality of Goodyear's work at the Great
Exhibition of 1851—exhibits which earned from the Jurors equal
praise with his own—yet the name of Goodyear is not to be found
between the covers of Hancock's book published in 1857. Certainly,
it is difficult to reconcile the sentiments expressed in the last sentence

[1] Alexander Parkes, English Patent No. 11147, 25 March 1846. This
process permitted the vulcanisation of single-texture garments, and certain
other small articles, by immersing them in a solution of sulphur monochloride
in carbon disulphide.

[2] On pp. 131-4, against the extract from the *Jurors' Report of the Great Exhibition of 1851*. Typescript in the possession of the Research Association of the
British Rubber Manufacturers, Shawbury.

[3] As is done in the Preface to the Centenary Edition of Hancock's *Personal
Narrative* reprinted in 1920 by order of the Directors of James Lyne Hancock,
Ltd., London. A publication by the descendants of Thomas Hancock naturally
commands respect and will probably be consulted by future scholars. It is
doubly important therefore that the reliability of this statement should not
remain open to question.

of Hancock's book: " Though called upon to do so, we have never interfered in the disputes on this question abroad, nor have we made any attempts to monopolise any portion of the rubber trade in America, or any other foreign country . . . " with the testimony submitted by him a year later when opposing the extension of Goodyear's American patent.   In this connection Goodyear wrote to Moulton in June 1858 : " I am happy to say that my patent is extended, enclosed I send you the testimony of Hugh Birley and Thomas Hancock.   This will form a nice appendix to the infamous Book of Hancock where the name of Goodyear cannot be found in it. Posterity will judge of the moral motives of the man when this evidence volunteered by the man himself is put together with the history of the facts in juxtaposition with that Book and another written by one Goodyear."

Whatever the merits of Hancock's invention, one fact is certain: the discovery of vulcanisation had opened the way to a new era in the history of this industry.

Chapter II

RUBBER COMES TO THE WEST COUNTRY

WHILST Moulton's journey to England in 1842 (he returned to New York in 1843) did not benefit Goodyear, it did nevertheless make Moulton increasingly aware of the commercial opportunities bound up with the growing use of rubber; so much so that in 1847 he returned to England ostensibly to take out and negotiate the sale of a new vulcanisation patent, ultimately to lay the foundations of the industry in the West Country. To become a rubber manufacturer, however, demanded more than commercial foresight. Unless Moulton chose to contest the Goodyear and Hancock patents in the courts his only hope was either to commence manufacture as a licensee or, and to this more profitable course he now directed his energies, to discover an alternative to the free sulphur patents of Hancock and Goodyear.

The first mention of an alternative vulcanisation formula was made in the Agreement of Co-partnership which was completed on 28 June 1847, between Moulton, the Rider brothers, and James Thomas, an American chemist.[1] This shows that in return for the chemist's scientific aid, and the use of the Riders' rubber factory in New York for practical experiments, Moulton undertook to share equally with them the proceeds of an English patent (No. 11567) for vulcanisation dated 8 February 1847. In addition, the agreement laid down the terms of all future investigations and experiments of the partnership. The origin of the English patent in which the hyposulphite of lead was employed in place of the free sulphur of Goodyear and Hancock is unknown, though the specification was drafted by Thomas, and William Rider referred to it as the "Thomas Patent". It soon became apparent, however, that it was a much easier task for Moulton to file a specification that would satisfy the English patent authorities than it was to translate it into production. The evidence available over the next two years does not show the employment of a new patented formula but rather the search for one. The specification drafted by Thomas, and deposited by Moulton in August 1847, was either incomplete or required for its employment a degree of skill and experience that neither the Riders nor Moulton possessed. In January 1848, William Rider wrote from New York:

[1] See Appendix II.

"Thus far we have not been able to get anything like a supply of Hyposulphite from Thomas, nor does he yet consent that we shall make it ourselves by letting us know how to do it." By February 1848, the trickle of compound that had passed from Thomas to the Riders' mill, with which the first samples had been made, had dried up: " Our whole operations here in Hyposulphite are stopped, or rather the supply of Hyposulphite is stopped by Thomas waiting he says to get your account. . . " wrote William Rider to Moulton[1]. The differences between Thomas and Moulton had been growing for some time and by 1848 the deadlock between them was complete. Moulton would not render an account to Thomas until he received the formula and Thomas would not render a working formula until he received an account of Moulton's financial activities in England. To all intents and purposes the Co-partnership Agreement of 1847 was a dead letter: " . . . I know not from Mr. Thomas, " wrote Moulton to the Riders on 30 January, 1848, "the meaning even much less the mode of making this sulphite . . . I should like to know whether you have gained more than I have from being told that a certain thing will do a certain thing without knowing at the same time why ? or by what means ? "

In the circumstances Moulton and the Riders might well have abandoned the English project, but these men were not to be daunted by the turn of events. If Thomas would not go on with them they must seek help elsewhere, and in March 1848 William Rider proposed to Moulton:[2] " . . . to set a good chemist to work to see if we cannot make the article and we will send you samples of some we had from Thomas for you to see what you can get done in England." Although Rider's greatest fear in this period of stalemate was that their patent would be superseded and all would be lost, by the autumn of 1848 Moulton's efforts[3] in England had met with some degree of success and he was able to announce the

[1] WR to SM 4 February 1848.

[2] WR to SM 10 March 1848.

[3] Of Moulton's efforts to find a practical formula for vulcanisation by lead sulphide see his letters to Professor Griffiths of St. Bartholomew's Hospital, London, 6 March 1848 and 24 March 1848; to Herepath of Bristol, 12 June 1848. On 2 June 1849 Wm. Shrapnell of Bristol, who had been making experiments for Moulton wrote : " I learn from Mr. Frost that there is no doubt now of the success of my trials so as to enable you to go on, and it will only remain for me to make . . . improvements in cheapness . . . " It needs to be remembered that although the Hancock and Goodyear master vulcani- sation patents were taken out in 1843-4 it was not until 1848 that either of these parties were able to vulcanise their wares satisfactorily.

discovery of a formula of a new compound which he called " Jenny Lind ". There was no rejoicing by his American colleague, only a word of warning: " We have often been where we thought we was sure, but time prooved we was wrong." In early October Moulton sent samples of articles cured by his new compound to New York. These were declared by the Riders to be: ". . . very clear from offensive smell [lessened in Moulton's case by the employment of Hyposulphite of lead rather than the crude sulphur of the Hancock and Goodyear patents], but are not so perfect as you seem to think, they do not stand the tests so well as could be desired. You must recollect that Goodyear and all the rest of us have frequently found we were wrong, therefore I would say do not reckon to sure." But Moulton had greater confidence in his discovery: " As to Jenny Lind," he replied " she sings admirably in England . . . " In fact by the end of 1848 Moulton had found a cure for rubber along the lines of his English patent. The next step was either for himself or others to prove the formula in manufacture. In later years he was to remember these days of trial and anxiety: " There is very little known about rubber and much time wasted in running after the chemist instead of the practical man . . ." He had written to a friend, which brought the retort: ". . . that the practical man would not have been in his present position had not the chemist stepped out of the crowd and shown him what could be done with rubber".[1] A generation later the backward state of British chemical knowledge was contrasted with the progress made by the Germans in their application of scientific methods and appreciation of industrial chemistry.[2]

It had originally been agreed between Moulton and his partners that if a sale of the patent could not be effected by samples alone they would have " . . . to prove to John Bull that the thing can be done . . . " by going into manufacture, but to the Americans this was to be the last ditch. The Riders had no illusions about the problem of rubber manufacture and it was their abiding concern that they should not become manufacturers in England :[3]

> I hope you will adopt my plan, and sell out before the machinery is built—this making money by manufacturing is too long winded for you and I, unless we think of settling down in England for life, which I hope does not for a moment enter

[1] W. Brown to SM, 2 September 1861.

[2] See article " The New German Immigration." *India Rubber Journal*, London, (hereafter referred to as *IRJ*), 10 June 1898.

[3] WR to SM, 4 April 1848.

into your calculations, for it does not in mine—let the sale, for instance, be conditioned that certain things be done, that is that machinery be put up, hands put into the works, and certain goods be produced at certain cost, make your calculations from what I have said to you heretofore.

Events on the eastern side of the Atlantic were not as the Americans saw them. Financial backing of an invention was probably easier to come by (which is the chief reason why Goodyear and Moulton had looked to the United Kingdom rather than to the United States) but just how far Moulton would have adhered to the Rider plan of "selling-out", if circumstances had favoured this course, is not known. Few of his letters covering this critical period remain, and without them one can only hazard the guess that instead of thinking in terms of negotiating the sale of his patent and returning to his family in America he inclined more to the prospect of settling down as a rubber manufacturer in England. Moreover, he came to doubt his partners' sincerity in pushing forward the English project on which, unlike them, he had staked everything. The turn for the worse in general trade conditions in the late 'forties, which made the Riders reluctant to press forward the English venture at this point,[1] left him little choice between the "long-winded" process of proving his patent by the test of manufacture in England or abandoning the venture altogether. Added to this, the Americans became increasingly absorbed in their own affairs and the Englishman was left to shift for himself. In May 1848, after Rider had refused Moulton's request for financial

---

[1] WR to SM, 15 November 1847: "... but I may ... wait ... until I get yours of 3rd now on the way, to know your views, and know how the great panic in the money market in England, has or is to affect our Rubber plans as to starting a Factory—If it affects your community as it has our money market, it may be desirable to wait a few months before we move with the Factory ... From the account from the other side I fear it will be a bad time to start a manufacturing business, and in particular a new one, but as you say nothing about the scarcity of money in England I presume it is only among business men, and therefore it will not affect your friend Mr. Palairett so but what he will be able to make payment for the Patent—therefore, I shall send brother John along as soon as he can get ready. From the accounts we get from the other side we should be led to conclude that all kinds of business was at a standstill, and that almost everyone had suspended payment, and this kind of belief has had a wonderful effect on our money market—so much so that we have not had it so tight for a twelvemonth, and from the fact that English Consuls have been selling at the Brokers Board, a thing never done before, the Brokers are fearful that we shall have a drain on the Banks through that kind of sale—hence everyone is looking for the next steamer with no little anxiety ... "

KINGSTON MILLS AND THE HALL
From a contemporary painting *circa* 1850

assistance with the English business, " . . . times arnt now as they used to was with us, and therefore we are obliged to husband every dollar we have at command . . .", Moulton replied that " I must work out my own plan, at my own risk and for my own gain, exclusively . . ." A few weeks later, at the age of 53, he took possession of the Kingston Mill at Bradford-on-Avon and set himself the task of forming the nucleus of a new industry—an event which did not escape the attention of Parliament.[1]

It is a matter of some conjecture why Moulton decided to locate the industry in the West of England. Whether his meeting with Captain Septimus Palairet[2]—landowner and philanthropist—was the occasion of his taking over the Kingston Mill, or whether he had already been attracted to Bradford before he met and enlisted the aid of this local benefactor is uncertain. Apart from the meeting with Palairet there are other circumstances that might help to explain Moulton's decision. His experience in the United States, as well as what he had seen of the Macintosh plant in Manchester, had convinced him that there were no serious drawbacks in converting a textile mill to rubber manufacture; and he not only got the mill at a favourable price but included in the sale was Kingston House (described by Aubrey in 1670 as " the best built house for the quality of a gentle-man in Wiltshire ")[3]—a suitable abode for his family. In addition, the river Avon, which ran beside the mill, provided cheap power and abundant water for washing and processing the rubber—vital factors in this industry; and the Somersetshire coalfields were only a few miles away. As for communications, Bradford lay close to the Bath and the Great West Roads linking the West Country with the metropolis; and—at the outset—as a producer of consumer goods, it was to the metropolitan market that both Moulton and his American partners looked for their future customers. Through

[1] The Chancellor of the Exchequer, speaking in the House of Commons on the state of the nation : " . . . I will mention here a curious circumstance, which shows the effect on the activity of trade, which is sometimes occasioned by the introduction of new descriptions of manufacture. At Bradford an abandoned cloth factory has recently been taken by a gentleman from a distance for the purpose of establishing a manufactory of articles of clothing &c. from India Rubber . . . " *Hansard* (Commons), 2 July 1849, Column 1180-1.

[2] Captain Septimus Palairet of Wooley Grange, Bradford-on-Avon, was a member of an old Somersetshire county family. According to a writer in 1887 (*Bradford on Avon Pictorial Guide, to which is added 50 yrs. of Progress, 1837-1887*, by C. Rawling) " he became one of the most popular and beloved residents that Bradford has ever had. His liberality to the poor and indigent was unbounded, and his munificence in works for the benefit of the neighbourhood unequalled ".

[3] Aubrey, *Natural History of Wiltshire* (c. 1670), 19.

nearby Trowbridge, Bath and Bristol (all important marketing outlets for the West of England cloth trade), Moulton could reach London, the Midlands and the North by rail; the construction of a railway line to Bradford was already projected, and a matter of yards from the mill itself was the wharf of the Kennet and Avon Canal, giving access to Bristol and the Somersetshire coalfields.

Moreover, there was an immediately available supply of displaced woollen workers, and the further decay of the staple woollen trade provided a reservoir of labour for future needs. Making allowance for the fact that it was intended to recruit key workers from America, (". . . We can send the force to start the factory "),[1] and that outside London and Manchester there were few operatives with any experience of rubber manufacture, the West County was as good a location as any other in England; better than most, as the factory system was already established there.[2] Finally, the town offered elbow-room for a young industry—a prerequisite stressed by the Americans (". . . put it in a place where room can be had for extending it").[3] There was not only room for expansion in Bradford but other empty woollen mills in the vicinity to facilitate its growth.[4]

The property acquired by Moulton on 30 September 1848[5]

[1] WR to SM, 22 September 1847.

[2] See H. R. Exelby, *The Industrial Revolution in the Textile Industries o, Wiltshire.* A thesis (unpublished) for M.A., Bristol University (1928). Also *Report of the Parliamentary Committee on the Woollen Industry* (1806), 6.

[3] WR to SM, 15 November 1847.

[4] In the 'fifties Moulton acquired the neighbouring Staverton and ' Middle ' woollen mills. At the end of the century the company purchased the ' Lamb', Church Street, and Abbey Mills, Bradford. See the author's article on the Wiltshire India-Rubber Industry. V.C.H., Vol. IV.

[5] By a conveyance dated 30 September 1848, the parties being : Maria Divett, Sarah Mackie, Mary Divett and Edward Divett Esq., of the 1st part, Russell Gray, John Ervine Clennie of the 2nd part, and Stephen Moulton of the 3rd part, subject to a Mortgage term of 100 years to secure £3000 with Interest at 5%. The following is a schedule of woollen machinery and equipment in the New Mill at the time of the sale and not included in the Conveyance :

2 Upright Gigs.	A 54″ spindle Billy.
A double washer.	A 56″ spindle Billy.
A cutter for broadcloth.	A 30″ carder—very good cards.
A large vice.	A 36″ scribbler.
A dyer's perpetual cutter.	A 36″ ditto—good cards.
A brushing up board table and scrawes (2).	A 36″ ditto.
	77ft. of leather strap—5″.
A 56″ Spindle Billy.	2 Gig scrawes and winding frame.
A 30″ carder.	A carpenter's bench.
A 30″ batten Engine—good cards.	

for a consideration of £7,500—£4,500 in cash and £3,000 on mortgage deed—consisted of the main Kingston Mill,[1] which has remained the core of the Moulton manufactory until the present day, a smaller mill known as the "Old Mill",[2] a dye-house[3] with an engine chimney, a counting house, four cottages, the "Great House" or Kingston House,[4] which was to become the home of the Moulton family, and nearly eight acres of land. The original cost of the mill property is not known but there are references to its having changed hands at an earlier date at £20,000 and in 1849 it was valued at £8,910.[5]

Although the early process of rubber manufacture has been described above, it might be well (before going on to discuss the conversion and equipping of this property) to outline again the principal stages of manufacture. These were, as Rider's "Estimate of Cost" given below makes clear, the cleansing, grinding, softening, mixing, calendering, and lastly, vulcanising of the rubber.

[1] Referred to in the Conveyance as the "New Mill". A five stories high building, fitted with a 20 horse-power water-wheel and solidly constructed of local West Country stone. It was built by Thomas Divett in 1811 for the manufacture of woollen cloth. According to SM/Amory & Co. 1 October 1849, the mill had been unoccupied since 1842.

[2] Erected in the second half of the eighteenth century and for some time past used as a flour grist mill. This mill was fitted with a 10 horse-power water-wheel, and in 1849 Moulton estimated its rental value at £200 per annum. See SM to Amory & Co. 1 October 1849. The woollen machinery in the building in September 1848 was as follows :

2 Cassimere Upright Gigs.
2 Indigo Pots.

[3] The schedule of equipment in the dye-house in September 1848 was as follows :

2 vat shutes.	2 vat shutes.
4 copper crosses.	4 tressles.
3 rakes.	A Kit Jack trench board spudgel
3 spudgels.	and one copper cross.
3 French cloths—1 net.	A washing basket, part copper.

[4] Formerly described as "the Great Hall or Manor House", it was probably built at the end of the sixteenth century by the Halls, a leading Bradford family since the days of Edward I. It subsequently passed to the Pierreponts, the Dukes of Kingston and the Manvers family. On 25 March 1805 it was sold by Viscount Newark and the Hon. Chas. H. Pierrepont to Thomas Divett, a cloth manufacturer who, in 1811, built the "New Mill" opposite the Hall. See *Wilts. Arch. Mag.,* I, 265., and Britton, *Beauties of England and Wales,* XV, 297.

[5] SM to Amory & Co., 1 October 1849. J. A. Cotterell to SM, 28 November 1849.

The first stage of manufacture was to rid the material of any foreign matter. The rubber was cut up by hand and the more obvious forms of adulteration, such as the large stones introduced by the native as good measure, removed. The rubber was then fed into a water-filled barrel or vat-like container, which like Hancock's original " pickle " or the rag-tearing machines already employed by the paper industry, was equipped with both fixed and circulating knives, the latter being fastened to a revolving inner drum. As the material became wedged between the two sets of knives it was torn apart—the cleansed rubber rising to the surface of the vat, the impurities such as sand, clay and stones sinking to the bottom. The next step was to plasticise the rubber before the various compounding ingredients were added. This problem was solved by grinding and compressing the material between two smooth-surfaced steam-heated cylinders along the lines of Chaffee's machine described in Chapter I. The machine was so arranged that one of its rolls turned faster than the other, thus providing a rolling and slipping motion which kneaded the rubber effectively. From this stage of manufacture, which took two or three hours of constant grinding, the material would either be passed to the " softening " machine (whose purpose was similar to the " grinder " except that it was at this stage that softeners such as camphene were added), or it could be fed into the " mixer " directly. It was in the " mixer " that the critical process of incorporating the chemicals (which would include softening ingredients if the " softening " machine had not already been used), took place. These were added to the rubber as it passed round the great cast iron rolls—the rubber being cut away from the roll by means of a sharp knife and fed back again between the rolls until the chemicals had been dispersed uniformly throughout the material. Although in appearance there was very little difference between the " mixer ", the " softener ", and the " grinder ", there was an essential distinction that ought to be mentioned: the " mixer " rolls (unlike the steam-heated rolls of the other machines) were water-cooled lest the friction heat of compressing the chemically treated rubber should result in partial vulcanisation.

When the material had been cleansed, ground, softened, and compounded it was ready for use. For articles built up from sheets of rubber, or for rubber-covered cloth or canvas, the next stage was " calendering ". The accompanying illustration of Moulton's original " Iron Duke " conveys some idea of the immensity of this machine. By altering the position of the cylinders, the calender pressed out the rubber dough (fed in between the two top rolls) in sheets of the desired thickness; or by altering the relative speed of one of the rolls (where rubber-covered cloth or canvas was required) it would " friction " the rubber onto the surface of the cloth fed in between the two bottom rolls.

After this there remained the last though perhaps the most important stage of early rubber manufacture: vulcanisation. The " vulcaniser " was not a machine but a steam-heated chamber along the lines of Rider's " Boiler Heater " mentioned below; and in principle not unlike the small brick oven by means of which Charles Goodyear had first effected vulcanisation. In fact the " vulcaniser " was a simple oven with a mobile rack on rails onto which the goods were placed prior to heating them, the steampipes taking the place of earlier experiments with wood or coal. In this last important stage of manufacture only an experienced worker was able to determine how long the articles should remain in the " vulcaniser," and what degree of heat should be applied to them.

In addition to this basic machinery, which met the needs of all rubber manufacturers whether producing clothing, footwear or mechanicals, Moulton needed certain secondary items of equipment—the most important of which were iron moulds. Without these, many of which were the patented property of his customers, the sharply defined outline of the railway spring, for example, could not have been obtained. To vulcanise the springs the heat was applied externally to the moulds which were clamped together securely before being run into the heater, and as the temperature rose—the degree of heat applied ranging between 100°–350° Fahrenheit—the heated rubber gradually accommodated itself to the shape of the inner contour. Steam-heated hydraulic presses and autoclaves only made their appearance in the last quarter of the century.

It would not detract from the drive and management shown by Stephen Moulton in these early days to say that the task of establishing this manufacturing process at the Bradford mill was made easier by the assistance he received from his American colleagues. To aid Moulton in his negotiations for plant and machinery William Rider had set out in one of his letters an "Estimate of Cost of a Rubber Factory" :

22 September, 1847.

Estimate cost here for a Rubber concern that will employ two

Hundred hands—say 160 Girls and 40 men, who can turn out from Ten to fifteen hundred Dollars worth of goods such as we have been making per day of 10 working hours.

1 Sixty Horse power with Boiler and setting ..	$6500.00
1 Spreading Machine	3000.00
1 Softening Machine	1500.00
2 Grinding Machine	1000.00
1 Mixing Machine	500.00
Shafting, Belting, Pipes, etc., for above ..	1200.00
1 Cutting and Washing Machine, Tube, Belts, etc.	600.00
1 Cyllender Boiler Heater 3½ ft. Diameter, 21 ft. long, with Car for goods, Valve, etc., etc. ..	1200.00
Steam Pipes for Heating Factory	1500.00
Fixtures for lighting Factory	200.00
Tables, Wash Tubs, Tools of all kind.. ..	2500.00
	$19700.00

An establishment with the above machinery and hands would require to be equal to Two Hundred feet long Forty feet wide and four Stories High, and should have a glass plat, or room on the Roof all equal to 150 feet sqr for suning goods—unless we get clear of that business—which I think we shall do—the establishment should have a good supply of water for washing Rubber—In putting up Factories, the expense always over runs estimates, then I think very probably the [average] Fixings will cost a cool $25,000 here.

W. Rider.

Our establishment now stands at a cost of $30,000 but our experience would enable us to get another up at much less expense.

This document is important not only because it lists the generally accepted equipment of a rubber manufactory of a century ago—indeed in basic principle of operation what rubber plants have remained until the present day—but because the manner in which the Englishman adhered to it in equipping his own mill suggests that there was no great difference in the rubber manufacturing processes of the two nations. It also indicates the highly capitalised nature of an early rubber undertaking.

In the spring of 1848 the Americans sent over a complete set of drawings for this machinery and an experienced engineer to superintend its purchase and erection :

It is very important [Rider had written on 15 November, 1847]

that we make our moves with the greatest care, and avail ourselves of all the skill we can in fitting up our machinery in
England, consequently, we have hired Mr. Frost the person who
built our machinery at the Vulcan Iron Works, to go out to
England and superintend the building of the machinery for the
new concern—I think in this way we shall not only get some very
perfect machinery, but be able to get it done on the lowest terms.

Events proved this opinion to be well founded. Frost arrived
in the following March (1848), with "what we consider the best
plan of rubber machinery . . ." and the first orders for the major
items of equipment—grained and chilled rollers—were placed
with a Staffordshire house as soon as Moulton had permission
to use the mill. The cutting machine, steam piping, gears, shafting,
pulleys, frames, fixtures, and other grain rolls were obtained from
Bristol.[1] The assembling of the equipment was done in the
factory, and Moulton must have had some extremely able millwrights to do this work, as there does not appear to have been any
undue delay in building the machinery once the parts had been
brought together at the mill. In all it probably took him five or six
years to equip the factory as he wanted it. In 1848, 1852 and again
in 1861 he purchased further sets of rolls from Bristol.[2] There was

[1] From Messrs. Thos. & Edwd. Bush, Engineers, Millwrights and Iron-
founders, Bristol.

[2] The measurements of the hollow grain rolls supplied from Bristol were
5 ft. long x 20″ diameter. A copy of an early invoice is as follows :

Messrs. S. Moulton & Co.   Bristol Iron Foundry,
   Bought of Thos. & Edwd. Bush.   29 September 1852.

		cwt.				
2 Hollow Rolls		112.2.0				
1 „ with additional						
round end		62.3.0				
		175.1.0	@	14/-	£122 13	6
Turning Necks—bodies—grooves and round						
ends on do			@	8/-	70 2	0
Turning out socket in both ends of each roll					8 0	0
Scouring the surface of body of each roll ...					18 0	0
Casing Rolls with Elmbd. & W.I. Hoops ...					2 6	0
					£221 1	6

The price charged in 1861 was the same as that of 1852 : 14/- per cwt. In
1873 (3 December) Bush & De Soyres of Bristol quoted £41 and on 3 April
1874 Crossleys of Manchester £56 (£90 if chilled) for a pair of best hard
grained cast iron rolls.

already installed in the mill a small boiler which enabled him to vulcanise his goods, but in 1854 he bought a new boiler heater like the one described by Rider in his estimate of 1847.[1]

The need of an adequate power supply to drive the heavy machinery and to provide the necessary steam heat for calenders and grinders is reflected in the history of all the early undertakings.[2] At Bradford the initial means of power consisted of two water-wheels (10 and 20 horse-power, which continued in use until 1910), and a 24 horse-power steam engine taken over with the mill. In 1853 a 40 horse-power engine was added, to be used conjointly with the water-wheels, and in the 'seventies further major alterations were carried out. But all this did not meet the needs of the industry and finally in the 'eighties still another engine was installed.

It might be added here that the steam coal for these engines came from the neighbouring Radstock mines at an average cost in the 'fifties and 'sixties of 12s. to 14s. per ton, and that there was little difference in the price of similar quality coal offered by other districts. On 11 May 1877, for example, the West Cannock Colliery Company offered Moulton " Best Bright Spirrs " at a competitive price of " 14/8d per ton ", and " Best Screened Shallow Kibbles at 14/8d and 13/8d per ton, 21 cwt. to the ton (no dust), less 1¼% disct. Delivered at Bradford Station . . . " In the 'nineties the Moulton Company—whose chief fuel requirements still came from the Radstock coalfields—paid an average of 22s. 6d. per ton for best steam coal.

The difficulty which Moulton experienced in obtaining some of this equipment—which reflects the difficulties met with by his fellow-manufacturers—throws interesting light on the early problems of the rubber machinists. With the grained rolls the foundry-men were tolerably successful, but the grinding of chilled cast hollow rolls for the calender proved to be an exacting task even to the

---

[1] G. Haden, Trowbridge (bought from a Staffordshire firm) 24 January 1855. " One Cylindrical boiler. 20 ft. long 6 ft. 6″ diameter with double fire-place into one tube 30″ dia. Del at Rly Station, Bristol. Weight 6. 15. 1. 7. @ £26.10.0 per ton = £179.5.8 ".

[2] Goodyear had written in 1853 : " It is want of adequate power and corresponding machinery for this purpose, and of that only, that the inventor is dissatisfied with the present state of the manufacture . . . " Until 1821 when he had " a horse mill put up " Hancock's only source of power at Goswell Mews, London, was the manual labour of his workers. In 1834 when it " became necessary to employ steam power it was determined . . . it should be done at Manchester ".

MOULTON'S 'IRON DUKE' CALENDER MACHINE

This was constructed for Moulton in 1849 to American design. The patterns were made at the Bradford Mill, the frame and other castings were supplied from Bristol and the rolls were made at Bilston, Staffs. It is possible that this was the first machine of its kind to be constructed in the United Kingdom.

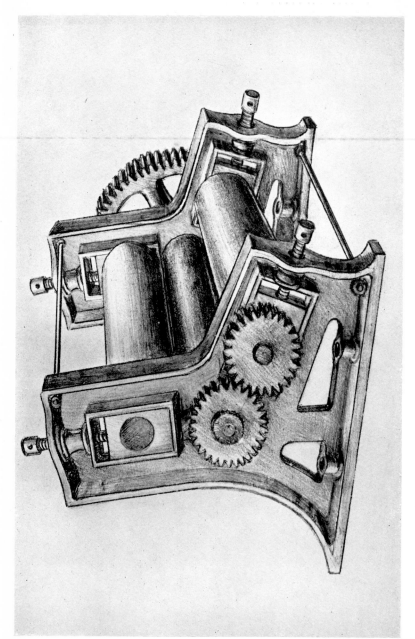

THREE ROLL MIXING AND WARMING MACHINE

Sketch of an early type of machine installed at Perfect dem &

important Bilston Foundry, as the following letter addressed to Moulton makes clear :

7th February 1849

I am extremely obliged for your hints respecting the grinding of the Chilled Rolls—The mode we propose is the Rolls to be placed on Frames thus in horizontal plane and turned round by cogwheels in the direction of the arrows, so that the surface of each rubs against the other ; and also to be at intervals moved sideways, water to be continually running on them, this we think will give an excellent and true surface without using emery.

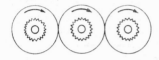

If you can give us any suggestions we shall be very much obliged for them as we hope soon to be able to commence the process . . .

On April 3, 1849, Moulton wrote to Bilston :

I am truly glad to hear that two of the rolls are finished— but how do you intend *to grind the third?* they must be *ground together in the same frame,* or otherwise, they will not be true . . . any mistake *now* would be indeed most serious *to me.* Perhaps you may think of grinding the remaining one with the spoiled one—but we think they should be all ground together on their frame, as *everything* depends upon the truth of the faces of the rolls.   Let me know your decision on the above suggestions . . .

Several months later in July 1849 (after " expensive experience " and " a very serious loss . . . if you could see the number of rolls strewing our foundry yard you would not complain . . . ") the foundrymen regretted to have to inform Moulton:

. . . we find the friction so very great, now that the rolls approach to a smooth surface, that we are compelled to abandon the machinery hitherto in use, and remove the rolls to another place, so that we may be enabled to have the direct power of another engine . . .

But they promised an excellent set of rolls : " . . . for the chill is so hard that coarse emery will not mark them . . . " and eventually, American technique (for the British had worked to American drawings and with the benefit of the accumulated experience of Moulton's American engineer Frost) combined with Stafford-shire skill and Staffordshire pig iron produced " a very fine sett of machinery . . . " that was the envy of the Americans themselves; " we cannot come up to you in finishing the face of goods or the lightness of Rubber put on—we shall be obliged to have some chilled Rolls from England for our machines here . . . " Yet even twenty years later Bristol and Manchester foundrymen were still bemoaning the risks bound up with the production of calender rolls.[1] A notable feature of Moulton's purchases of equipment after the 'sixties is that they were not made in the West Country but with a group of rubber machinists growing up alongside the chief concen-tration of the industry in the Manchester area; one of whom (Crossley Bros.) in 1874 claimed to be able to " come within 1/3000th part of an inch of absolute accuracy in the best and hardest chilled rollers . . . "

At this distance it becomes extremely difficult to apportion the different outgoings incurred in converting and equipping the Kingston Mill; a difficulty increased by the absence of a proper set of account books prior to May 1853, when the first ledger (based on double-entry book-keeping) was begun. Rider's " Estimate of Cost " included the installation of machinery, but Moulton's method was to buy the parts and erect them on the site. There are grounds for suggesting, however (and here the invoices given above and the accounts in Appendix VII are the best evidence available) that the work cost much less than appears in the American estimate. According to the invoices for 1849–50, for example, the cost of conversion, exclusive of the payments made for labour and machinery, cannot have been more than £300; and the greater part of this was for fixtures and fittings bought in Bristol and timber from Bath. On this score, even if a generous allowance is made for

[1] On 31 March 1874 Bush & De Soyres wrote from Bristol : " . . . The roll we had on the lathe has proved a waster, making the third . . . " And when in 1875 Moulton complained of the price asked by Crossley Bros. of Manchester they replied : " . . . rolls never seem worth their money. They are very risky things to make . . . " (Crossley/SM, 4 February 1875).

labour charges the total outlay for converting the mill was much
less than the Americans had expected to pay.

In turning to the early capital supply for the Bradford mill it is
noteworthy that unlike the cotton and woollen manufactures there
was no domestic stage in the evolution of the rubber manufacturing
industry.   Quite apart from the need to supervise the manufacturing
process and the special problems connected with the supply of raw
materials and power the financial outlay required to establish a
rubber manufactory made a concentration of the manufacturing
process inevitable.

American estimates of the capital requirements of the Bradford
mill ranged widely from an absolute minimum of $25,000[1] to
£100/200,000 suggested by William Rider in his " Plan for a
Company " sent to Moulton in November 1847.[2]   Rider did well to
add that the figure of £200,000 " may look to large for your
capitalists " for the Englishman found it difficult to raise even a
tenth of this sum.   Other than the contribution made by Moulton,
which was in the region of £5,000,[3] the source of capital for the
Kingston Mill was threefold.   Firstly, there was the supply of capital
from outside the industry by loans and the sale of part of Moulton's
patent—a source chiefly employed in the purchase of buildings and
equipment.   The principal supporters were Captain Septimus Palairet
of Bradford-on-Avon, who in September 1847 advanced £5,000 for
a fourth share of Moulton's patent, and George Holgate Foster, a
London merchant, who by May 1851, had advanced £11,000 on the

---

[1] WR to SM, 22 September 1847.

[2] WR to SM, 15 November 1847 :
   PLAN FOR A COMPANY.

Make a stock in shares £20 each		£100,000
Of the stock give to Patent...	£40,000	
Sell £20,000 of stock for cash and give it		
Patent as bonus	£20,000	
Sell the balance and use it for Factory and		
working Capital	£40,000	
		£100,000

   Perhaps you will think it would be better to make the Capital
   £200,000 instead of £100,000, if so it should be divided as above—I
   think it should be the larger amount, but it may look to large for
   your capitalists.

[3] The only evidence in support of this is the item of £5,617. 4s. credited as
" Capital " to Stephen Moulton's account in the Company's first ledger on
May 12th, 1854.

security of the Kingston estate and mill equipment.[1] It was one of Moulton's London distributors who first interested this merchant in the Bradford mill, and the original loans were made as security for goods delivered by Moulton to the distributor. In this union of agricultural and mercantile capital the merchant played a most active role. Unlike Palairet, who was content to receive a steady return on his money, Foster did not put one penny into the business until he was satisfied that the venture was worthwhile.[2]

Of the other efforts to obtain financial support from outside the industry Moulton's application in 1849 to a London firm of discount merchants (Amory & Co., of Throgmorton Street), for a loan of £7,500 is of singular interest in that it directs attention to the question of collateral security. The only available security left to the manufacturer after the Kingston estate had been mortgaged was his own bond which he did not hesitate to offer as collateral security for the loan; in this instance (the money being " not readily obtainable at 5% ") without success. In 1851 there was mention of turning to an American commission house in London, although there is no evidence that this source was used.[3] In addition, there were the

[1] George Holgate Foster was the senior partner of G. H. Foster & Co., General Merchants, Moorgate Street, London. On the 7 January 1851, Kirkman, Brown, who had already advanced a certain amount of working capital wrote : " We placed the arrangement before Mr. Foster in this light : for them to advance Kirkman, Brown & Co., of Bradford £1,500 upon £2,000 of their manufactured goods for 4 months bearing interest at 5%, and they charging 2¾% for Commission upon the Invoice. They holding the goods as security and we, K.B. & Co., would . . . give a cheque for the value (of any goods) we should take away, and should the 4 months arrive without any sale having been made we would pay back the £1,500 with the 5% I, @ 2¾% Commission."

[2] A statement submitted by Moulton to Foster caused the latter to write to Kirkman, Brown on 25 January 1851 : ". . . In their account of Stocktaking I find 290 lbs. of Gum valued @ 5/- : £72-10-0 3,500 @ 2/6d : £437-10-0. Chemicals @ £50 — £560. The rest consists of manufactured articles valued £2,564-15-0 . . . I was informed that the articles were valued a little below the selling prices . . . I perceive at full selling prices ; net profit £3,088-16-6d. taken as realized, the great profit which they tell us they gain upon goods unsold. *You cannot submit profits not realized.*" Foster's comment that " It may be difficult to get them into the quiet, sober, jog trot, habits to which we have been accustomed " casts an interesting light on the commercial capitalist's attitude to the rising industrial capitalist.

[3] SM to Thomas Scutt, 10 October 1851 : " My plan of action is this—if our best friend Mr. G. H. Foster will not go on with us—I shall ask him to hold the £11,000 on the security of the mortgage in his hands—and this I will use every endeavour to take up as speedily as possible if he wishes it. Then I think

advances made by the trade itself in anticipation of the supply of manufactured goods. Although Moulton sold his goods to the retailer as well as to the wholesaler the amount of short-term capital provided by London merchants was considerable, and it is doubtful if the Kingston Mill could have commenced manufacture without it.[1] That this accommodation was given against the manufacturer's bond alone (save in one instance where a mortgage of the Kingston estate was demanded), and without any exclusive rights of distribution, provides the strongest evidence of the growing demand for rubber commodities. The chief drawback to this arrangement as far as the manufacturer was concerned, was the attempt made by some distributors to dictate his selling policy. Although this channel of financial assistance appears to have been at its greatest during the first five years of the industry's life, letters written in the early 'sixties show that Moulton was still dependent on these men for a certain amount of working capital.

Some idea of the part played by the country (rural, that is) banks in the financing of a new industry can be gained from a study of Moulton's relations with the Wilts. & Dorset bank at Trowbridge. As this was a pioneering venture it is not surprising that the bank played no part in financing its establishment; nor, at the outset, did it share the opinion of a Bradford correspondent who, in replying to Moulton's letter dealing with the reluctance of the Trowbridge bank to discount his promissory notes, in the spring of 1851, wrote :

> . . . it seems to us almost certain that within a few months we shall not require aid from your Bank but that the business we can get all the credit we want, through an American Commission House here of good standing. The Partners know the nature of our undertaking, and the certainty of its success, by their own knowledge of its just reputation on the other side of the Atlantic. This even if I should succeed would be a poor substitute for Mr. Foster . . . "

[1] Assistance was given by several houses and not always without dispute, e.g. Kirkman, Brown & Co. 28 March 1850 : " . . . why you should be drawing upon us for Wages and etc. when you ought upon the showing of the last statement . . . to be in possession of at least £1,200 passes our comprehension . . . " Price, Coker's letter 14 September 1850 shows them to have advanced (" for no other than manufacturing purposes ") £5,593.7s. and to have received on a /c of sales £346.11s.—Braithwaite & Co. 4 July 1851 : " your observation about the £500 being the dearest you ever borrowed sounds rather like an imputation on our fair dealing, which I am sure you cannot mean. It would strike a casual observer that your paying it back in goods, mostly at Mill prices with the exception of imperfect goods, that it was a very profitable and easy loan to yourself . . . "

D

which must grow out of the Mill will be a great benefit to
the Bank.

In fact the Bank's charges for interest and commission in the
autumn of 1851 show that Moulton was receiving accommodation
in the form of loans, overdrafts, and the discounting of bills and
notes to the extent of several thousand pounds.[1] A fact which
needs to be emphasised here is that these advances were made only
against the security of easily realisable stocks of crude rubber.[2]
Indeed there were periods when every scrap of crude rubber that
Moulton possessed (at the factory as well as in London warehouses)
was in the bank's hands;[3] and occasions when the flow of raw
material to the Kingston Mill was made possible only by the bank

---

[1] Prior to 1851 no important sum was paid to the Wilts. and Dorset Bank
for interest and commission.   For the period 1851-60 the annual totals are as
follows :

1851	£172.19s. 1d.
1852	£ 78.12s. 8d.
1853	£425.10s.
1854	£284.12s.11d.
1855	£237. 6s.10d.
1856	£298.18s. 8d.
1857	£236. 7s. 4d.
1858	£197. 4s. 6d.
1859	£314.19s. 6d.
1860	£422.12s. 3d.

The accommodation in these years ranged from approximately £2–8,000.
On 28 November 1853 the " Balance due to the Bank " was £4,150 ; on 10
May 1854, £5,542.6s.8d. ; and during 1859-60 it was between £6/8,000.
The London and Westminster Bank granted accommodation in 1853 for
£3,000 @ 5%. Source : Cash Book No. 1 and Ledger No. 1. Moulton MSS.

[2] Samuel Provis, Wilts. and Dorset Bank Manager, to SM, 5 September
1854 : "Owing to the Bank £4,452.3.11.   Warrants held as collateral security
[Rubber] to the supposed value of £4,800."   The bank did not hesitate to
realise this collateral if it thought it necessary to do so.   For instance,
Provis to SM, 26 July 1854 : " The Directors will agree to your terms as
to the part due bills of S. Moulton & Co., if L. Bunn & Co., will accept the
bills. They will also renew for three months the note to C. R. Thompson if
he and they (T. & Co.) will consent to the arrangement. But they do the
above on the understanding that the Java Rubber be forthwith sold and the
produce paid to the credit of the Rubber a/c. If you cannot procure sales
for this, the Directors propose to employ their own Broker to sell . . . "

[3] Provis to SM, 28 November 1853 : ". . . it appears necessary that we should
grant you a temporary accommodation of about £1,000 above the value of
the Rubber lodged—this £1,000 I understand you will be able to liquidate
in about eight or ten weeks and that you will give us a lien on the Rubber in
your Mill as security in the meantime with an undertaking to dispose of the
same for our benefit when required."

granting the manufacturer temporary accommodation. Only in 1859 when the business was relatively stable did the bank invest a portion of its capital in the Bradford mill.[1] One conclusion which ought to be recorded regarding the bank's control of the industry's raw material is that the bank did not abuse its power or impede the industry's growth in any way. There were times, however, when the manufacturer thought he was being charged an excessively high rate of interest.[2]

Before leaving the subject of capital supply for the Bradford mill two further points remain to be mentioned. The first of these concerns the temporary loans obtained by Moulton in the 'fifties by the use of promissory notes. These loans were made simply on Moulton's undertaking to pay the money back again; and the bulk of them were made by men who were fully aware of the manufacturer's difficult financial position.[3] The other refers to the influence of the British money market on the establishment and expansion of the Bradford and other early British rubber undertakings. Investigations show that unlike in the United States, where much short-term credit was used for long-term investments, the fluctuations in the money market, especially in the 'forties, did not have the same disturbing effect upon the British as upon the American industry. It was Moulton's ambition to become financially independent of the bank and the mortgagee, and slowly but surely this ambition was realised until by the end of the 'sixties his capital requirements came from ploughing back the profits of his own business. By the 'sixties the manufacturer had done more than place his business on a sound financial basis, he had kept faith with himself.[4]

[1] The outstanding mortgage of £6,000 on the Kingston estate was transferred from the executors of the will of G. H. Foster to the Wilts. and Dorset Bank on 1 July 1859.

[2] Wilts. and Dorset Bank to SM, 11 July 1861: " ... The charge of 6% p.a. is an exceedingly moderate one, the Bank of England minimum rate for the same period averaging 6¾% within a fraction ... if any question be raised upon this point we shall be compelled to call upon you to repay the advance ... "

[3] Ch. VIII.

[4] SM to Thomas Scutt, 18 October 1851: "I must, I will, I can struggle through my present difficulties, great as I feel they are ... and if our business has come through ... what will it not do with our Order Book over-ful in the next 12 months ? And where is the risk to anyone in the assisting us ? Have we not made money the first six months—where is the factory that does this ? Who can expect to make large returns and profits all at once, with a little business and a little capital ? But I will not talk ... "

Having discussed the problems met with in founding the Bradford manufactory a word might be said concerning the tendency towards combination in the early rubber industry.

In the United States the movement can be traced to the earliest days.[1] The Goodyear Shoe Association (of dealers in rubber footwear) and the Union India Rubber Company (a holding company of manufacturers of general rubber products operating under Goodyear licence) were formed in 1848. Moulton had been quick to describe the latter as " . . . a little like a Wall Street cornering. The big ones refuse to pay Goodyear Tariff, so he and they combine together to make the little ones pay the *Union* . . . " But William Rider contended that the holding company, of which he was the treasurer, was not " . . . to use up the little ones . . . " but rather " . . . to help all hands along . . . " Similar forces were at work in England. According to the brief held it might be argued that the Macintosh group were trying to establish a monopoly by threats of proceedings at law under the Hancock patent, or these threats could be interpreted as an appeal to " the respectable portion of the Trade".

Moulton's American partners had no desire to fight a trade war on either side of the Atlantic. In 1847, looking forward to the time when they would iron out the practical difficulties of the hyposulphite patent they urged Moulton to consolidate forces with the Manchester house. Especially, as William Rider insisted in October 1848: " . . . if we go for the big prize, and at the same time look to the security of the matter". If the Macintosh group could be brought to terms, Rider continued, the American and English businesses would " be joined under one head, or divide the business among the three [Moulton, Goodyear, and Macintosh] or combine the Patents and form a Mother concern like the Union Company here giving to others the right to specific articles while the Mother concern sells out rights . . . " If the Macintosh group would not come to terms with Goodyear and Moulton then it would be necessary to consolidate American interests in England.

These letters appear to have had little influence on Moulton. In his opinion there was nothing to be gained at this stage by joining forces with Goodyear, and he was aware of threats made

---

[1] One of the most interesting early American rubber combinations was that formed in 1852 between seven Goodyear licensees whose purpose was to fix minimum prices, discounts, agencies, freight charges and the conditions of barter. See the terms of combinations reprinted by *IRW*, 15 June 1894.

by his own countrymen.[1] Moreover, throughout 1849 the Riders and Moulton (Thomas by this time having dropped out of the picture altogether) were becoming increasingly absorbed in their own separate pursuits, and Moulton came to realise that his chances of success depended not so much on joining forces with others as upon his own enterprise. Yet he erred in thinking that the Riders would give up their share in the English project so easily. To his declared intention to go on alone William Rider wrote in May 1850 :

> . . . The Kingston Mill must make some arrangement with us, or with Goodyear through us, or it will never prosper —Think of this and make up your mind that half or even a quarter of a loaf with security, is better than none—for you will yet be glad to take that, or I am mistaken . . .

Behind this was the agreement of 1847 which the Rider brothers had the power to enforce; but before this letter arrived a new arrangement had been reached with John Rider in England whereby for the next four years the Rider Brothers and Stephen Moulton became partners and joint traders in the manufacture of rubber goods.[2] The next step was to come to terms with the Goodyear group, of which William Rider was a powerful figure, so that they might be a match for Macintosh & Company. " Hence let us study our own interest," Rider wrote, " but we have plenty of time yet." In this he was wrong. Scarcely two years had passed after the signing of the new agreement in May 1850, when the English group struck at Moulton for infringement of patent.

[1] R. Jacques to SM, 20 April 1849 : " Brokerton [Brockedon, Director of Chas. Macintosh & Co.] has told the Chief Clerk of Leaf & Co. that he intends stopping you as soon as you commence and moreover he remarked you have not a leg to stand upon."

[2] It is a matter of regret that the agreement of 1850 has not been preserved. The only evidence of its existence and content is contained in the correspondence of the time.

Chapter III

THE MATERIAL

INDIA-RUBBER is the produce of tropical and semi-tropical regions. Its chief source during the past century and a half has been the *Hevea brasiliensis* tree. Yet, whereas the bulk of nineteenth-century supply came from the wild hevea tree of the northern districts of South America, especially from the Brazilian province of Para, the principal source of supply during the present century (as a result of the transplanting of the hevea species from the Western to the Eastern hemisphere, and its conversion to a plantation industry), has been the tropical regions of the Far East, especially the Malayan Archipelago.

Although many plants yield rubber, indigenous to the temperate as well as to the tropical zone, only a few give enough to be of any commercial value, and it will suffice here to mention the principal forms of nineteenth-century supply.

The chief source of crude rubber in the West was the *Hevea elastica* tree, flourishing in the moist, clayey lands of the Amazon basin and extending over a large district of Central and South America.[1] The most productive of Central American trees was the *Castilla (Castilloa) elastica Cerv.*[2]

Small quantities of this rubber had been landed at British ports since early in the eighteenth century. Out of an approximate total of 6,640 cwts. of all kinds of rubber landed in 1840 (the figure had been in the region of 112 cwts. two decades earlier) 5,912 cwts. came from Brazil. In 1850 Brazilian imports into the United Kingdom amounted to 5,967 cwts. out of a total of 7,617 cwts.; a lead which Brazil retained until 1910,[3] in spite of the relative inaccessability of the dense jungles of the lower regions of the Amazon river, and of the inadequate

---

[1] Including Para, Ceara, Pernambuco, Maranham, Cartagena, Guayaquil, Bahia, Columbia, Cayenne, Peru, West Indies, Colon and Panama, Guatemala, Nicaragua and Mexico.

[2] Belonging to the families Euphorbiaceae and Moraceae.

[3] In 1910 world exports of wild rubber reached an all-time peak of 83,000 tons. The peak year for the whole of S. America was 1912 with total exports reaching 44,000 tons, the bulk of this being " fine hard Para ", the best and highest priced rubber. Cmd. 1678 (1922).

labour supply.[1] Exports to the United Kingdom grew from 5,967 cwts. in 1850 to 228,003 cwts. in 1900.[2]

Except for certain years such as 1869[3] when Para imports showed a sudden decrease—due to a diversion of supplies to North America —receipts at British ports grew throughout the century. In contrast, the exports from other parts of South and Central America—other than Brazil—were small and relatively unimportant. Imports into the United Kingdom from these areas were unenumerated in 1850 and had reached a mere 15,955 cwts. by the end of the century. A marked characteristic of these imports, and an especially serious drawback of Western supply, obviated by the transference of the industry to the Eastern hemisphere, was the seasonal fluctuations dependent, in the main, on climatic conditions. This is brought out in the following table:

IMPORTS OF PARA-RUBBER INTO THE UNITED KINGDOM, 1863-9*

	1863	1864	1865	1866	1867	1868	1869
	tons	tons	tons	tons	tons	tons	tons
January	41	100	340	170	355	515	95
February	285	—	—	90	4	280	285
March	160	215	360	180	130	300	155
April	110	330	130	90	215	400	440
May	210	—	270	300	250	480	195
June	197	195	225	155	—	150	100
July	10	75	190	130	325	90	60
August	23	195	40	—	172	65	55
September	95	125	215	235	37	145	185
October	65	35	—	145	180	150	80
November	178	190	60	145	115	120	120
December	120	130	60	240	185	260	155
Totals	1494	1590	1890	1880	1968	2955	1925

* Extracted from Wright, Roberts & Co's *Prices Current*, 19 January 1870.

[1] In contrast with the future developments of plantation rubber in the Far East an adequate labour force was Brazil's chief problem. Attempts were made to encourage migration of labourers not only from other S. American provinces, but also from Europe and Asia. See: 'Chinese Labour in Brazil', *IRW* 15 June 1893.

[2] Unless otherwise stated the figures in this Chapter are taken from the *Annual Statement of Trade and Navigation of the U.K. with Foreign Countries and British Possessions*. Unlike the records of the American Department of Commerce (whose annual Statement of Trade is calculated from July to June), the British figures cover the calendar year.

[3] A decrease of 1,030 tons from the previous year's imports. Total exports from Brazil increased from 2,785 tons in 1868 to 4,850 tons in 1869.

In the East[1] the *Ficus elastica* tree and *Urceola elastica*,[2] a vine-like plant of the East Indies, yielded the greatest supply of rubber. Ficus is a genus of many species distributed throughout the Indian Archipelago and the islands of the Pacific Ocean. Records exist of the receipt by the Society of Arts in London[3] of specimens of this rubber in 1798. Imports of Asiatic rubber into the United Kingdom however, remained unimportant[4] until the late 'fifties when a rapid increase in deliveries took place from approximately 10,000 cwts. imported in 1857 to 21,808 cwts. imported in 1900.

Commencing in 1885, the official returns of imports into the United Kingdom distinguished between supplies from foreign countries and British possessions. Britain's imports from these possessions (largely in the East) in 1885 amounted to 37,476 cwts., roughly one-fifth of her total rubber requirements. By 1895 they met almost half of her needs, but during the next five years, due to the rapid growth of the rubber manufacturing industry, the proportion declined to about one-sixth: 77,256 cwts. out of a total of 436,030 cwts. Unimportant as these figures are when compared with the gigantic rise in demand in the twentieth century they were, nevertheless, prophetic of future developments and represented a concentration of the world's production of wild rubber in the British Colonies unmatched by any other industrialised nation.[5]

[1] Asiatic supplies came from Assam, Borneo, Rangoon, Penang, Java, Sumatra and British East Indies, including the British Territories in Continental India, Singapore and Ceylon.

[2] Belonging to the families Moraceae and Apocynaceae respectively. One of the first references to this plant is contained in a paper contributed by James Howison, surgeon in Prince of Wales Island, to *Asiatic Researches*, Calcutta, in 1798 entitled: "Some account of the Elastic Gum Vine of Prince of Wales Island, and of experiments made on the Milky Juice which it produces, with hints respecting the useful purposes to which it may be applied." V, 1798.

[3] *Transactions of the Society of Arts*, XXX, 191-2. See especially a letter from James Amos, 12 December 1811, also *Official History of the Royal Society of Arts* by H. T. Wood (London, 1913), 102-5, containing an extract of a letter, 22 February 1811, from Dr. Roxburgh, Superintendent of the Botanic Gardens at Calcutta. In 1838 a report was submitted on *Ficus elastica* by Mr. Wm. Griffiths to Capt. Jenkins, agent in Assam to the Governor-General of India. See *Mechanics' Magazine*, I, No. 30, 425, (1838).

[4] According to the *Mechanics' Magazine*, for Saturday 25 November 1837, 128, "The London Caoutchouc Company impressed with the idea that a large supply ... might be procured from India ... sent an offer of a premium of £50 for the first 1 cwt. of E. India caoutchouc which should be shipped for England."

[5] Evidence of the extraordinary rise of shipments from Rangoon during the last two decades of the century is to be found in the Moulton Company invoices.

By 1920 these possessions met almost two-thirds of the world demand for rubber.

The sources of African rubber were various[1] but unlike the American and Asiatic supplies most African rubber (generally regarded as of inferior quality, although certain kinds such as Madagascar and Mozambique came to be highly valued) was the produce of the giant vines of the *Landolphia* and *Clitandra* species.[2] Small parcels from the coastal settlements and from the Portuguese colony at the mouth of the Zambesi had reached British ports in the early part of the century. The development of this source, however, had to wait until the interior of the continent had been explored by such men as Livingstone and Stanley, who directed attention to the possibility of enlarging the African rubber supply— although the latter was rebuked by the industry for doing so.[3]

African rubber first appears in the official returns in 1864 (Moulton had been buying it since the early 'fifties) when West African imports into the United Kingdom amounted to 3,267 cwts. Official records of East African and South African imports date from 1877 when the following quantities were received: 6,404 cwts. and 2,410 cwts. respectively. Thenceforth imports grew swiftly until by 1900 they stood second only to those from South America.[4] In spite of the enormous problem of communications the penetration and the development of the rich Congo basin was undertaken by a Belgian trading company,[5] and the imports of Congo rubber into the United Kingdom at the end of the century (they first appeared in the official returns in 1889) grew at an unprecedented rate. The extraordinary progress of the growth of African supply is shown

[1] Madagascar, Mozambique, Angola, Congo, Niger, Accra, Sierra Leone, Gambia, Senegal and Mauritius. Historically African rubber dates back to the 1760's when caoutchouc-yielding plants were discovered by Pierre Poivre, French intendant of Mauritius, and by M. Coffigny in Madagascar. Mainland rubber was first mentioned in 1805 by the French botanist Palisot de Beauvois.

[2] Belonging to Apocynaceae. The Landolphia vine was classified by Beauvois in honour of Capt. J. F. Landolphe, a member of the French expedition into the Niger basin.

[3] 15 June 1890, *IRW* : "With all due respect to Mr. Stanley in London . . . how does he know exactly how intensive the Amazon forests are ? The shortness of the Rubber crop coming from the Amazon is never due to the scarcity of trees. It is simply due to the laziness, the incapacity or the scarcity of labour. . . . The world must still look to the Americas for its best rubber."

[4] The figures are : African, 101,739 cwts.; South American, 243,189 cwts.

[5] Société Anonyme Belge pour le Commerce du Haut-Congo, formed in 1883.

by the fact that the imports received by the United Kingdom increased almost tenfold between 1870 (10,369 cwts.) and 1900 (101,739 cwts.).

The supply situation at the outset of the twentieth century may be summarised as follows :

WORLD SUPPLY OF INDIA-RUBBER IN 1900 [1]

	Tons
Amazon District (Brazil, Peru, Bolivia) ...	25,000
Rest of South America	3,500
Central America and Mexico	2,500
Java, Borneo and Eastern Archipelago ...	1,000
E. & W. Africa	24,000
Madagascar and Mauritius	1,000
India, Burma and Ceylon	500
	57,500

Until the coming of the automobile in the twentieth century the supply of wild rubber was able to meet the limited demands of rubber manufacture. In certain years in response to price rises the supply was capable of rapid adjustment, as for example in 1868 when total imports into the United Kingdom were almost twice the amount of the previous year.[2] Serious glut and famine were avoided. The chief fault of wild rubber was its variability rather than inadequate supply. Moreover, the method (or methods, for there was the greatest variation from ordinary tapping to the felling and draining of the trees), of collecting the wild rubber led to a wanton destruction of trees and the exhaustion of certain areas.[3]

[1] *Vice-Consul Temple's Report to the British Government on the State of Amazonas*, 4 June, 1900. (Cd 2-13). Also Temple's *Report on the Trade of Para for the year* 1900, April 3, 1901, Foreign Office, (Cd 129-38).

[2] Total imports of crude rubber into the United Kingdom in 1867, 79,756 cwts. ; 1868, 145,584 cwts.

[3] As for instance with the rise and fall of exports from Java which were slightly less (69,493 lbs. as against 70,336 lbs.) in 1893 than they had been in 1833. In 1863 they had reached an all-time peak of 1,035,200 lbs. " The reason of this state of affairs", wrote a correspondent from Amsterdam in 1867 (Dunlop and Mees to SM, 22 June) "is a very plain one. Rubber has been collected plentifully near the coasts and near the rivers of Java, but the trees having been wantonly destroyed in collecting the Rubber these supplies have ceased altogether. Now the natives are forced to go very deeply into the forests and into the interior, and this they will not do, unless paid very high wages. It is a positive fact that stocks in Holland and Java, and the quantities afloat do not amount to more than ten tons. Two years ago the quantities were near 300 tons . . . " And the same process was being repeated in Africa and America. See also C. R. Markham, *Peruvian Bark* (London, 1880), 441.

Although the advent of the plantation industry in the present century lies outside the scope of this book (production of plantation rubber in 1900 amounted only to 4 tons out of an estimated total production of 53,890 tons),[1] the foundations were laid during the 'seventies of the last century and should not pass unnoticed.

There is abundant evidence in the Moulton papers of the inadequacy of wild rubber but no suggestion of an alternative Eastern plantation suppply.[2] The first steps in this new development were taken by those who knew little or nothing of the day-to-day problems of rubber manufacture,[3] and it is due rather to the foresight and enthusiasm of a small group of botanists and loyal servants of the Government of India that this great enterprise was got under way—a point which needs to be emphasised lest too great importance be given to Sir Henry Wickham's exploit in bringing *Hevea brasiliensis* seeds to the Botanical Gardens at Kew in 1876.[4] If particular credit is owing to any group of individuals for the introduction of this industry to the East it should go to Sir Clements R. Markham, botanist and senior official of the India Office, to Sir Joseph Dalton Hooker,[5] Director at Kew, and to the group of men who worked with them. Markham had already transplanted the quinine-yielding chinchona tree from South America to India and in 1870[6], working closely with Hooker, he turned to the cultivation

[1] F.M.S. Information Agency Handbook, *Rubber Planting* (1922), 21.

[2] The only reference to plantation rubber is the invoice (24 October 1900, Hecht, Lewis & Kahn) for: " 5 lbs. of Plantation Java Rubber @ 3/1 lb.". Wild Java rubber was selling at this time at 2s. per lb. Moulton Invoices, October 1900.

[3] Thomas Hancock was an exception, *op. cit.* 76-77. A very much earlier reference is contained in an article published in *The Bee or Literary Weekly Intelligencer* of Edinburgh on 23 March 1791.

[4] H. L. Fisher, *Rubber and its Use* (London, 1941) 17 : " The Plantations were made possible through the courage, sagacity, and shrewdness of Henry A. Wickham." Also Sir John Clapham, *An Economic History of Modern Britain,* (3 vols., Cambridge, 1926-38), III, 143 : " Back in the 'seventies ... an Englishman had smuggled the seeds of Hevea brasiliensis out of its native country ... " The "smuggling " story does not seem to have grown up around the exploits of James Collins or John Cross who returned to Kew with seeds and plants from Central and South America before Wickham. The latter's account of his exploits is given in his *On the Plantation, Cultivation and Curing of Para India Rubber* (London, 1908). Markham in his writings makes only passing reference to Wickham.

[5] Strangely enough this aspect of his work is unmentioned in *The Dictionary of National Biography*.

[6] C. R. Markham, *op. cit.* 441.

of rubber.   James Collins, formerly Curator of the Museum of the Pharmaceutical Society, was commissioned by the India Office to make preliminary investigations.   In his report, published in 1872, Collins recommended[1] the establishing of plantations in Assam of the indigenous *Ficus elastica* tree and the introduction into India of the South American species.   Supported by the Inspector-General of the Forests of India (and by the Duke of Argyll, Secretary of State for India in the Gladstone Cabinet), effect was given to the former recommendation in 1873.   Markham next turned to the problem of cultivating the hevea and castilla plants.   Preference was given to the latter as it was thought that more suitable sites could be found for them in India and Burma,[2] and in 1875 and 1876 the noted botanist Robert Cross was sent out to Central and South America to collect specimens and report on their requirements regarding climate and soil.[3]   The plants and seeds which he brought back with him,[4] along with those delivered by Wickham, also acting under instructions of the India Office, were soon distributed through the Botanical Gardens at Kew to the tropical colonies.[5]   " Against the apathy and indifference of the Government of India ", wrote Markham in 1894,[6] unheralded and almost unnoticed the nucleus of the plantation industry was formed.

The story of the distribution of these supplies in the nineteenth century is illustrated in the trade circulars and market reports found

[1] *Report on the Caoutchouc of Commerce* by James Collins to the Under-Secretary of State for India, 1872.

[2] C. R. Markham, *op. cit.* Appd. A.

[3] *Report on the Investigations and Collection of Plants and Seeds of the India Rubber Trees of Para and Ceara and Balsam of Copaiba*, by Robert Cross to the Under-Secretary of State for India, 29 March 1877.

[4] Cross collected 600 young castilla plants in 1875.   134 of these were successfully cultivated at Kew and sent on to India in the course of 1876.   In November 1876, he returned from his second expedition with over a thousand hevea plants of which only 34 survived the journey.   In addition he brought 42 ceara plants and 700 seeds.   Wickham's consignment consisted of 70,000 hevea seeds of which 4% germinated.   See " The Caoutchouc Supply from British India", by C. R. Markham, *IRW*, 15 March 1894.

[5] The reports of the Royal Botanical Gardens at Kew, Calcutta and Ceylon 1880-1, quoted by A. M. and J. Ferguson in *India Rubber and Gutta Percha* (Colombo, 1882), 72, 92, 107, show to what extent they were used as the distributing points and experimental stations for new tropical plants.

[6] C. R. Markham, *op. cit.* 462.

among the Moulton papers. It is in part the story of Britain's role as the leading mercantile nation; her ships carried the bulk of the trade and her commodity markets became the distributing points of all types of rubber to Europe and the New World. Born in an era of growing free trade there were few restrictions to impede the development of the industry. Even before the price increases at the end of the century, rubber was a valuable cargo and freight charges never prevented the functioning of a world market.

In the 'fifties most of Stephen Moulton's purchases of Para rubber came from London, while a decade later they came from Liverpool. Although there is abundant evidence of Liverpool's growing importance in American and later the African types of rubber, London's control of the Eastern trade from the mid-century onwards remained almost undisturbed. Neither market secured complete control over the distribution of Western or Eastern rubber, but by 1875 Liverpool had become the principal port in the United Kingdom for this trade :

IMPORTS OF CRUDE RUBBER IN CWTS.

	ENGLAND						SCOTLAND	
	Total*	Liverpool	London	South-ampton	Hull†	Man-chester	Leith	Glasgow
1875	153,564	111,106	28,216	11,766	774	—	1,463	140
1885	180,141	138,068	34,340	1,627	1,161	—	1,385	1,973
1895	341,553	281,411	46,813	3,421	2,763	1,625	1,642	1,870
1900	513,286	387,987	48,100	12,117	44,215	—	10,267	3,203

* Including small shipments not listed here.

† The extraordinary rise of Hull at the end of the century not only reflects the growing volume of trans-shipment of rubber from Continental ports, but also the extent to which Hull was becoming an important gateway to Lancashire and the Midlands.

Liverpool's experience confirms the dictum "Trade begets trade". Merseyside led in this field because the trade pattern was already established before the rise of the rubber industry ; for it was the general contents of the vessel (of which, until the last quarter of the century, rubber formed only a small part)[1], that determined the port

[1] In 1868, 2 tons was the least amount of rubber landed by any one ship at Liverpool, whilst 100 tons was the highest. The heaviest shipload in 1869 was 150 tons. By the 1870's rubber cargoes of between 100/250 tons

of destination. It was to be a very different story with the coming of Eastern plantation rubber during the first World War, and the decline of Western and African supplies. Eastern supplies were landed in the Thames, not in the Mersey, and by the early 'twenties of the present century London (aided by its financial strength and by its excellent warehousing and insurance facilities), had become the leading world market for natural rubber.

Unlike the early London manufacturers who looked to the Thames for their supplies of rubber, as those in Manchester looked to the Mersey, the Edinburgh houses to the Firth of Forth, and the Glasgow establishments to the Clyde, the branch of the industry founded at Bradford-on-Avon did not look towards the neighbouring Severn; for Bristol, once Britain's second port, had little to do with the development of the rubber trade.[1] Indeed, with the constant shift in the centre of gravity of the economic life of the nation to the North and North-West the tide of events had ebbed for Bristol just as surely as it had flowed for Liverpool. While the nucleus of the rubber industry in the West Country found shelter in the abandoned woollen mills along the side of the Avon and its tributaries, it turned more to the Mersey and to the Thames for its raw materials, and as an outlet to its foreign markets, than to the Avon. In this respect the Bradford manufactory was closer to the London natural rubber market than its chief competitor in Manchester—much more so than the principal Scottish house in Edinburgh. Where Liverpool and the growing American trade was concerned Bradford-on-Avon was at a disadvantage. Yet as it cost more to transport the finished product than the raw material, nearness to the metropolis was of greater importance to Moulton than nearness to the supplies of crude rubber.

Although by the end of the century Liverpool had become the chief market for rubber, it would be false to assume from the

were not unusual, and in February 1875 *S.S. Paraenese* brought to Liverpool the largest rubber cargo ever shipped in one vessel, viz. : 524 tons. In this month there arrived also *S.S. Cearenese* with 242 tons and *S.S. Augustine* with 285 tons. Thenceforth rubber cargoes became of increasing importance to the shipping lines. (Moulton MSS.)

[1] There are, however, examples in the Moulton papers of rubber being dealt in at Bristol. Gwyer & Son of Bristol/SM (10 July 1854) offered Moulton " . . . a parcel of about 5 tons African . . . at 1/- per lb. . . . we have very often some of it for sale". And on 22 August 1860 Messrs. Barnard, Thomas & Son of Bristol auctioned 14 casks of West African rubber, part cargo of the *James Hey* just arrived from the West Coast of Africa. *Bristol Advertiser*, 14 August 1860.

figures of total deliveries at British ports given above that the influence of the Liverpool commodity market over internal distribution was in proportion to Liverpool imports. It is impossible to say precisely what part of these imports found their way to the London market, but a comparison of the stocks of rubber held in London and Liverpool on the 1st January for the ten years 1871–80 shows that London played a much more important role in the home trade than the landing figures would suggest :

LIVERPOOL [1]

	1871	1872	1873	1874	1875	1876	1877	1878	1879	1880
Para	190	970	450	1,250	685	870	825	820	555	575
African ...	145	70	75	100	175	85	100	75	75	60
Sundries ...	75	95	120	105	15	60	56	—	20	9
Tons	410	1,135	645	1,455	875	1,015	981	895	650	644

LONDON

	1871	1872	1873	1874	1875	1876	1877	1878	1879	1880
E. India and Madagascar...	383	346	606	906	823	861	806	792	661	274
W. India and Para ...	82	112	162	200	125	93	116	167	122	30
Tons	465	458	768	1,106	948	954	922	959	783	304

While these figures leave no doubt about Liverpool's predominance in the American trade Mincing Lane never abandoned its traditional right to handle this or any other branch of ' Colonial produce '. In 1867 Stephen Moulton was assured by a London house that: " We can and *must* do as well for you as at Liverpool " ; and where quotations for Fine Para differed on these two markets, London was always prepared to make a bid, even if it meant cutting prices, to retain a share of the Para trade. The London market, relying on Liverpool for American deliveries,[2] retained an important part of the home

[1] Extracted from *Melchers Runge & Co.'s Circular*, 1 January 1880. (Moulton MSS.)

[2] The impression gained from the *Trade Circulars* and *Market Reports* is that about one-third of the rubber landed at Liverpool was sent on to London by rail.

trade in all kinds of rubber, just as it continued to be a centre for re-exports. It is also evident from the sales notes and the merchants' lists of the time that the London market held a much more exclusive control over the sale of the Eastern types than Liverpool did over the Western. Only rarely in the nineteenth century was East India rubber landed at a northern port or handled in any quantity by a northern market—an important factor when the development of the eastern plantation industry diverted shipments to the port of London.

A decisive influence in the British crude rubber market in the second half of the nineteenth century was the extent and direction of the export trade. According to the *Expositor* the figures for the earlier decades of the nineteenth century are as follows :

Year	Imports	Exports
1820	112 cwts.	46 cwts.
1830	1,322 ,,	364 ,,
1840	6,148 ,,	1,345 ,,

Year	Total Imports of Crude Rubber into the U.K.[1]	Total Exports of Crude Rubber from the U.K.
1850	7,617 Cwts.	1,048 Cwts.
1860	43,039 ,,	12,895 ,,
1870	152,118 ,,	50,737 ,,
1880	169,587 ,,	76,732 ,,
1890	264,008 ,,	142,524 ,,
1900	513,286 ,,	293,624 ,,

Taken over the whole period about one-half of the total imports were re-exported to other countries. In the 'fifties the proportion was much below this. In the last decade of the century, stimulated by the demands of the growing transportation and electrical industries overseas, Britain's exports of crude rubber were almost three-fifths of her total imports. Whatever the factors tending to

[1] Source : *Reprint of the Statistical Abstract and Annual Statement of Trade of the U.K.*

increase or decrease the general level of European industrial activity they were quickly reflected in the demand for crude rubber from Britain.

The relative share of London and Liverpool in this export trade can be seen from the following table :

TOTAL EXPORTS OF CRUDE RUBBER FROM LONDON AND LIVERPOOL, IN CWTS.

Year	London	Liverpool
1850	Unenumerated	Unenumerated
1860	7,238	1,303
1870	13,928	25,394
1880	27,613	31,967
1890	28,446	91,956
1900	23,566	182,558

Of these overseas sales, those to the United States were of singular importance. Enjoying an unparalleled development in the rubber manufacturing industry America quickly became the world's greatest consumer of rubber, and remained so; and unlike the British, American re-exports were negligible. The position in 1900 was as follows :

CONSUMPTION OF CRUDE RUBBER[1]

	Tons
United States and Canada - -	21,000
United Kingdom - - - -	21,000
Rest of Europe (excepting U.K.) -	15,500
	57,500

Until the Civil War interrupted the flow of commerce, approximately one-half of Britain's exports of natural rubber were absorbed by this market. In 1864 the figure had fallen to about one-sixth, 4,825 cwts. out of a total of 29,107 cwts. It recovered rapidly under the impetus of the post war boom, fell again during the business recession of the early 'seventies—in 1875 it stood at one-tenth of Britain's total exports—and then grew steadily until by 1886 America again took one-half of Britain's exports, 51,766 cwts. out of a total of 111,437 cwts. This level of demand

[1] Vice-Consul Temple's Report (Cd. 129-38).

E

continued for the remaining years of the century. Whilst these changes arose in part from speculative influences as well as the attempts of certain American importers to obtain supplies directly from South America, they are largely to be accounted for by the changing course of general business activity.

The decisive nature of the American trade is reflected in the numerous references made to it in the trade circulars and correspondence of the time. The falling off in total imports from Para into the United Kingdom, as in 1869 and 1878, was a direct result of the sudden growth of American demand. " India-Rubber is all on the move ", wrote a London merchant, " since a telegram reached us yesterday from Para stating that the Yankees had paid as much as 2/1d for Fine Para in order to cut out the European buyers—there being very little Rubber available."[1] And the same house wrote several years later: ". . . the market is practically not dependent, or at least only to a slight extent, upon the requirements of the home trade, but principally upon the consumption in the United States ; the latter being nearly double the quantity of ours here . . ."[2] Whilst American activity on the British rubber market stiffened demand, there were occasions—due to speculative influences—as in 1868 when American action in returning consignments to the United Kingdom caused a break in prices.[3]

The principal markets on the Continent in the nineteenth century were Germany, France and Russia. Given below is a list of Britain's chief markets for crude rubber throughout the half century.

The chief shipments went to Hamburg, Amsterdam, Rotterdam, Le Havre and St. Petersburg, though with the exception of the supplies sent to St. Petersburg (centre of the Russian industry) it is not known what proportion of these shipments were in transit to the European hinterland, particularly those sent to the Dutch and German ports. One of the characteristics of this Continental trade was that some of the less enviable kinds of rubber—such as pressed Guayaquil and Carthagena because of their bad reputation for false

[1] Heilbut, Symons & Co. to SM, 28 June 1878.

[2] H. S. & Co. to SM, 6 August 1885.

[3] W. Wright to SM, 18 January 1868 : " American stocks became almost into one hand, who for the moment ruled the market . . . in November and December the Cable between this [country] and the United States brought into requisition the large stocks held there, and Rubber for the first time was sold for shipment per steamer, which rapidly caused a decline . . . "

packing—were exported almost completely.[1] Thus Continental buyers were often the first to make experiments with new grades.[2]

PRINCIPAL COUNTRIES OF EXPORT FOR CRUDE RUBBER FROM THE UNITED KINGDOM

	1850 cwts.	1860 cwts.	1870 cwts.	1880 cwts.	1890 cwts.	1900 cwts.
Russia	349	688	7,710	16,189	20,148	55,897
Hanse Towns ...	441	—	—	—	—	—
Prussia	—	1,963	1,445	—	—	—
France	5	4,325	8,318	9,920	12,022	15,600
Germany	—	—	—	18,921	38,282	55,534
Sweden	—	—	—	—	—	4,076
Hanover	—	1,776	—	—	—	—
Denmark	—	—	—	—	—	1,613
Holland	55	—	4,595	7,182	8,482	6,613
Hamburg	—	2,771	15,908	—	—	—
Belgium	198	872	2,335	—	1,853	8,059
Bremen	—	—	1,702	—	—	—
Portugal	—	—	—	—	—	719
United States ...	—	314	7,853	21,941	57,863	134,987
Italy...	—	—	—	—	3,285	5,375
Spain	—	—	—	—	—	316
British Possessions...	—	—	—	—	108	276
Austria and Hungary	—	—	—	—	—	2,920
Others	—	186	871	2,579	481	1,639
Total (cwts.) ...	1,048	12,895	50,737	76,732	142,524	293,624

Small quantities of rubber were exported from the Continent to the United Kingdom but with the exception of those from Rotterdam and Amsterdam the majority were indirect shipments.

[1] See *Wright, Roberts & Co.'s Circular,* 19 January 1870 : " *Carthagena.* Owing to a system of false packing which prevailed more or less in the year's [1869] imports, manufacturers refused to purchase. The sales made in this description have been entirely for export." Also *Wright, Roberts & Co.'s Circular,* 20 January 1871. It is a noticeable fact that the average price of crude rubber imported into the U.K. was higher than the average price of that exported (in 1889 for example 231s. cwt. against 209s.) which suggests that the British manufacturer normally retained the superior and exported the inferior kinds.

[2] G. L. *Newmann & Co.'s India Rubber Statement,* 12 February 1866 : " The foreign manufacturers were the first, who appreciated the virtue of this Rubber, and not till a few years ago, English Mills began to masticate West India-rubber."

Although the receipts from Holland were unimportant in volume, they cast an interesting light on an older phase of Dutch history. With the British the Dutch can claim to have been one of the first to have undertaken the sale and distribution of this commodity in Europe, and the rubber market, founded at Amsterdam in the 'forties, was watched closely by British traders.[1]   The impression existed that the Eastern supplies sold by the Netherlands Trading Company were of better quality than those coming onto the London Market: " . . . from observations I am led to the conclusion that the quality shipped direct from Batavia to Holland by Dutch Houses is better than that shipped to this port . . ."[2] concluded a London broker in 1860.   The Dutch had a good name not only in the quality of their Eastern rubber, but also in the African sorts.   " Mr. Norris assures me ", wrote another dealer in 1868,[3] " that the Ball African he has got from time to time from Rotterdam is vastly superior to anything he has had from either the London or Liverpool markets in point of quality"; and to secure these supplies, English and Scottish houses were often prepared to pay a higher price in Amsterdam or Rotterdam than in London or Liverpool.[4]

The last decade of the century saw the rise of Antwerp[5] as a distributing centre, especially for Congo rubber.   This development is not only important because of the inroads made into the Liverpool trade but also because the interference of the Belgium Government in the distribution of Congo supplies foreshadowed the action of other governments in the twentieth century.[6]

[1] " My chief object was to let you know how the [Dutch] market looked at the moment . . . as it was my duty to let you have any information received from Holland . . .", wrote Moulton's London broker in 1859.   A little earlier he had asked for " . . . instructions to secure some more Fine in Holland at a given price laid down here . . ."

[2] J. Brown/SM, 8 December 1860.

[3] Peacock & Co./SM, 25 January 1868.

[4] J. Brown/SM, 8 December 1860 : " It would be well to consider their points [The Dutch were asking 1d. lb. more than the London market].   The Dutch have the pick of nearly all the Rubber produced and therefore the best comes from Java direct."

[5] The deliveries at Antwerp (chiefly African sorts) had grown in the last decade of the century from practically nothing to 5,000 tons in 1900.

[6] The growing belief that those who controlled the source should also control the distribution of crude rubber was reflected in the increased shipments not only to Antwerp at the end of the nineteenth century, but also to Le Havre, Lisbon and Hamburg.

Variability and shifting price levels made the proper choice of wild rubber one of the greatest hazards of early manufacture. All sorts and conditions of rubber came on the market, depending on the source, the season, the method of gathering and even of transporting the produce. There was no guarantee that two packages of the same consignment would be alike. Whilst many methods were employed in selecting rubber the only true test of its suitability for a particular purpose was to use it in manufacture; and this was true not only of certain grades of African and Asiatic rubber but also of the celebrated Para.[1]

The following list shows the principal descriptions of rubber offered for sale in 1879 :

1 Fenchurch Avenue,
London, E.C.

24th March, 1879.

Messrs. S. Moulton & Co.
Bradford on Avon.

Gentlemen,
    Below we beg to give you our to-day's quotations for INDIA RUBBER, and solicit the favor of your commands.

Yours respectfully,

MELCHERS, RUNGE & Co.

RE-WEIGHTS ON DELIVERY

AFRICAN	s. d. s. d.		s. d. s. .
Ball Congo	—	Tongues, Medium and Bold	1/2 1/2
„ Small...	1/2 1/2	Tongues, Small	—
„ Soft	11	Thimbles	1/10
Mixed (Ball and Flake) ...	1/3		
Knuckles	10	ASSAM	
Lump	10	Ball, Prime	1/– 1/2
Flake	8 1/2	„ Good	1/5
Negrohead Loanda ...	—	„ Fair	1/4
„ Sierra Leone ...	1/5	„ Ordinary	1/1 1/3

[1] Para rubber normally consisted of three chief types : " Fine ", " Entrefine" and " Negro-head " or " Seramby." " Fine " rubber was well smoked (achieved by the native revolving a wooden paddle above a smoke-fire until several layers of dried latex formed themselves into a "ball " or " biscuit " of hard rubber), and was therefore free of water and proteid matter which encouraged putrefaction and reduced elasticity. " Entrefine " rubber had been insufficiently smoked, or even burnt by the native and fetched a slightly lower price. " Seramby " or " Negro-head " consisted of scraps and strips of latex peeled off the bark of the tree, and was generally suspected of heavy adulteration.

RE-WEIGHTS ON DELIVERY—*continued*

	s.d. s.d. s.d.		s.d. s.d. s.d.
Slab, Prime ... ... —		MOZAMBIQUE	
„ Fair ... ... —		Ball, Picked 1/5 1/2	
Mixed (Ball and Slab) ... —		„ Good 1/5	
		„ False Packed ... 1/2 1/2 1/3	
BAHIA —		Sausages ... ... —	
		Liver ... ... —	
BORNEO			
New 1/3		NICARAGUA	
Old 1/4		Sheets, Thin ... ⎫	
		„ Medium ⎬ 1/9 1/2	
CEARA		„ Thick ... ... —	
Scraps ... ... —		Scraps, Prime ... —	
		„ Fair 1/7 1/2	
EAST INDIA		PARA	
Singapore ... ... ⎫		Fine, spot, New ... 2/1	
Penang ... ... ⎬ 1/8		„ „ Old ... —	
		„ Delivery 2/1	
GUATEMALA —		Entrefine 2/-	
		Negrohead, spot, New 1/5 1/2	
GUAYAQUIL AND CARTHAGENA		„ „ Old —	
Pressed ... ... —		„ Delivery... 1/5 1/2	
Slabs 1/2 1/2			
		RANGOON	
MADAGASCAR		Ball, Prime ... ⎫	
Pinky 1/- 1/2		„ Fair ... ⎬ 1/5 1/2	
Black ... ... —		Slab, Prime ... ⎬	
Mixed, Pinky and Black —		„ Fair ... ⎭	
		Mixed (Ball and Slab)... —	

On arrival in the United Kingdom the rubber was disposed of by private or public sales, the commodity markets of London and Liverpool being the centres of this trade. The Liverpool auctions were held either at the brokers' office or in the Public Sales Room at the Exchange building. London sales were normally held at the Commercial Sales Rooms, Mincing Lane. The procedure was usually the same: the lots were briefly advertised in the Press and auction lists sent to the trade. No mention of weights (which varied with case, cask, bag, and basket from 80-300 lbs.), was made on the auction list; and whether the sale was by inspection (which meant that the goods could be examined in the different warehouses), or by sample, the buyer ran heavy risks.[1] On occasions even the

---

[1] Jackson & Gardner/SM, 23 September, 1869 : " The owners will not sell by sample but by inspection, which makes it very risky to buy, as it is impossible to say to what extent it may be false packed."

experts refused to predict the outcome of a sale.[1] In addition to the purchase price the buyer was expected to pay " Lot Money " (a small charge made by the auctioneer at a public Sale), brokerage, rent[2] (if the goods remained stored at the docks), and (where a specific consignment was bought " to arrive "), Landing Charges.[3] Allowance for tare varied from 3% to 15% of the weight of the parcel. The accompanying invoice illustrates the conditions of purchases made in 1850 from a London house. If Moulton's purchases were representative most trade was done by private sales from store.[4] Nevertheless the public auctions served a very real purpose in that they set the standard for the rest of the market.[5]

Until the appearance of a futures market at the end of the century Moulton either bought rubber from ' spot ' (i.e. current) supplies or ' to arrive '. As it was generally understood that the importers or merchants would supply the manufacturer with a particular type of rubber at a fixed price as soon as it became available, the earliest

[1] Kirkman Brown/SM, 26 March 1850 : " Any opinion as to value would be quite useless as everything must necessarily depend upon the competition . . . ", and two hundred tons expected to be taken up at a Liverpool auction in 1866 were withdrawn for want of bidding. Jackson & McCullochs/ SM, 27 September 1866.

[2] Where the rubber was allowed to remain in dock warehouses, either for want of storage space at the factory or because it was intended to resell it, the broker made a charge for " Rent and Commission " at ⅓d. per cwt. per week. J. Brown/SM, 15 April 1862.

[3] In 1886 details of these Landing Charges were as follows :
" Landing, Piling and Weighing 5½d. per cwt. gross. Taring (only 1 bag in 20 to be tared), 1/3½d. per bag. Sampling (only 1 bag in 20 to be sampled), 2/- per bag." Hecht, Levis & Kahn/ SM, 14 January 1886.

[4] W. Wright & Co./SM, 20 March 1875 : "Total imports (into Liverpool) for the last 3 months are 2,265 tons, while the total sales only represent 562 tons, it is thus perfectly evident that large quantities of Rubber, especially Para, must find its way to the manufacturers without coming on the open market, the result no doubt of forward contracts so that considerable quantities must have been forwarded from store."

[5] Jackson & Till, Liverpool to SM, 9 April 1861: " Buyers with us are waiting to see if our present prices will be maintained at the coming sales . . . " and on 20 November 1875, W. Wright & Co., wrote : " In order to test the market fairly importers resolved some little time ago to revive the old practice of offering by auction . . . to be repeated monthly, which will give buyers and manufacturers the opportunity of selecting from larger quantities than are generally offered by Private [sales], and also establishing the current price of the day."

contracts for forward delivery bore no delivery date.   The following English and Dutch contracts illustrate this :

(English Contract)   18, Hackins Hey, Liverpool,
                                                    18th August, 1868.
Messrs. S. Moulton & Co.

WE HAVE this day bought for you the following Goods :—
5 Tons African Ball Rubber @ 1/2¼d. lb. from the quay to be delivered out of the first arrival of Ball Rubber on sellers account and to be the usual current quality known as Ball Rubber.

Customary allowances and Public Sale Conditions.
Payment—Cash within 14 days, and before delivery, if required, less 2½% discount, from delivery.
Any dispute on this Contract to be settled by arbitration here in the usual way.

Your obedient Servants,
JACKSON & GARDNER, *Brokers.*

(Dutch Contract)

BOUGHT FOR a/c of Messrs. Stephen Moulton & Co., off Mr. N. Breelaart agent for Messrs. Goll & Co., Amsterdam.

About Five (5) Tons (More or less) Java Rubber expected to arrive per " Philip Van Marnix " from Java to Amsterdam at Two shillings and one penny (2/1d.) per lb. English nett weight. F.O.B. a steamer (at Amsterdam) for London or Hull ; at the buyer's option : the quality guaranteed to be fair average, and merchantable condition—if inferior in quality to the above guarantee or damaged, the Rubber is to be taken by the buyers at an allowance which is to be settled by the arbitration of sworn Brokers in Amsterdam, in the usual manner.

To be paid for by buyers acceptance payable in London at Two (2) months from date of shipment per steamer to London or Hull.

Any dispute that may arise, to be settled by the arbitration of sworn brokers in Amsterdam in the usual manner.   If the vessel be lost this contract to be void, as also for any portion not arriving.

London.   25th October, 1860.   J. BROWN.

Of necessity, rubber sold "to arrive", unlike "spot" sales which could be inspected and sampled, was sold by description, the seller guaranteeing that the quality would be "fair average, and merchantable condition," or "a fair average sample of the season". The minimum unit of contract was (and still is) five tons. The manufacturer did not enter into a forward contract (it became increasingly common during the last quarter of the nineteenth century for a delivery date to be inserted into such a contract), in the hope of making a profit or avoiding a loss. He was concerned with the physical delivery of the commodity, not with the hedging of price risks. In fact, the market for rubber futures, as distinct from that for "spot" sales or forward delivery, is a relatively new development arising out of the rapid growth of the industry at the end of the nineteenth century. Before the 'eighties the manufacturer obtained his supplies in the "actuals" market for "spot" or forward delivery.

The chief needs of the Bradford house were met from "spot" supplies, despite the fact that on occasions the price for forward delivery was a fraction below that for "spot". Moulton not only preferred to see what he was buying,[1] he also shared the view that forward contracts were responsible for sudden price fluctuations; and there is a good deal of evidence available to support what appears to be a rather paradoxical opinion.[2] In 1870 forward contracts "created a fallacious demand . . . as deliveries become due, sellers are compelled to come into the market and purchase on the best terms they can . . ."; and the comparative calm of 1871 was explained by their total absence.[3]

By the 'nineties the buying and selling of futures, chiefly by the non-manufacturing interests, had become an accepted practice.[4] It reduced the inherent price risks borne by all branches of the trade, and enabled the manufacturer to safeguard his supplies over a longer period. Like the market for forward contracts (discharged by the

[1] J. Brown/SM, 22 February 1859: "I well know your determination not to buy for arrival . . ."

[2] Wright, Roberts & Co./SM, 20 January 1871. *Annual Report.*

[3] Wright, Roberts & Co./SM, 19 January 1872. *Annual Report.* In 1870 Para ranged from 3s.7½d. to 2s.8d. The prices in 1871—in the absence of forward contracts—showed a range of only 5½d. from the highest to the lowest quotations ; and even that was attributed to the large export demand felt in June and July.

[4] *IRW.* 15 September 1892, " Selling Futures in the Rubber Trade ".

delivery of the rubber), the market for futures contracts[1] (normally fulfilled by taking out another contract and settling the difference in cash), was stimulated by the growing uniformity of rubber which the twentieth century plantation industry made possible. Of greatest significance to the manufacturer was the fact that the improved trading procedure enabled him to carry smaller stocks of crude rubber.[2]

In addition to the purchases of " spot " and futures contracts there were occasions when Moulton bought parcels of rubber lying at Para, subject to being unsold before the vessel sailed, but this type of contract was an exception. One very good reason why the early rubber manufacturers rarely bought direct from Brazil was the fact that Liverpool prices were frequently below the corresponding price quoted in Para. There is no evidence that Moulton made such direct purchases either from the United States or from the East.

Until now nothing has been said of the rubber broker, but in all these transactions he was the manufacturer's constant guide and ally, and there can be no doubt that in the early years of this industry (whilst Moulton sometimes attended the public sales at Liverpool and London himself),[3] he was an essential link between the manufacturer and the raw material. He not only reported but appraised and assessed changing market conditions, and there were few days when he did not send some item of market intelligence to Bradford. No aspect of the home and export trade, or conditions, in the

[1] Whilst futures had been available since the last quarter of the nineteenth century (there can be no doubt that futures contracts grew out of the market for forward contracts, and at times in the early correspondence it becomes difficult to distinguish between the two), the London Rubber Exchange, controlled by the Rubber Trade Association, did not commence operations until 1921. In this market the continuous adjustment of futures contracts is made through the Settlement House.

[2] Which meant a considerable economy in the use of circulating capital : J. Brown /SM, 21 September 1853. " As you say you have Rubber on hand for a twelve month . . . " But thirty years later two or three months' stock was normal. For instance SM/Hecht, Levis & Kahn, London, 30 July 1886, " . . . we should not again be in the market before September." In this connection it has to be remembered that the rubber had to be dried for several months on arrival at the factory.

[3] There is in the Moulton MSS. a Liverpool sales sheet for 1855 with the top corner turned back, and on it is written in Stephen Moulton's handwriting " Had a row with the Birleys and bought the lot." Clearly the orthodox approach to a study of market conditions can have its limitations.

producing countries, escaped him. On his advice the manufacturer entered or withdrew from the market. "There is a prospect of Rubber being dearer", wrote Moulton's broker in 1863, "and I therefore write to prepare you—if an order even of 30 tons was to come onto the market a start of 1d. or 2d. (per lb.) might be the immediate effect . . ."[1] There were also occasions when he was not afraid to exercise his own judgment in order to catch the market on the turn :

> If I had not bought but had run the risk of another post . . . and if prices had gone up, and you had blamed me for not taking the responsibility upon myself, of course I could shield myself by simply referring you to your letter of instructions. Fortunately for me the market is firmer . . . I did not like to let the parcel slip as you approved the quality and there is not much good Rubber here . . .[2]

The broker played a vital role both in the buying and selling of rubber :

> From information that I have just received I fear that in about a week we shall have an arrival of about 150 tons of Para Rubber in one ship . . . as you say you have Rubber on hand for a twelve-month I should imagine you would act wisely to get out of any super abundant stock that you may hold . . . if therefore you forward me per return a few of the Warrants of the parcels at Smith's Warehouse and if you like to send back the bottles and scrap which you last purchased I will house them for you in another Warehouse and will do all in my power to assist you with whatever you want to get rid of. I fear we shall have a sudden and heavy fall in prices as soon as the news oozes out. Act with promptitude and all will be right . . .[3]

Sometimes he sold rubber not to avoid price falls but because it had proved unsuitable in manufacture: "The 65 cwts. of African Ball Rubber received from you on May 13th we should like to sell again as it does not suit us . . .", wrote Moulton in 1871. In addition, the broker's help in arranging credit terms (discussed in Chapter VIII below) must have been of considerable importance to the small manufacturer with limited capital resources.

[1] J. Brown/SM, 7 January 1863.
[2] J. Brown/SM, 3 August 1861.
[3] J. Brown/SM, 21 September 1853.

One of his most important functions was to safeguard the manufacturer from the worst abuses of adulterated produce—in one instance from " 5 cases of infernal deception ". The inability of the trade to classify raw rubber according to its quality provided the manufacturer with his most serious grievance. Whilst Moulton normally expected a loss of say 10—15% on Fine Para to 30—45% on parcels of Mozambique and African, the extraordinary variability of this produce made it impossible for him (or his broker) to estimate (prior to washing it) what the cost of the dried rubber would be; and the higher the price the more keenly did he feel the loss of buying an uncertain amount of mud, sand and stones. In the case of certain kinds such as Ceara and Assam (and on the Continent for African varieties as well) classification according to quality had been achieved by the end of the century, but for the most part (until the more uniform supplies of the plantation industry made themselves felt), the buying and selling of wild rubber continued to be a most hazardous undertaking. It was not the lack of good will in the rubber trade that occasioned these difficulties but the extraordinary character of the produce handled. As late as 1899 the *India-Rubber Journal* was moved to describe some of the rubber imports as: " . . . not rubber, but dirt and mud with just sufficient rubber to keep it together . . . "[1] The fault lay in the methods of collecting the latex and in the extensive adulteration taking place in the producing areas. To remedy this the broker was as helpless as the manufacturer himself.

In addition to the losses entailed in cleaning adulterated rubber there was also the problem of rubber drying in storage.[2] It was not unusual for rubber on its way from the East to lose 25-30% of its weight ; while storage in the docks, even for as short a period as a fortnight, could result in a further loss of anything up to 10%. As the custom was that all East India supplies were sold at landing weights, (" a stupid one we must confess ")[3] there was no telling what the loss in weight might be until the rubber was reweighed at the factory. The manufacturer's grievance was that he often paid for a larger quantity of rubber than he eventually received. In this problem, as in others, the manufacturer turned to his broker for assistance: " We will lose no opportunity ", wrote Moulton's

[1] *IRJ*, 10 July 1899.

[2] As the latex issues from the tree it consists approximately of 2/3 water and 1/3 dry rubber content. Other constituent elements of the fluid are resins, proteins, phosphates and carbonates.

[3] Heilbut, Symons & Co./SM, 21 June 1860.

broker in 1865, "to try to establish reweighing [on delivery from the docks] as a custom, but it is very difficult to disturb old practices."[1] But customs arising out of the inherent conservatism of the East India trade eventually gave way before constant protests, and in the late 'seventies East India rubber was sold subject to reweighing on delivery.

For these and many other services the broker was paid 2% of the invoice shared equally by buyer and seller. The relation between broker and principal, however, went beyond the buying of the cheapest and best rubber. Moulton treated his broker as confidant and friend. At times he entertained him in his house and fed him at his board. In sickness he supported him, and when the broker died he arranged with the importers from whom he had bought the bulk of his supplies to continue paying brokerage to support the widow—a generous act in any age.

The last quarter of the century saw changes in this field of commerce as in many others. Three or four of the largest importers came to dominate the trade[2] and attempts were made to exclude those who stood between importer and manufacturer. An importer wrote to Moulton in 1872:

> We will charge you neither commission nor brokerage and you will clearly see from our offer and terms that we are anxious to have direct transactions with you. It happens so often that we sell imports and other lots in the market to buyers who purchase on your orders, and therefore must earn a further commission, that we cannot help thinking a direct intercourse must prove to be of mutual advantage . . .[3]

But the importer (whilst prepared to sell without commission or brokerage) was neither able nor prepared to give the guidance and support which the broker had rendered in earlier days:

> We regret that with your late purchases you have not been fortunate, but we hardly think you can blame us for that.

[1] J. Brown/SM, 23 March 1865.

[2] H. J. Green & Co., brokers, London/SM, 21 May 1886 : " We may mention that this lot is not in the hands of either of the two large Hebrew houses who so largely control the trade, and render the efforts of young beginners in the trade so hard a nut to crack."

[3] Hecht, Bros., London/SM, 5 September 1872. Also T. Stiff & Co., Brokers, London/SM, 28 April 1876 : " We have in this instance given you the sellers' names, but never again ask us to pass names as we do not do it. We never before gave up our seller but once and then the buyer was un-handsome enough to do the business in future direct."

Knowing the great uncertainty of the movements of the rubber market we are at all times unwilling to express an opinion, much less offer advice. All we can do is to put before you the facts as they present themselves, leaving it to you to decide whether to act upon them or not . . . [1]

At the end of the century an established manufacturing business with a plentiful supply of capital could afford to dispense with some of the services which the broker had rendered in earlier times. The variability of rubber had not lessened but improvements in manufacture, such as the wider use of ' fillers ' and reinforcing agents, and the extension of the market to commodities such as lower grade footwear, made it practicable to employ a greater quantity of the inferior grades. The buying policy of the Bradford company was well expressed in a letter written in 1886: " We have always made it a rule not to run about trying to better ourselves which we are constantly being advised we can. We never change for change sake . . . "[2] A policy which applied to aspects of supply other than rubber.[3]

In the case of textile and chemical supplies there is little that calls for special comment. Apart from the direct imports of cotton duck fabric from his American partners in 1850, Moulton's requirements of sheeting and fabric were met almost exclusively by the same Manchester wholesalers.[4] Prior to the American Civil War which cut off the chief source of raw cotton, Moulton purchased best cotton fabric at 2s. to 3s. per yard. In August 1862 the price was "3/6 per yard *today* ". By November it had risen to 4s.; and in October of the following year (1863) " it was impossible to give a quotation to hold for more than a day".[5] In the search for a substitute material experiments were made with jute and flax, but as soon as the war was over these materials were quickly abandoned in favour of cotton. The same continuity of relations is found in the supply of chemicals. These came from Bristol and London

[1] Heilbut, Symons & Co./SM, 2 October 1885.

[2] SM/Hecht, Levis & Kahn, 10 May 1886.

[3] Moulton's other requirements such as calico thread, eyelets and bindings, iron moulds and foundry work, timber and sacking, soap and string were all obtained in Bradford-on-Avon itself or in Bath or Bristol.

[4] Messrs. Outram & Co., Armitage & Sons, and Hall & Udall. The exception was Messrs. James Englefield of London.

[5] On 24 February 1862 Moulton announced to the Great Western Railway Company that in view of the high price of cotton he was compelled to raise the price of belting $17\frac{1}{2}\%$.

firms of manufacturing chemists and wholesale druggists,[1] and a study of the invoices reveals no important change throughout the half-century.[2] With the exception of the famine prices paid for textiles during the American Civil War there was an abundance of both chemicals and cotton, and the manufacturer who purchased these articles knew none of the uncertainty as to price and quality that characterised the supply of raw rubber.

Although the production of synthetic rubber has become possible only within recent years, reclaimed rubber—manufactured in the main from waste vulcanised scrap which was ground and mixed with the pure fresh material—has engaged the attention of the industry from the earliest days.[3] By the end of the century American consumption (stimulated by rising price levels) equalled that of the natural product, and the *India Rubber Journal* most significantly voiced the opinion in 1898 that " without reclaimed rubber . . . prices [of natural rubber] would be perhaps double ".[4]

[1] Louis Berger & Co., and Hubback & Son, both of London, and C. Hare of Bristol.

[2] A representative list of the chemicals purchased in this period by Moulton is as follows : Sulphur and Sulphurette, White Lead, Whiting, Carbon Lamp Black, Lead Hyposulphate, Litharge, Oxide of Zinc, Black Lead, Camphene, Magnesia, French Chalk, Fine Soda, Talc and Turps.

[3] A. Mason, " Waste Rubber ", *50th Anniversary Copy of IRJ*, 1936, has antedated the origins of this branch of the industry. According to the Moulton Papers £20 per ton was offered for scrap by Ford & Co. of London on 5 June 1856, and as much as £37 by T. Bryant of Chelsea in March and April 1860. But even £37 was not much against the £200–£250 for a ton of natural rubber.

[4] *IRJ*, 8 March 1894 and 26 August 1898. It is impossible to confirm these estimates. Moulton & Coy's consumption of reclaimed rubber is too small to warrant consideration, but it is noteworthy that supplies came from France or America. An analysis of reclaimed rubber offered to the Moultons at 8d. lb. in 1893 is as follows : Moisture .54 ; Insoluble Matter .94 ; Oxides of Iron and Alumina .55 ; Sulphate of Lead 17.70 ; Carbonate of Calcium 14.05 ; Sulphate of Calcium 18.17 ; Sulphur .41 ; Rubber 47.64. At the end of the century the French supply (Fabrique de Produits chimiques, Chauny, France) was handled by their United Kingdom agent, Somerville & Sons, Rubber Manufacturers, of Liverpool and Leicester. The American produce came to Moulton from a number of importing houses : Sgal & Co. of Liverpool, The Anglo-Russian Oil Co. of Bristol, and T. B. Peacock & Co. of Edinburgh. Samples forwarded by Somerville to Bradford on 26 July 1894 were as follows :

      10 lbs. A.A. Drab @ 3½d. per lb.
      14 lbs. B.B. Drab @ 4¾d. per lb.
      1¼ lbs. Red pneumatic tyre stock without cloth @ 11¼d. per lb.
      2 lbs. with cloth 10d. per lb.

Until the introduction of the alkali process in 1899 reclaiming was normally done by treating waste rubber with acids;[1] the object being to reduce the waste to a plastic state, free from sulphur and oils and fit for remanufacture. Progress in these developments was made on both sides of the Atlantic, but especially by the Americans, who undertook the earliest production on a commercial scale. The first important English company to attempt the reclaiming of waste rubber (whose managing director, incidentally, was Stephen Moulton), was formed for the working of American patents.[2]

The increasing demand for rubber in the nineteenth century—particularly for bicycle tyres in the 'nineties—resulted in a rising price level. In 1830 Para rubber changed hands at 7¼d. lb.; in 1900 it was over 4s. In 1850 African was available at 4½d. lb.; in 1900 it sold at almost 3s. But the rise, as the graph (Fig. 1) on page 64 shows, was neither continuous nor even; sudden price fluctuations remaining one of the greatest hazards of early manufacture.[3]

[1] Earliest patents for reclaimed rubber were those of A. Parkes, No. 11147, 1846, T. Hancock and R. Phillips, No. 12007, 30 December 1847, and C. Goodyear's U.S. patent No. 2933 of 16 December 1853.

[2] The London I. R. Company, Ltd., formed in 1860 with a capital of £75,000. The manufacturing manager was the American H. L. Hall, and his British patents, entered under the name of Nathaniel Shattswell Dodge, and dated 30 July 1858 (No. 1728), 2 November 1858 (No. 2449) and 23 May 1859 (No. 1274), were transferred to the Company. The project was short-lived as the works were completely destroyed by fire a few weeks after production had begun.

[3] Two examples must suffice : Wright, Roberts & Co. /SM, 20 December 1869 : " . . . contrary to all anticipation and even to those most interested in the trade for the last 25 or 30 years, the price has advanced from 3/2d. to 3/5d. in the past month . . . "; Heilbut, Symons & Co. /SM, 2 October 1885 : " That events have falsified the expectation is only another proof of the uncertainty of our market." One of the heaviest losses sustained by Moulton can be seen from the Bradford Stock a/c dated 1 January 1856 :

> Recapitulation.
>
> | | | | |
> |---|---|---|---|
> | Raw Materials in Mill Cost | ... | £2,388 | (incl. £492 Java). |
> | Java Rubber in London | ... | £1,885 | |
> | Moulds, Tools, etc. ... | ... | £961 | |
> | Manufactured goods nett | ... | £3,160 | |
>
> £8,394

Then follows : "Note.—The above Java Rubber is now depreciated in market value £1,000 or thereabouts." And the Trade Account for that year shows a resale to Heilbut, Symons & Co., the importers, of 209 packages of Java

INVOICE ILLUSTRATING CONDITIONS OF PURCHASE IN 1850

Between the lowest point on the price curve, 1858, and the highest point, 1883, there was a three-fold increase in the average price of first quality Para.

The scarce factor in this supply situation was not rubber but the labour to collect it; and until the systematic development of plantation rubber in the present century made its collection and transportation a comparatively easy task the growing demand for crude rubber could only be met at an increased cost.[1]

Within certain limits, as a glance at the Fig. 1 will show, high prices attracted increased supplies (" The great and sudden advance in prices in November and December", wrote Wright, Roberts & Co. of Liverpool to Bradford on 28 February, 1866, " . . . stimulated arrivals from two producing districts into Para, which were immediately shipped off to this country and New York. The effect has been to paralyse the market . . ."), although it took some months before the high prices made themselves felt. Conversely, a sharp fall in prices such as occurred in 1870 and 1882 resulted in smaller shipments, the producers responding quickly to price changes.

The demand for raw rubber appears to have been closely allied to general business activity. Yet prices rose more than the average (from 1857-66 there was a 100% rise in the average price of all kinds of rubber), in the period of general rising prices 1849-74, and fell less than the average in the period of falling prices 1874-96, a tendency to be explained largely by the preponderant influence of the United States.[2] There were occasions such as in 1870 and 1894, to take but two of several examples, when the course of prices was contrary to that followed by most other commodities. In the

Rubber valued at £661.0.0. The Directors of the North British Company, meeting on the 29 January 1867, noted the : " . . . rise in the price of the Gum during the past year has been ascertained to be £20,000 more than if the Gum had been at a normal price . . . " (North British MSS.)

[1] See Layton and Crowther, *The Study of Prices*, 89-90. The astonishing fall in the cost of freight to the seaboard which had benefited the American grain trade was not feasible in the case of South American rubber.

[2] The analysis of the rise in prices of other commodities between 1846-50 made by Layton and Crowther, *op. cit.* 75, 88, shows the average rise to be about 25%, whereas rubber rose 125%. In the case of falling prices in the period 1874-96 the relative change in commodities between 1871-75 and 1894-98 shows the average fall in price to have been 40% ; rubber did not fall in this period, but, on the contrary, showed a rise in the region of 80%.

F

former year, in spite of the enormous increase in industrial activity, rubber prices (no longer able to maintain the inflated levels reached under speculative pressure), preceded the general fall by several years; conversely, in 1894 they preceded the general rise.   The

TOTAL ANNUAL IMPORTS OF CRUDE INDIA-RUBBER, 1850-1900

Showing the average yearly price of para-rubber

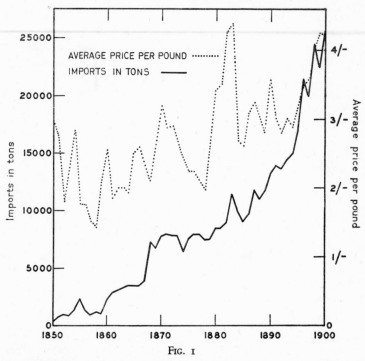

FIG. I

Sources : Import figures from the Annual Statement of Trade. Prices are based on the quarterly average figures for first quality Para contained in the *London Mercantile Price Current* (1850-64), *Prices Current* of Jackson and Gardner, Jackson & Till, Wright, Roberts & Co. Ltd., Liverpool (Moulton Papers, 1865-66), *London New Price Current* (1867-70), and from the *Public Ledger* (1870-1900).

tendency for rubber prices to rise more and fall less than others arose in part from the special circumstances of the trade; from the fact that as there was no real substitute for rubber the growing demand was relatively inelastic, and (in the case of the mechanical trade) the price changes in the raw material had little influence on the total cost of the final product for which rubber parts were used. The price rise in 1894, which preceded the general movement in 1896, needs little explanation beyond the boom in the bicycle industry. In this connection it is worth noticing that the uses for rubber grew most rapidly in a period of rising rather than falling prices.

A most important influence in these fluctuations was the peculiar speculative element operative in this trade from the earliest days. The concentration of so much of the rubber in the Amazon valley, coupled with the growing demand for this commodity, made the rubber trade an attractive field for the speculator, who operated to the discomfort of the legitimate trader.[1] Some indication of this movement is given in a letter from a Liverpool house in June, 1869 :[2]

> . . . the mode and operation of our transactions in this description seems to be that the outside holders are cleared at the current rate of the day, the buyers having thus secured the market in their own hands, resell tomorrow at ½d or 1d advance, and this being repeated from time to time, we have reached the present high figure . . . There is no scarcity of rubber, no extraordinary demand, and consequently nothing to warrant such an extraordinary high price, which in the end must work its own cure . . .

Under these speculative influences, Para reached a record price of 3s. 5d. lb. by December 1869, and in April 1870, at the top of the price rise, 3s. 8d. was paid. For a brief period in 1882 5s. 2d. lb. was asked, a price not to be reached again until the first decade of the twentieth century.

Another feature of this speculative tendency was the manner in which price changes in the 'eighties were attributed to the manoeuvres of an American group upon whose movements the market depended.

---

[1] Kirkman Brown/SM, 13 November 1861 : " I never knew it otherwise than starving follows high speculative prices. Look at the state of the rubber market, the prices are such that for an investment [you] may just as well put your hands into the fire to get out a hot coal . . . " Dealing with the speculative trend in 1879 which caused a rapid rise in prices another broker wrote : " My friends with others have been doing their best to lower prices . . . a steady market and moderate prices suit their business best." J. Brown/SM, 5 December 1879.

[2] W. Wright/SM, 17 June 1869.

If, however, the market has lately followed a declining tendency [wrote a London House in 1885],[1] in spite of the favourable position, this to be ascribed solely to the manipulation of the American clique of speculators who for some time past have had an interest in getting prices down and have used every means at their disposal to achieve this object ... The main question now is : when may it suit the ends of the Americans to see prices go up again ? As soon as this becomes the case, you may depend upon it that we shall witness an immediate advance.

In 1878, 1882 and 1891 attempts were made by a European syndicate of speculators operating under the title of the Empreza Industrial du Gran Para at Rio, and the Companhia Mercantil at Para, with offices in London, Paris and New York, and linked with some of the oldest merchant bankers in Europe, such as the house of Barings, to gain control of all South American stocks and so rule the world market. Because of inadequate capital, and an inability to prevent the increasing flow of African and Asiatic supplies reaching the market, these attempts failed, but not until (having gained control of 80-90% of the available supply), they had forced famine prices upon the trade and an awareness of the need for concerted action. Reports made in 1882 from New York to the Manchester house of Macintosh & Company show that the American manufacturers (" entirely ignorant of English moves to end speculation ") were determined to end the matter even if it meant shutting down certain branches of the industry.[2] In Britain there was no such common

---

[1] Heilbut, Symons/SM, 30 July 1885.

[2] H. C. Birley reporting on 20 October 1882 from New York to Macintosh & Co., in Manchester wrote : " *Price of Rubber*. There are constant meetings taking place between the principal Rubber Manufacturers to consult as to what course must be adopted to break the present corner which speculators have successfully made. It is now pretty well decided to establish a company with a capital of $5,000,000 to buy direct from Para and should it be found necessary, which is expected, they will proceed up the river and actually organise the collection of Rubber and if possible elbow out the speculators. It seems a gigantic undertaking. Some of the manufacturers are extremely irate. For some weeks speculators have recommended them to abstain from buying as prices would be lower before long, and they adopted their advice then the speculators bought very largely and now hold stocks and are enabled to run up the price. These manufacturers who have contracts on their books for which they are not provided are in a fix, and some of them talk of closing their works for a time ..." And further on 23 October 1882 : "... Dodge (the Manager of the Mineralised Rubber Company, U.S.) knows some of the operators in R. (Grace Bros.) and informs me that this summer one of

action, most manufacturers limiting their purchases to cover immediate needs.

For the industry as a whole, these speculative phases had their uses. Whilst they plagued the manufacturer with high prices and low quality produce—for adulteration was at its worst in periods of scarcity prices—they also gave an added impetus to the development of alternative resources in Africa and the East, and to the search for substitute rubber.

them went over to England to negotiate with Heilbut, Simmons for a big corner . . . " (Birley MSS.)

Heilbut, Symons & Co., 10 September 1883 : " The Lot No. 133, altogether 306 bags of Assam, was sold today for speculation at secret prices"; and from the same house on 19 November 1889 : "... speculators are trying to make capital out of the revolution in the Brazils, spreading the report that supplies of Para Rubber will be affected ..." See also letters from J. Brown, especially 7 January 1859, 22 February 1859, 26 April 1859 and 1 February 1872. (Moulton MSS.)

Chapter IV

MANUFACTURE

THE growth of industrialisation in the second half of the nineteenth century, coupled with the discovery of the vulcanising process, greatly accelerated the application of rubber mechanical devices. In contrast to the footwear and garment trade—the original see ds of the industry—rubber mechnicals represented the bulk of Moulton's output, which will be apparent from a study of the items produced at Bradford throughout this period :

ANALYSIS OF OUTPUT: 1857-90

	1857 £	1860 £	1870 £	1880 £	1890 £
I *Mechanicals*					
Hose & Tubing ...	1,646	5,746	1,371	466	2,126
Packing & Washers ...	4,233	6,980	5,528	4,518	4,313
Springs & Rings ...	3,572	8,927	15,011	41,639	57,720
Belting	697	1,870	106	93	—
Rollers	—	—	260	17	—
Draft Stopping ...	—	—	—	820	878
Diaphragms	—	—	—	—	2,067
II *Clothing, etc.*					
Coats, Capes & Leggings	5,992	4,828	630	274	—
Blankets & Aprons ...	132	—	—	—	—
III *Medical*					
Beds & Cushions ...	154	126	83	23	—
V *Others*					
Piece Goods	614	587	234	112	—
Sundries	696	458	1,138	430	379
Annual Total	17,736	29,522	24,361	48,392	67,483

Source : Sales Books, Moulton MSS. The figures cover the period 1 January 1857 to 31 December 1890, (for which complete figures are available for the Bradford Mill), and represent Moulton's annual sales for the year indicated. The choice of the beginning of each decade is arbitrary.

The absence of footwear from these lists is not due to Moulton's inability to anticipate the greatest single employment of rubber in the nineteenth century, but rather to the intense competition which sprang from the more highly specialised and experienced American manufacturer operating from the United States, as well as from Scotland after 1855; and also from the inability of the British shoe dealers to agree among themselves, which Hancock said spoiled "an excellent and profitable trade".[1] In addition the patent law restricted severely the scope of the English shoe manufacturer.[2] The manner in which the Bradford company became highly specialised in one branch of rubber manufacture by the 'fifties (the general waterproofing trade was abandoned entirely after 1883), was more representative of the American than the English scene.

By 1860, of the many mechanical devices manufactured at Bradford, the most important single item was the rubber railway spring, which took the form of a number of simple rubber discs separated by metal plates. Whilst there can be no denying the improvement in physical properties effected by vulcanisation, the Moulton correspondence shows that these springs were in use prior to the introduction of the vulcanising process.[3] By the end of the century rubber railway springs were employed in many parts of the world. Cheaper and lighter than steel, flexible, yet able to withstand heavy pressure, they played an important part in the extension of modern transportation.[4] In 1861 in an attempt to add to the resisting power of rubber Moulton patented his embedded

[1] Hancock, *Personal Narrative*, 55, 62.

[2] See Chapter VII.

[3] Correspondence in the *Mechanics' Magazine*, No. 776, (23 June 1838) 80, and No. 778, (7 July 1838) 231, also points to this conclusion. Some of the more famous English inventions are linked with the names of H. C. Lacy (Patent No. 5423, 18 November 1826) ; W. C. Fuller (Patent No. 10894, 23 October 1845) ; De Bergue (Patent No. 11815, 26 July 1847) ; J. E. Coleman (Patent No. 14193, 28 June 1852) and R. Eaton (Patent No. 2752, 20 November 1856). The principal stages in the evolution of the railway spring since 1852 can be traced through the following patents of G. Spencer : Patent No. 13951 (1852); 1733 (1853); 758 (1877); 3906 (1886) and 19011 (1894). See also *Practical Mechanics' Journal*, 6 October 1852 and 27 April 1853.

[4] In steam shipping as well as in railways. R. Eaton (8 February 1850) writing to Bradford after his arrival in North America: "Bye the bye I found some large India-Rubber Springs in use on board the *Canada* for to perform the return stroke of the cut off valve . . ." And on 11 April 1861 the Great Western Railway Company wrote from Paddington : " The *Great Eastern* is expected in Liverpool about the 15th of next month by which time I shall be obliged if you will have ready 32 Ind. R. valves : 19″ x 14½″ x ¾″ 64—do— 19″ x 8½″ x ¾″ thick . . . "

steel and rubber bearing spring (see the accompanying diagram), consisting of a hollow rubber cylinder 5″ dia. by 5″ long with a 2″ hole in which was embedded a helical coil of ¼″ steel wire. Other mechanical devices were valves, washers (soon extensively used for the repair of burst steam joints in place of the lengthy white lead and gasket process), and packing for steam engines. Hitherto not even the inventive genius of James Watt had succeeded in devising a substance that would resist high temperatures and prevent the loss of air, gas, water or steam. A foundryman wrote to Moulton in 1849 :[1] "Did you ever know of any rubber rings being put in a steam engine piston, I should much like to try one. It would want something to stand the steam and wear . . ." Scepticism such as that expressed by the editor of the *Practical Mechanics' Journal* (15 November 1848) ". . . that the frictional effect made vulcanised India-Rubber unsuited as a packing material . . ." was quickly disproved by rising sales. These small rubber parts not only enabled the engineer to conserve power but to harness it to a still further degree.

As rubber-covered canvas (power and conveyor) belting was one of the first items to be produced by the American industry it is not surprising to find it being manufactured at Bradford in 1849. Moulton sold it to almost every branch of industry: to paper and saw mills, mines, machine shops, and grain elevators. Cheaper (in 1859 Moulton claimed that the price of the wide rubber belts was at least one-third less than leather of equal strength), and yet as strong as leather, it was soon adopted by many trades ; but the intense competition that developed in this particular line— a consequence of its simple construction—led Moulton to abandon its manufacture in the 'eighties. This did not happen in the case of rubber hose and tubing, which remained important for Bradford throughout the period, and was employed for every conceivable purpose[2] where the conducting of air, liquid (including acids),

---

[1] G. Gough/SM, 8 January 1849.

[2] "The pit to the present", wrote Coulthard & Morland of Plymouth to SM on 23 April 1860, dealing with the drainage of a Cornish clay mine, "is drained by means of wooden pipes 4½″ in dia. He (the mine owner) wants to know, if, as the pit is sunk deeper, the hose could be joined to the wooden pipe in the first instance, and as it again becomes deeper if the next length of hose could be joined to the first and so on . . ."; and on 24 November 1860 : "The hose seems to answer the purpose very well and although the pressure is about 170 lb. to the sq. inch I have not seen any sign of its giving way at any point . . ."

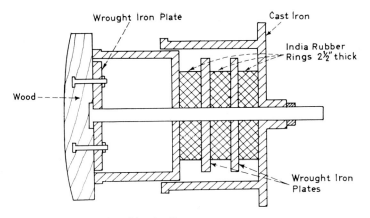

Rubber buffers in use 1836-46

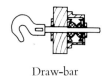

Draw-bar

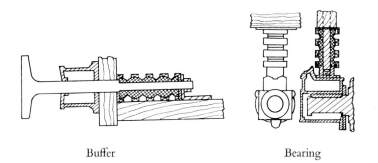

Buffer   Bearing

RAILWAY SPRINGS MANUFACTURED AT BRADFORD-ON-
AVON TO THE ORDER OF GEORGE SPENCER AND COMPANY,
MARCH 1855

Rope Packing, 10ft. Lengths.

$\frac{1}{4}$ $\frac{3}{8}$ $\frac{1}{2}$ $\frac{5}{8}$ $\frac{3}{4}$ $\frac{7}{8}$ 1 $1\frac{1}{8}$ $1\frac{1}{4}$ $1\frac{3}{8}$ $1\frac{1}{2}$ $1\frac{5}{8}$ $1\frac{3}{4}$ $1\frac{7}{8}$ 2

Socket Washer.

Flange Washer.

SECTION

WASHER AS APPLIED TO A SOCKET JOINT

SECTION

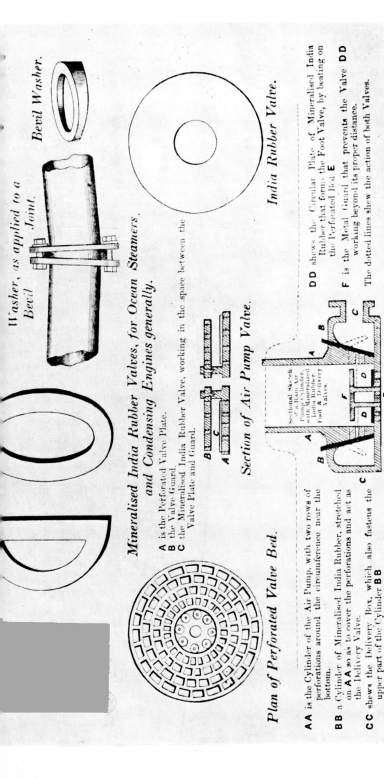

Bevil Washer.

Bevil Washer, as applied to a Joint.

Mineralised India Rubber Valves, for Ocean Steamers, and Condensing Engines generally.

A is the Perforated Valve Plate.
B the Valve Guard.
C the Mineralised India Rubber Valve, working in the space between the Valve Plate and Guard.

Section of Air Pump Valve.

India Rubber Valve.

Plan of Perforated Valve Bed.

AA is the Cylinder of the Air Pump, with two rows of perforations around the circumference near the bottom.

BB a Cylinder of Mineralised India Rubber, stretched on **AA** so as to cover the perforations and act as the Delivery Valve.

CC shews the Delivery Box, which also fastens the upper part of the Cylinder **BB**

Sectional Sketch of a Ram Air Pump Cylinder, with Mineralized India Rubber Foot & Delivery Valves.

DD shews the Circular Plate of Mineralised India Rubber that forms the Foot Valve, by beating on the Perforated Bed **E**

F is the Metal Guard that prevents the Valve **DD** working beyond its proper distance.

The dotted lines shew the action of both Valves.

SOME EARLY MECHANICAL APPLICATIONS OF INDIA-RUBBER

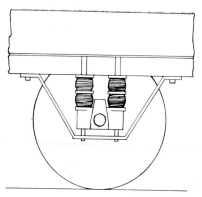

Bearing springs made to the order of Brown Marshall and Company
Wagon Builders, Birmingham, July, 1852

Stephen Moulton's embedded steel and india rubber spring
Patented in 1861

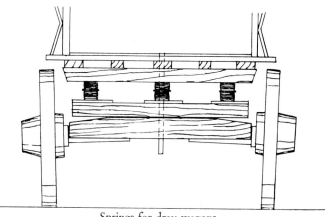

Springs for dray wagons
Supplied by the Bradford Mill from 1850

steam and gas were concerned.   The volume and tone of correspondence with the mining industry leaves no doubt that the economic
effect of this improved means of drainage must have been considerable.

The introduction of rubber into the practice of medicine and
surgery dates from the earliest days of the industry in Europe.
Plastic, soft, flexible, yet resistant to chemicals and easy to sterilise,
rubber was bound to attract the attention of the medical faculty.
Whilst it is true to say that their demands upon the industry never
reached the proportions of other branches of the trade there can be
few articles of commerce to which modern surgery owes so much—
and the debt is owed not only by the doctors but, in their use of hard
rubber for dental plates, by the dentists as well.[1]

Whilst the numbers of rubber workers in 1851 were too few to
appear in the census returns of that year, the application of rubber
was already widespread, and its employment was increasing.
A decade later in the early 'sixties the number of manufacturing
establishments had probably doubled, and the working force
quadrupled.   According to the census of 1861, there were more
than a thousand rubber workers in England alone, the majority of
them in the Manchester and London areas; probably half as many
again were employed north of the border.   It is an indication of
the highly capitalistic nature of rubber manufacture that the majority
of these workers were employed by three or four of the pioneering
companies[2] who, at the end of the century still operated from the
original centres of the industry.

On this side of the Atlantic most of the early manufacturers

---

[1] Hard rubber, vulcanite, or ebonite was prepared by increasing the proportion of sulphur in the mixture and subjecting the whole to prolonged heating.
It was first described in Hancock's Patent of 21 November 1843 and is most
important perhaps in its work as a resistant to chemicals and an insulator of
electric current.

[2] A valuable source on location and employment is the *Report of the Commissioners on the Employment of Children and Young Persons,* C. 3548 (1865),
Second and Fourth Reports, which brings out most forcibly the disparity in
the size of the early manufacturing units.   In 1861 (of the total of 1,290
employed in rubber manufacture in England and Wales) half were employed
by the chief Manchester house (Macintosh & Co.) and by the chief London
house (Wm. Warne & Co. of Tottenham).   The other units ranged from 70
to 200 workers. The North British Company of Edinburgh with a payroll
of 300 employees was one of the largest rubber factories in the United
Kingdom.

aimed at a general rather than a specialised market.   With certain exceptions—telegraphic cable insulation[1] (which required highly specialised machinery), rubber footwear (largely in the hands of the Americans),[2] and contraceptives (a " stealthily conducted trade" which has flourished since the 'fifties of the last century)[3]— most goods were made at Bradford in the early years.   Yet the Kingston Mill did not remain typical of the industry as a whole. By the 'sixties it was committed to the production of railway mechanicals, and this specialisation was increased in the 'seventies with the growth of the carriage cushioning and draught-stopping trade.   The introduction of the suction brake on the railways in the 'eighties brought with it a demand for rubber diaphragms. Though solid rubber tyres had been made at Bradford since the 'forties the company played little part in the developments dependent upon the re-discovery by J. B. Dunlop of the pneumatic tyre in 1888.[4] Regarding this discovery it needs to be emphasised that there was

[1] According to a correspondent writing in the *Mechanics' Magazine* on 9 January 1861 (Vol. 67, 28), the first wire insulated with pure rubber was put down in Russia in 1837, and applied to submarine telegraphy by the British in 1846.   Ousted by gutta-percha (whose mechanical and electrical properties were superior to those of rubber) in the 'fifties, experiments were still continued at Bradford.   Even in the 'eighties rubber was not despaired of for use in insulating Atlantic cables : G. Le Doux & Co./SM & Co., 31 July 1882. For all land work, and the tropical underwater cables, rubber was unrivalled as an insulating material until the recent developments in polythene.   On this see G. R. M. Garratt, *One Hundred Years of Submarine Cables* (H.M.S.O., 1950).   The *Report of the Privy Council Committee with Minutes of Evidence on the Construction of Submarine Telegraph Cables*, 1861, is a valuable source of information on this subject.   See also *The Telcon Story*, published by the Telegraph Construction and Maintenance Company Ltd. (London 1952).

[2] The first house in the United Kingdom to manufacture rubber footwear exclusively was the Liverpool Rubber Company formed by the American-trained William Somerville in 1859.   Between 1855 and 1859 Somerville had directed the Canadian Rubber Company from Liverpool (whose chief concern had been the importing of Canadian footwear), but in that year, after the lapse of the Hancock patent, he turned the ' Canadian ' into the ' Liverpool Rubber Company', and the manufacture of rubber footwear in Liverpool was begun.

[3] The only reference which the author has discovered either in original MSS or nineteenth century trade papers is an article " The Trade in Questionable Rubber Goods" by T. J. Buckingham published in the *IRW* 15 March 1892. One of the first to mention the use of rubber associated with birth control was De Pauw in his *Reserches philosophiques sur les Americains* (Berlin, 1768).

[4] See J. B. Dunlop, *The History of the Pneumatic Tyre* (Dublin, *c.* 1925). Provisional English patent granted on 7 December 1888.   Final patent granted 8 March 1889, No. 4116.

nothing remarkable about a rubber tyre at this time.[1] The first patent for a pneumatic tyre had been taken out by R. W. Thomson in 1845[2] but had proved to be a crude and impracticable affair and was soon forgotten. The solid tyre, however, in spite of its defects—the chief problem was to keep the tyre fixed firmly to the rim of the wheel—continued in use, and the increase in cycling in the 'seventies and 'eighties did something to stimulate Moulton's sales.[3] Yet Dunlop's invention in 1888 marked the beginning of a new phase. Two years after the original Dunlop Company began its spectacular career in 1889 with an authorised capital of £25,000,[4] they purchased for £200,000 W. E. Bartlett's ' Clincher ' patent,[5] which established the principle of an easily detachable pneumatic tyre held securely in position by air pressure alone. In 1896 when Dunlop's nominal capital stood at £5,000,000,[6] the *India Rubber Journal* wrote :[7]

> There is certain to be some new invention which will arise and take the place of the pneumatic tyre at no very distant date when the vast amounts invested in the pneumatic tyre

[1] *Mechanics' Magazine*, XLV, 188 ; XLVI, 289-90 ; L, 522-3. On their application to railway engine and carriage wheels see Daft/SM 4 August 1854: " I wish I could say the Railway wheels were established but I may have some very prejudiced people to get over before I can set them fairly going . . . " A century later the principle was introduced by the French railways.

[2] English Patent No. 10990, 1845. See A. Du Cros, *Wheels of Fortune*, (London 1938), 41 *et seq.* ; and H. C. Pearson, *Rubber Tyres and All About Them* (New York, 1906), 34 *et seq.*

[3] It is an indication of the quickening of this trade that the first copy of the *India Rubber Journal*, published in 1884, contained seven notices of improvements in the manufacture of the solid tyre.

[4] Arthur Du Cros, *ibid.* 81-4 ; J. B. Dunlop, *ibid.* 34-5. The original company, the Pneumatic Tyre and Booth's Cycle Agency, Ltd., resulted from a combination of tyre interests with an established cycle agency. The original 15,010 £1 shares allotted to the public were not fully subscribed.

[5] English Patent No. 16,783 granted in 1890 to W. E. Bartlett, whose company (the North British Company), continued to manufacture the tyre on payment of a royalty. Dunlops also bought the patent granted to C. K. Welch (No. 14,563 dated 16 September 1890) in May 1892. These patents saved them from serious embarrassment when the courts declared J. B. Dunlop's original patent invalid. On this see Arthur Du Cros, *ibid.* 106-10.

[6] In 1939 the nominal capital of the Company stood at £16 million. *Dunlop : Fifty Years of Growth* (London, 1939).

[7] *IRJ* dated 12 May 1896 ; a view shared by Charles R. Flint, a leading American rubber manufacturer, who gave his opinion in 1892 that " Pneumatic tyres will not generally be used on carriages, but instead solid rubber tires, for their greater durability . . . " *IRW*, 15 October 1892.

business will be practically sunk, if not altogether lost . . .
The cycle craze is only a nine days' wonder . . .

Far from being a " nine days' wonder " the cycling craze was
undoubtedly a turning point in the long history of the rubber
industry.[1] By 1894 the cycle trade ranked next in importance to
footwear in its consumption of rubber. The number of rubber
workers in England and Wales increased from 10,621 to 18,516
between 1891 and 1901. By 1924 the total had reached 48,087 of
which approximately half were engaged on tyre work alone; and,
as might be expected, the centre of gravity of the industry, which
until now had rested on the textile regions of Manchester and
Greater London, was shifting to the vicinity of the bicycle and
motor-car industry in the Coventry and Birmingham areas. The
relative importance of the tyre trade in the opening years of the
twentieth century is best seen in the fact that the value of tyre
production in 1907 was £2,834,000 as against £8,908,000 for the
entire industry.[2]

While these developments did not leave the Kingston Mill
undisturbed the railway mechanical trade was its chief staple and
remained so. The policy of sticking to its own last brought
security[3] and a steady degree of progress; conversely, it denied the
Moulton Company the remarkable expansion of the tyre companies
in later days. When the time came for decision in the 'nineties,
Stephen Moulton and his two lieutenants, his sons Alexander and
Horatio, were dead.   Only John Moulton remained at the Bradford
mills and he did not respond to the commercial challenge of a new
age.

When the rubber industry was introduced to the West Country
in 1848 the basic problems of manufacture had been overcome.
Suitable machinery had been devised, and the industry had passed

---

[1] The progress of the pneumatic tyre is best seen in a comparison of the
solid and air-filled tyres fitted at the Stanley Cycle Show in London in 1890
and 1895 :

| 1890 Pneumatic Cycle Tyres | 20 | Solid 1,543 |
| 1895 Pneumatic Cycle Tyres | 1,588 | Solid 3 |

[2] *The Final Report on the First Census of Production of the United Kingdom* (1907).

[3] "The history of the tyre trade", wrote the *IRJ* on 30 April 1890, "is an
unbroken record of notorious financial promotions, amalgamations, litigation
and failures, and is a striking illustration of the inability of a new industry to
cope with a sudden and continual demand for a certain article, although the
obvious obstacle—the lack of working capital—does not exist ".

from the simple stage of manufacture with the aid of solvents[1] to the more critical and complicated vulcanisation process based on the employment of sulphur and heat. Apart from the use made of " cold vulcanisation" (invented by Parkes in 1846) for thin articles, this process was as vital in 1900 as it had been shortly after its discovery by Goodyear in 1839. The next most important advances —the introduction of organic accelerators[2] and the use of carbon black[3]—were made in recent years. There was in fact no fundamental difference between the manufacturing process of the 'nineties and the 'fifties. Improvements and changes were effected,[4] but the

[1] Moulton employed solvents at the outset, but in 1851 his insurance policies were amended to cover a process of rubber manufacture that did " not make use of Camphene, or any similar oil, or Naptha . . .", one of the primary hazards of fire.

[2] Chemical ingredients which accelerated the vulcanisation process, enabling it to be done at a much lower temperature, and improving the quality of the manufactured product. Litharge (important also for its ability to improve certain grades of low quality rubber), red and white lead, zinc oxide, lime, and other substances were all employed in the nineteenth century. The real advance came in 1906 with Oenslager's discovery of the value of certain organic substances.

[3] An all-important reinforcing agent employed in tyre manufacture. See F. Burnham MacLeary, *Natural Gas, Soot, and Better Rubber,* privately printed by Godfrey L. Cabot, Inc. (Boston), 1940. Of the " toughening " ingredients used by Moulton, zinc oxide—which acted as an accelerator as well as a reinforcing agent—and magnesia were by far the most important.

[4] Such as H. H. Waddington's " dry heat " vulcanising stove (Patent No. 15,680, dated 16 November 1887), whereby rubber-proofed cloth was passed by means of rollers through a zinc-lined wooden chamber and submitted to hot air at ordinary atmospheric pressure. With the adoption of Waddington's invention for double-texture garments the industry now had four vulcanisation processes at its command : steam cure, in which the articles were exposed to high pressure steam in the vulcanising boiler as described above ; cold cure (most suitable for thin single textures), along the lines of Parkes' discovery ; press cure (as in the case of Moulton's railway springs), where the articles were subjected to heat under pressure in moulds. When H. C. Birley went from Manchester to study American methods in 1882 he reported on 16 October that "water vulcanising is almost unknown in America", and that the rubber clothing manufacturers were already using Hot Air as a vulcanising process, in preference to water and steam . . . " Though on 4 November he thought fit to warn his partners that " the way that they [Americans] vulcanise, hanging the cloth or coats in a stove is not as good (for finish) as lapping face to face on a drum, and vulcanising in Steam as we do."
The reports posted back to England by Birley at this time cast interesting light on the condition of the industry in the early 'eighties : " . . . Williams got some very useful hints [Birley wrote on 23 October] about gearing. He tells me that their mixing and warming up rollers do not take anything

essential process of milling, compounding, moulding, spreading and vulcanising were the same as Goodyear, Hancock, Chaffee, Macintosh, Parkes and the other pioneers had made them. The important changes in this industry were changes in products—not processes—arising out of the developments in mechanical transportation and the advent of electrical power. The experience of the Bradford mill makes it abundantly clear that whilst the principles of modern rubber manufacture were established by Goodyear and the rest they were not very widely understood until many years later. The art of rubber manufacture was acquired slowly; and in acquiring this art Moulton and the others drew upon the Americans for practical knowledge, as the French at an earlier date had drawn upon the English. This marked dependence of Europe upon America reveals an unsuspected degree of reciprocity in the flow of ideas and technique between the Old World and the New. Unless it should be thought that the British were taking all and giving nothing during this period it is worth remarking that even as late as the 'eighties American manufacturers were engaged in transplanting British methods of waterproof garment manufacture.[1]

In these circumstances secretiveness (especially in the case of jealously guarded compounding formulae), characterised the early rubber undertaking :

> You ask whether the different densities are caused by different compounds or by different treatment in curing the same compounds [Moulton wrote to G. Spencer & Co., in 1859], We beg to say that it would be doing ourselves an injustice to make known the actual details of our own process of manufacture which must be considered in the nature of private property . . .[2]

like so much power to drive them as ours . . . "   And (27 October) whereas buttons were sewn on by hand in the Manchester works, they were put on by machinery by the Americans "in ¼ the time"—a method (and a machine) introduced to the English works post-haste. The same is true of the rubber-thread cutting machine which " beats the lot" (28 October). His visit to the Goodyear Company's works at Naugatuck greatly impressed him, and that night (27 October) he penned a detailed report for his colleagues in Manchester on all that he had seen there. (Birley MSS.)

[1] C. M. Depew, ed., *One Hundred Years of American Commerce* (2 vols., New York, 1895), II, 502.

[2] SM/G. Spencer & Co., 27 January 1859.   Conversely, certain formulae appear to have been common knowledge, as for instance those published by

These practices provided a tradition which has died hard,[1] as nineteenth-century empiricism gave way to twentieth-century laboratory control.

For Moulton the most critical and exasperating problem was the vulcanisation process itself. In spite of the use of hyposulphite of lead (provided for in his patent of 1847), which reduced the risk of sulphur bloom and burning,[2] it was not possible to predict with accuracy the durability of the manufactured product. Without rhyme or reason the same mixture and vulcanisation treatment produced articles of totally different quality, and often the disparity did not become evident until the goods had been put to use :

I had a piece of rubber sent to you a few days ago [wrote Daniel Gooch of the Great Western Railway to Moulton in 1853[3]], as a sample of the state it gets into after only a few

the *Mechanics' Magazine*, Vol. 65, 279, 324, 397, 446 and 539, in 1856 for the manufacture of high quality mechanicals, e.g. :

Para Rubber	25	lbs.
Java Rubber	5	,,
Zinc Oxide	16	,,
Magnesia	6	,,
China Clay	3	,,
Red Lead	2	,,
Sulphur	1⅛	,,

58⅛ lbs.

[1] Early British rubber manufactories (the American-directed North British Co. was an exception to this rule), were normally jealously guarded places. Stephen Moulton never gave permission for outsiders to inspect his mill and processes ; and the same policy was followed by the Manchester house of Macintosh & Co. Yet in 1882 when H. C. Birley went to study progress in the United States he was treated most liberally by manufacturers there. " Contrary to my expectations," he wrote to his partners from New York on 23 October " we were most cordially received. I think we must have seen nearly everything . . . We have detailed memoranda of what we saw." Later on he was agreeably surprised that a Massachusetts Company should have " received us very cordially", particularly as the manager of the Company had recently been " refused admission into ours . . . " (Birley MSS.)

[2] " Bloom " is a greyish patch of uncombined sulphur appearing on the surface of the vulcanised article. It was most displeasing when it appeared on garments. " Burning " or " scorching " resulted from exposing the article to too high a temperature during vulcanisation ; it reduced the life of the commodity considerably.

[3] Daniel Gooch (later Sir Daniel Gooch), Chief Engineer of the Great Western Railway,/SM, 17 October 1853. See also, for example, the Ebbw Vale Iron Company's letter to Moulton on 6 October 1854 (reproduced below facing page 78).

weeks work. If this is the best you can make I fear we must discontinue its use as it is much more troublesome and expensive than the steel springs. Will you be good enough to let me know if you can do any better for us.

By trial and error Moulton did do better, and the railways became the mainstay of the Bradford house, as well as one of the greatest consumers of rubber products. The problem of varying quality in rubber mechanicals, however, was not transitory. In 1870 when a London house wrote : " We have sent two six inch No 1 valves by Rail for your inspection, one of which has been at work only six weeks, in the same place and doing the same work as another which worked twelve months . . ." Moulton replied :

We can assure you as far as we know the materials and heats are exactly the same as for many years past. The valve returned to us is as perfect a one as we possibly could make . . . we are at a loss to account for its failure . . .

Some of these failures were attributable to the uncertain quality of the raw rubber supply as well as to wrong timing in the vulcanisation process; others were the result of faulty compounding, and the growing practice of meeting the rising cost of natural rubber by substituting whiting, chalk, china-clay and other ' fillers'. The needs of the industry could only be met by modifying the simple compound of rubber and sulphur with the addition of other ingredients,[1] and by a more scientific method of inspecting the final product.[2]

Many other problems tested the ingenuity of the early manufacturer; not least was the effect of oils and grease on rubber :

We have been compelled to relinquish the use of India Rubber in all places where it would be subject to the action of oil or grease . . . [wrote the Vale of Neath Railway in 1855].[3]

[1] For instance, the toughening properties required in a shoe " mix " were provided by adding large proportions of French chalk, whiting or china-clay ; strength and resistance for a mechanicals " mix " from lamp black, magnesium carbonate or zinc oxide.

[2] Many of the complaints in the 'fifties were put down to defective workmanship and lack of supervision. " If the goods supplied from your Mills had always been the same," wrote Greenhill Fry & Co., London to Bradford on 7 November 1850, when submitting a claim for £51.19s.6d. for defective sheeting returned from a consignment of £100.11s. "had always come up free from punctures, strains and other defects or been the same measure they were professed to be sent out from the factory . . . no returns would have been necessary . . ."

[3] Vale of Neath Railway, Neath,/SM, 2 April 1855.

LETTER FROM WILLIAM ADAMS
Giving specifications for the manufacture of rubber valves

In reply to Frank Pearce & Co., who wrote to Bradford in November 1874 of the damage done to rubber by oil, Moulton admitted (as the industry was compelled to do until the recent introduction of synthetic rubber brought some measure of relief), that ". . . There is no rubber that will stand oil or grease for any length of time . . ." Another problem was the effect of high temperature on rubber,[1] and the extension of the market to regions of extreme climate accentuated this difficulty.[2] Other difficulties met with at Bradford concerned production flow,[3] the welding of steel for Moulton's combined rubber and steel springs,[4] the 'bonding' of rubber with other materials, and perhaps one of the weakest links in the manufacturing process—until the development of the German aniline dye industry in the 'eighties—the colouring of rubber. By the 'eighties most of these problems had been overcome. The largest buyers of rubber mechanicals not only insisted upon uniform standards of quality for all goods (in the case of Government contracts with such vexatious conditions as to make the contract hardly worth while), but also a 2-3 years' guarantee of efficiency. The fact that Moulton could "work to about 1/32 of an inch . . ." in 1871 is striking evidence of the progress made by the industry in a matter of two or three decades. Especially so when it is remarked that until the end of the century the manufacturer worked to roughly drawn sketches, many of which appeared as part of a customer's letter such as the one from William Adams which is reproduced facing page 78.

[1] Ebbw Vale Co., Newport,/SM, 14 November 1856: "I cannot get my hose pipe to stand the heat coated with India Rubber, which peels off the hose outside, being apparently acted upon by the boiling water coming from the oven and then it cracks at the places where it kinks in handling . . . "

[2] G. Spencer & Co., London,/SM, 30 October 1879: "In March 1877 you supplied us with a lot of car springs which were used in St. Petersburgh . . . these . . . will not stand the severe cold of the Russian winter, but become hard blocks, and shake and injure the cars . . . The I. R. springs of *Russian* make are said to stand the cold, but the price is so high that our English supply is preferred if it can be made to equal the Russian in utility."

[3] The garment and footwear industry was particularly subject to seasonal trade. When Moulton got behind with his orders, customers (Windeler/SM, 14 September 1852) demanded £5 a day penalty for non-delivery; and Spencers (24 September 1884): "We hope you will be able to keep the supply up . . . as promised as the waggon builders are under heavy penalties to deliver the waggons."

[4] Cornforth Bros. Birmingham,/SM, 26 April 1862, 12 July 1862, 16 July 1862 and Monmouthshire Railway & Canal Co./SM, 2 July 1862, 17 July 1862.

Little more than a hundred years ago the application of rubber was confined to the waterproofing of cloth and the provision of crude footwear. Of the events that resulted in the growth and technical progress of this young industry none perhaps was of greater significance than the demands made of it by the engineers of the day. The letters written by Britain's leading railway engineers such as Gooch and Brunel to Bradford illustrate how the successful extension of the use of rubber in the nineteenth century was dependent on the closest relations existing between manufacturers and consumers—between those who made the rubber goods and those who where prepared to investigate their extraordinary properties.

Leaving the subject of general price fixing for more detailed discussion in Chapter V, it is the intention here to illustrate certain aspects of the manufacturing costing practice of the rubber industry a century ago. As far as Moulton was concerned the true trading position of the Bradford mill was only revealed with the casting of the half-yearly ' Working of the Factory ' account, an example of which is given on the next page.

This document is interesting not only for the analysis of expenditure and the rate of profit enjoyed by the business, but also for the postscript which follows it :

> Remarks on the Factory *Expenditure* for the six months ending 30 June.
>
> Out of the Expenditure of £5,933 only £3,050 or about *one-half* was incurred for the expense of Rubber, Clothes and Chemicals, almost exactly *one-fifth* of the whole expense was for Wages, *One-sixteenth* for Salaries, *One-twentieth* for Interest of Money paid.[1]
>
> Altogether the cost of production may be taken thus :
>
> | | | |
> |---|---|---:|
> | One half, Rubber and other materials, say | .. | 1/– |
> | One half, Mill Expenses | .. .. .. | 1/– |
> | | | |
> | Cost, Money out of Pocket .. | .. | 2/– |

---

[1] The evidence of these early papers (Moulton, Macintosh and the North British) is that the rate of net profit earned on sales was sufficient to make the changes in the rate of interest of little importance in the policy-making decisions of these companies. One example must suffice here :

After submitting a detailed estimate of the probable outlay in plant required to begin an elastic web weaving department the secretary of the North British Company in his report to the meeting of directors on the

WORKING OF THE FACTORY TO 30 JUNE 1858

Dr.					Cr.		
	£	s.	d.		£	s.	d.
For India Rubber ...	1,631	11	1	Goods Sold 1st Janu-			
Cloths and Duck	1,068	11	6	ary to 30th June	6,803	14	2
Chemicals ...	350	6	4	(See Sold Book).			
Sundries ...	151	7	6	Nett increase in stock			
Iron Castings &c.	25	3	9	30th June...	583	0	0
Coals	112	16	4				
Iron, Iron Wire							
& Iron Pipes ...	152	17	2				
Paint, solder and							
lead	29	15	9				
Boards for Pack-							
ing Cases ...	44	19	3				
Insurance ...	70	7	6				
Carriers A/c. ...	96	3	8				
Rates and Taxes	122	14	10				
Commission to							
Clayton ...	18	18	9				
Rent of London							
Office	60	0	0				
Interest Paid ...	226	10	8				
Wages	1,194	12	6				
Salaries	368	0	0				
London Petty Ex-							
penses Discounts							
and Deficiencies	80	16	2				
Alld. for damaged							
goods returned							
& cash discounts	89	7	11				
Gas for 6 months	38	14	6				
	£5,933	15	2				
Expended to produce							
£7,386.14.2 Nett							
Profit, as per Ledger	1,452	19	0				
				Goods Produced			
	£7,386	14	2	value: ...	£7,386	14	2

12 April 1865, concluded : " Or say for an outlay of £800-850 we could produce 250 yards per loom per week or 3,000 yards in all, which at 3/- per yard would amount to say £450, or say the net monthly production would be £1,500." On the 27 January 1866 the manager reported " that after a careful estimate of the Elastic Fabric Department up to the end of last year he had found it yielded a net profit of about 12½% on the sales . . . " which at an approximate figure of £1,500 per month=£18,000 a year @ 12½% = £2,250, i.e. about three times the original capital outlay. (Minute of meeting of Directors of the North British Rubber Company, Ltd. for these dates). The estimated rate of profit on sales was the determining factor in capital outlay in this industry, and not the movements of interest rates.

by which is intended to be conveyed the idea that to know the actual cost *out of pocket* the amount for materials must be doubled.

It will be noticed from this account that in arriving at his net profit Moulton neither made an allowance for the rent of the mills used by the company nor for depreciation of machinery; he regarded both these assets—mills and machinery—as his own private property.[1]   In valuing his net increase in stock at existing market prices he followed a practice which did not meet with the approval of the merchants who, at an earlier date, had financed him.

In contrast to the rule-of-thumb practices of the small manufacturer, a large establishment like the North British Company was able to assess the position of its different manufacturing departments by means of a detailed fortnightly " Statement of Consumption and Output ":[2]

It is true that the cost figures in this instance do not represent total costs (and from discussion at board meetings these statistics played no part in pricing policy), but they did provide a fairly efficient guide to the progress of the different departments. Of greatest importnce to the directors was the fact that these returns threw light on the special labour charges of each department.

Both systems—the Bradford account of total costs and receipts, and the Edinburgh account of prime (direct) costs, to which was added an allowance for overheads—were concerned with giving a general picture of the entire business. Other methods were used to assess day-to-day profit or loss on a particular product, or to help in fixing a new price. Except for the first attempt to value

---

[1] At the foot of a stock sheet of the Bradford mill dated 5 February 1851 appears the following note : " The Mill is rented by S.M. & Co. from Mr. M @ £750 per annum, he being bound to keep the machinery in repair."

[2] Extract from the Minute of Meeting of Directors of the North British Rubber Company Limited, 29 August 1864. The Manchester house appears to have ascertained the relative expenses of buying, manufacturing and marketing a product by costing summaries :

Summary of Cost of Washers—March 17/1851.

Material 14d. (incl. rubber and chemicals).

Making 7¼d. (incl. labour as well as indirect standing expenses calculated as 20% of direct costs).

Sale Expenses 8¾d. (incl. an allowance for discounts).

2/6d. per lb.   (Macintosh MSS.)

STATISTICS FOR FORTNIGHT ENDING 10 AUGUST 1864

Shoe Department

	£ s. d.	£ s. d.
Rubber used 9,804 lbs.	770 0 2	
Mixtures	95 0 10	
Textile Fabrics ...	720 14 6	
Special Labour ...	346 4 0	1,931 19 6

Clothing and Air Goods

Rubber 760 lbs. ...	61 8 8	
Mixtures	5 16 4	
Fabrics	148 16 1	
Special Labour ...	37 1 3	253 2 4

Mechanical Rubber

Rubber 12,989 lbs. ...	1,050 3 2	
Mixtures	82 2 3	
Fabrics	538 3 3	
Special Labour ...	195 17 1	1,866 5 9

Productions

44,037	Pairs Boots and Shoes, various kinds.
445	Garments various kinds.
400½	Piece Goods.
844	Bags and Air Goods Articles.
12,183	lbs. Packing.
19,141	feet Belting.
11,335	feet Hose.

his goods by seeing what the market would bear Moulton and the other manufacturers appear to have followed a fairly uniform costing procedure. In the case of a new article, or a new composition, for which a price had to be fixed, the first step was to prepare a cost analysis of a trial batch or short-run production period, as is done below:

Estimated Cost of 1,200 lb. Nett of Spring Rubber, being about *One* day's Manufacture for the Kingston Mills supposing the Works to be *fully and wholly* employed in making that description of Goods :

				£	s.	d.
Para Rubber, (including Dock Rent, Carriage &c.)						
		300 lb. @ 1/10d.		27	10	0
Java Rubber	...	300 lb. @ 9d.		11	5	0
Whiting ...	...	300 lb. @ ¼d.			6	6
Chemicals ...	...	336 lb. @ 3¼d.		4	11	0

£43 12 6

				£	s.	d.
Wages	...	...	...	...	2	12	0
Cost of Packing Materials ...		...	...	0	10	0
Breakage of Moulds...	...	...	...	0	7	0
Coals for Engines	...	...	...	0	14	0
Office and General Expenses		...	1	13	4
Salaries to Sundry	...	...	...	1	15	0
Interest on Capital and on Mortgage		3	8	0

10 19 4

£54 11 10

If 1,200 lbs. = 13,102d., one pound, say 11d.

It is noteworthy that the manufacturer should have thought fit to add :

> It must be understood that the basis of the above calculations is founded upon the idea that by incessant grinding during the 24 hours, without a moment's respite, and excluding all other descriptions of Manufacture, the above results might be obtained, but it will be borne in mind that no allowance is made for Rubber occasionally spoilt in curing, as well as loss by heavy adulterations of sand with the rubber, beyond the ordinary average—paper statements in such cases being fallacious.

However fallacious this or other cost estimates may have been, they evidently were relevant to price fixing. Moulton's calculation based on this estimate for spring rubber (which allowed for a profit margin of 20%, and a discount of 30%),[1] shows a selling

[1] As Moulton's discounts were much below this figure it is difficult to understand why he made such an allowance, unless he included with the discount his selling charges. It is worth adding here perhaps that in his " Stock A/c." for the years 1850-4 the manufacturer made a similar discount allowance (30%) against stocks of manufactured goods. From 1855 onwards stocks of manufactured goods were entered as " Nett."

price of 1s. 5d. lb. In actual fact the first springs sold by Moulton
later in the year were priced at 1s. 6d. lb. To have sold them below
11d. lb. (minimum unit costs) would not have even covered money
"out of pocket". The extent to which he could sell his goods above
this figure in order to allow for the anticipated profit margin on the
average product was dependent on the limits of market strategy,
which in this instance are not known.

Although the practice of preparing a cost analysis of a short-run
production period, or a trial batch, was common to these early
companies, the Manchester and Edinburgh houses were prepared
to add a fixed allowance for indirect costs—termed " Expenses ",
or " Standing Expenses "—as is done below :[1]

COST OF 538 VULCANIZED SHOES, 19 JULY 1849

121 lbs. 10 oz.	Spread Rubber	@ 3/- =	£18	5	0	
105 lbs. 0 oz.	Stationers' ,,	@ 2/- =	10	10	0	
52 lbs. 8 oz.	Corrugated ,,	@ 1/- =	2	12	6	
						£31 7 6
20 lbs. of Varnish	@ 1/- =					1 0 0
1 Gallon of Naptha	@ 2/- =					0 2 0
Wages paid...						5 7 0
36 yards of Cotton Check }	=					3 12 0
48 yards of Woollen Check }						
39 lbs. 3 oz. of leather... ...	@ 1/6 =					2 18 9
						£44 7 3
	20% for Expenses					8 17 6
						£53 4 9

How the early rubber manufacturer gauged his position in the
case of a commodity already on the market, and for which the price
was known, is clear from the example given below, where an attempt
was made by the Manchester house (still on the average cost basis)
not only to estimate the cost of a pair of rubber shoes but also to
discover the profit per pair :

ESTIMATED COST OF A PAIR OF RUBBER SHOES

August 27, 1849.

	d.
Rubber and Varnish ...	24.1
Check lining	2.0
Leather	3.0
Wages	5.0
	34.1

[1] Macintosh MSS.

Expenses 20%
    inclusive Rent, Heating and Lighting,
    Overlooking, Lasts &c. and Royalty :
              6.9

            41.0 per pair average.

		$d.$
Average Price ...	...	63.0
20%* ...	... ...	12.6
		50.4
Charges 10%* ...	...	5.08
		45.32
		41.00 cost
		4.32 Profit per pair.

*It is reasonable to assume from other examples that the 20% and 10% deducted from the average price are liberal allowances for discounts and selling costs respectively.

In these calculations the manufacturer appears to have been concerned primarily with the average cost and the supposed average gain or loss on one product, whether it was a pound of spring rubber or a pair of shoes, average unit costs being regarded as constant for different levels of output.[1] This method might not have been precise, but it was at least simple and straightforward, and it told him what he certainly appears to have been concerned to find out : the gross profit margin on the average product.[2]

[1] Several years later, on 24 March 1853, the Manchester house prepared an estimate of the direct costs for a New Material Composition for Rubber Over-Shoes along slightly different lines :

			s.	d.
8 lbs. Pickled Rubber Bottles ...	@ 17d.		11	4
6 lbs. Zinc....	@ 3d.		1	6
6 lbs. Whiting	@ ½d.		0	3
1 lb. Sulphur	@ 1½d.		0	1½
3 lbs. Lamp Black—uncalcined ...	@ 1½d.		0	4½
			13	7
Mixing and Spreading will cost 3d. lb.			6	0
			19	7 x 12

= 235d., divided by 24 (No. of lbs.) = 10d. lb.

(Macintosh MSS.)

[2] H. C. Birley (27 October 1882) writing to Macintosh & Co. from New York referred to the practice of a Massachusetts company of calculating " the total cost of this place, rent, taxes, wages, power, everything in fact, at 6d. per lb. of the thread produced." (Birley MSS.)

Chapter V

MARKETS

THE market for manufactured rubber commodities has passed through three stages. Firstly, there were the crude attempts at waterproofing clothing and footwear before the advent of the vulcanisation process in 1839. Secondly, from the 'forties, when Moulton entered the English market, to the end of the century rubber was applied to many uses (particularly in the field of railway mechanicals), where hitherto it had proved unsuitable. The third and most expansive stage of the industry's growth has lasted from about the turn of the century to the present day and is bound up with the enormous demands of the pneumatic tyre industry. In entering the trade when he did Moulton was spared the trials of those who had worked with the unvulcanised rubber, and in concentrating on the growing demands for engineering products his ultimate success was assured.[1]

At the outset most of Moulton's markets were found for him by the general merchants, who not only provided working capital for the Bradford mill but also the channels of distribution :[2] "We have had our travellers out", wrote one of them in 1850, "and resumed expensive advertisements in *The Times,* the *Medical Times,* and the *Lancet* newspapers, together with the distribution of circulars." As long as Bradford products consisted of general items, such as articles of clothing, the merchants were able to handle the trade fairly efficiently. By the middle 'fifties, however, the direct trade with collieries, engineers, foundrymen, the Government

[1] Yet when he entered the market a century ago much of the prejudice against the use of rubber still remained, and he had to educate not only the general consumer, but the technician as well. J. A. Jacques /SM, 13 May 1850 : " I mentioned to the Engineers by using our Packing [for steam engines] they did not require to face their joints, the answer was, let your packing be ever so good we should not think of turning our work out unless the joints were faced. "

[2] Price, Coker & Co., /SM, 12 August 1850. Goods sold outside this channel were to be accounted for by the manufacturer to the merchant : " furnish us with particulars of all goods sold by you, that we may pass them through our books according to our Agreements." The terms of this agreement were a commission of 10% to be paid on all London transactions passing through their hands, which accords with the terms offered by Braithwaites/SM, 22 October 1851.

and the railway companies, outweighed the indirect distribution through the wholesalers and the general distributors.

Until the changing circumstances of the last quarter of the century resulted in a London middleman becoming responsible for the distribution of almost the entire output of the Bradford mill,[1] Moulton's selling policy is sufficiently clear and continuous to bear summarising. In the absence of an existing system of distribution of rubber products his aim was to widen his market and achieve independence from the general merchants. Whilst he preferred the direct trade with the large consumers, such as the railway companies, he was prepared to accept orders—in spite of the protests from different sections of the trade[2]—from whatever source they came to him, including " a good coat for a respectable yeoman ";[3] a policy which involved him in certain administrative difficulties such as problems of debt, credit supply, accounting, and dispatch of small orders, and a good deal of correspondence. But it gave him greater control over his own business and kept him in touch with the changing needs of the market. In an attempt to break new ground in the more remote areas of North-Eastern England, Wales, and Scotland, Moulton employed commission agents (the Welsh agent was paid 2d. per lb. on all orders obtained; the Scot and the Tynesider 5 % on the value of invoices), whose special task it was to introduce to industrial consumers the different mechanical adaptations of rubber. Outside these areas—in the regions south of the Tees—he employed his own travellers[4] (normally paid on a

---

[1] Below, p. 110.

[2] To J. C. Harding, wholesale clothiers of Hereford, who protested (6 December 1856) that Moulton was supplying his customers direct the manufacturer replied : " How are we to know or guess who are your customers ?— especially in S. Wales. We can't refuse to supply shop keepers at our list prices when they apply for our goods. We allow you the handsome discount of 15% and often a four months credit, yet you do but a small business with us in return for requiring the monopoly of the retail trade throughout England and Wales." Copy reply written across Harding's letter.

[3] P. & A. Pumphrey /SM, 12 April 1853, whose letter suggesting that Moulton should " . . . open up no new accounts within 10 miles of Birmingham and refer any applicant to us . . . " went unheeded. Though, as a letter from SM to his traveller on 13 June 1868 illustrates, this policy could be altered when circumstances demanded it : " don't cross the Tees as we have a large customer in Newcastle-on-Tyne to whom we must give up Durham and Northumberland."

[4] J. C. Wills, /SM, 19 August 1868, was allowed 21 /- per day expenses. Eaton,/SM, 23 April 1868, was appointed at a fixed salary of £350 p.a., expenses paid. Sometimes these men would be on the road for weeks at a

commission basis of 10% with an expenses allowance), whose reports, along with those of the commission agents, were his chief source of market intelligence.

An interesting feature of the early rubber market was the opening of retail and wholesale stores and warehouses in the metropolis. Moulton's London salesroom, opened at No. 2 St. Dunstan's Terrace in 1850[1], was probably the first of its kind in Great Britain, although he himself was following the example set by the American manufacturers. The chief explanation for this was the manufacturer's desire to add the merchant's profits to his own. Other reasons were the novelty of the products, their appeal to the general consumer (that is at the outset when articles of dress represented the bulk of the trade), the need to combat prejudice, and to offer the public a specialised personal service. The salesroom was an important link between the Bradford factory and the London market. It was the centre of all operations there and a barometer of general as well as special trade conditions.[2] Yet by 1868 the need to economise, coupled with the administrative worry of the London establishment and occasional irritating differences in policy between London and Bradford, led Moulton to dispense with its use.

Other contacts were made with the public through advertisements in the Press, which until the cycling craze of the 'nineties were largely of an informative nature, the manufacturer being content to announce his existence and list his chief products. There were exceptions, such as the advertisement describing Moulton's

time, submitting daily reports to the factory and using the General Post Office at their next town of call as their address. When Moulton's first traveller, Oliver Kirkman, worked the Fen country in the spring of 1851 the men of Brandon " had never even heard of such a thing as rubber banding", and " a great many very uncouth dogs at St. Ives " laughed at him. Oliver Kirkman/SM, " Wednesday," May 1851.

[1] Moulton's chief competitors, Macintosh & Co., and the North British Company Ltd., were not long in following his example : W. Charles, London,/SM, 20 October 1857 " Mac opens a beautiful shop . . . " It is believed this was at 73 Aldermanbury, London ; and W. Goodwin/SM, 6 January 1864 : " The North British have opened a retail shop in Ludgate Hill."

[2] The offices and showrooms of the early manufacturers, including the North British Company of Edinburgh, were concentrated in one area. According to Moulton's London manager writing in 1866 : " Cannon Street has now become the Street of the Rubber trade " and " We shall do more business in one year there than we do here in five." W. Goodwin/SM, 21 and 23 August 1866.

patent springs and inking rollers, as well as those directed at members of the armed forces, but on the whole the notices give the barest details of manufacture. The amount spent by the Kingston Mill on this account was inconsiderable.[1] Advertising as a selling technique had not been developed by the industry as it was to be in later years; the most important factors determining a diversion of trade from one manufacturer to another were the quality and the price of the goods offered. As regards engineering products for the Government and the railways, the recommendation of leading engineers such as Brunel, Gooch, Craig,[2] or the support of a house such as Boulton & Watt, was worth all the newspaper advertisements put together.[3] The large Government contracts arising out of the Crimean War[4] coupled with the demands of the growing railway network helped to put the Moulton business on its feet.

Prior to the Crimean War the extent of government patronage to the industry was small, although Moulton always kept before him William Rider's advice " to drive at the Government for

[1] The most complete account is for the year 1870 when the amount spent was £71 against total sales of £24,400.

[2] Haigh Foundry, Wigan,/SM, 22 March 1851 : " Mr. Gooch of the G.W.R. informs us that you supply vulcanized I. R. washers and of a quality to bear high pressure steam of almost any temperature &c. . . ." C. E. Balleras & Co., London,/SM, 4 November 1856 : " Mr. Craig of the Manchester-Sheffield Railway has favoured us with your name and recommended you to us for I. R. Buffer Springs &c. . . ."

[3] Moulton was an exhibitor at the Great Exhibition of 1851, where he was awarded a Prize Medal for his manufacture. The earliest reference found to rubber goods being displayed at a public exhibition occurs in the *Rapport du juri sur les produits de l'industrie belge exposés à Bruxelles dans les mois de Septembre et d'Octobre* 1835. (Brussels, 1836).

[4] Many thousand waterproofed capes and sheets were supplied by Moulton in 1855. Whilst there can be no denying that the Crimean and American Civil War provided a stimulus to this industry the correspondence of the time shows that the manufacturers preferred the prospects of peace to war. Spencer T. Parmelee writing to his partner Henry Lee Norris in London on 19 January 1856 : " . . . I am sorry to hear that the prospects of peace is to deprive us of a few thousand pounds of cheap rubber, but for our own sakes, and for the vast benefit which peace would be to the world, I think we had better willingly lose the little advantage in the Rubber Trade while we have brighter prospects in peace than war can possibly furnish . . . " (North British MSS.) The desperate plight of the Confederacy during the American Civil War is reflected in the terms offered for hospital sheeting and other rubber goods : three times the gross amount of the invoice, paid for in cotton, Confederate 8% bonds, or in Confederate treasury notes. (Moulton MSS.)

business instead of at the general market . . . "[1] Yet the record of his relations with the War Office and the Admiralty shows that the authorities were alive to the possibilities of this new material, and his suggestions for the use of rubber in military and naval equipment always received full and fair consideration.[2] It was not at the highest levels that he had reason to complain, but once the plans had been approved in principle (and particularly when he had supplied the goods and was waiting for his money) he was then faced with a long administrative wrangle with government officials that was as exasperating to the manufacturer of a century ago as it is at the present day. "I find you are quite correct in your opinion of the Government officials ", a correspondent wrote to Bradford in March 1855. "They are very troublesome people and scarcely worth seeing." Yet the fact that the early rubber manufacturers did not turn aside from government patronage suggests that the venture was not without its profit. Coupled with the charge of incompetence of junior government officials was that of bribery. It is not suggested that bribery in the allocation of contracts was any worse in the period under review than in any other; though the conviction that it was a growing influence resulted in the War Office Contracts Inquiry[3] of September 1900, and the passing of the Prevention of Corruption Act of 1906: " I am told that I might have avoided much delay ", wrote H. E. Coles to Bradford in March 1855,

> . . . and many obstacles in this matter by feeing the officials ; but this I neither could afford to do, nor would I do, upon principle.[4]

[1] WR/SM, 15 November 1847. And on 10 February 1848 : " We should be showing our samples to the English Government and East India Company . . . then the French Government should not be neglected . . ."

[2] 31 January 1847. Lord Fitzroy Somerset appointed a Select Committee of senior officers to examine Moulton's exhibits of a knapsack, canteen, haversack and cornsack. See SM/His Grace the Duke of Wellington, 8 May 1851. In 1863 an Admiralty committee examined Moulton's proposal to use rubber for a gun recoil. Admiralty/SM, 18 May 1863.

[3] The IRW, 1 October 1900, commented : " Is it not rather like affectation to ignore the fact that bribery in some form or another is rampant in business generally . . . "

[4] H. E. Coles /SM, 14 March 1855. See also the autobiography of the engineer David Napier (1799-1869) (London 1912), 25, who explained his reluctance to handle government contracts " from an inherent dislike to bribery, which I believe to be generally pursued in one way or another by those who obtain Government employment . . . "

Another correspondent wrote to Moulton on the same subject in 1855:[1]

> So we go on—Moses, Son, and Davis got the contract for the water-decks, sample you saw at the Tower at 3/2d. The cloth cost them 2/-. I tell you a Jew never entered a trade but what he damned all those in it.

Conversely, the early correspondence shows nothing but respect for the railway technicians. They appear as a group of conscientious and highly efficient workers—down to the storeman himself—who knew what they were about and, contrary to the habits of government officials, talked the same language as the manufacturer himself. Unlike the tenders for government contracts, which normally laid down the materials to be used and the standards to be attained, the railway companies applied the only test that mattered—fitness for the job for which the goods were designed.[2] It was Moulton's good fortune to win the confidence of the railway engineers through the quality of his products,[3] and it was on this foundation that the Bradford mill established its reputation.

One of the strongest incentives drawing Moulton to England was the growing market for rubber products. In the United States several manufacturers competed for the trade, whereas the English market in the 'forties was dominated by the Macintosh group who, possessing Hancock's master patent for vulcanisation, held a temporary monopoly of the manufacturing process. Moulton challenged this group when he began to manufacture under his own patent in 1848, and his example was followed in 1855 by a group of Americans (the North British Company) who were

---

[1] W. Kirkman/SM, 27 April 1855. Also H. E. Coles/SM, 8 February 1855.

[2] Until the 'eighties (when Government procedure came to be increasingly adopted by the railway companies), orders were obtained by Moulton's commodities proving superior to his rivals under severe test—granting that they were also of a competitive price. Spencers/SM, 16 April 1887 : "A railway company is going to test our rubbers against Moseleys and the account will be settled one way or another on the result, so we need hardly point out the great importance of the affair." But in the 'nineties Spencers had much sharp criticism of railway specifications, describing their tests as " absurd . . . and one which rubber will not stand . . . "

[3] In 1857 Moulton became a member of the Institute of Civil Engineers with the support of Isambard Kingdom Brunel. (Copy of nomination form signed by I. K. B., 14 January 1857.)

wise enough to locate their industry in the Scottish capital beyond the reach of the English patent law. All three companies (Macintosh, Moulton and the North British), unlike the American firms, were multi-product manufacturers, and a rough idea of their relative size a century ago can be gained from a comparison of their annual sales. In 1860, for instance, Moulton's total annual sales were approximately one-tenth of Macintosh's sales, which stood at £300,000; while those of the North British were probably in the region of £150—180,000.[1] In terms of economic weight the Manchester company was larger than either of its rivals in the 'fifties and remained so for several years, though the Bradford house found it possible to sell its wares (akin in most respects to those of the other two companies) in the same market, while the Edinburgh company was soon to make a bid for price leadership. The sharp decline in United States exports of rubber products to Great Britain following upon the establishment of the Moulton and North British companies suggests that these companies made substantial inroads into the American market in Britain.[1]

In the five years 1850-5 Moulton's sales grew rapidly from £2,000 to £30,000; but, as the accompanying chart (Fig. 2) shows, 1855 was a high-water mark. The rise was soon halted (in fact with the end of the Crimean War in sight at the fall of Sebastopol in September 1855, sales fell as quickly as they had risen), and not until 1872, by which time Stephen Moulton had established himself as a specialist in the manufacture of rubber parts for the railways, did the record sales of the middle 'fifties recur. The trend in Moulton's sales may be partly accounted for by general factors outside the industry. The rapid increase in the early 'fifties (accompanied by a rise in the total imports of crude rubber into the United Kingdom from 15,000 cwts. in 1851 to 45,000 cwts. in 1855) might be regarded as part of the general upswing in commercial and industrial activity culminating in the collapse of 1857. In the same way the effect of the business crises of 1857 and 1866 in curtailing the demand for most products, is reflected in Moulton's sales chart for manufactured rubber. Conversely, the commercial crisis of 1873 was too short-lived to have had an important influence on the trend of his sales, though in this (as the declining imports of crude rubber from 157,000 cwts. in 1873 to 129,000 cwts. in 1874 bear out) he was probably more fortunate than his rivals. In spite of the growing market for rubber goods the impact of the business

[1] See p. 105 ff.

MOULTON'S ANNUAL SALES, 1850-1890

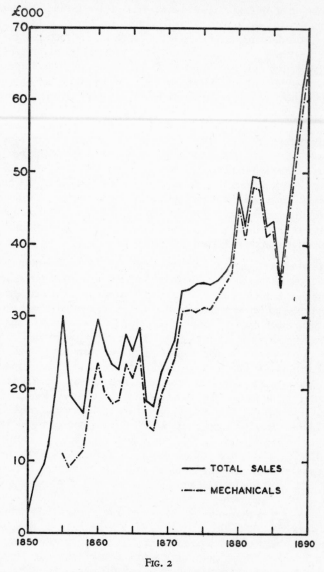

FIG. 2

Source: Moulton's Sales Ledgers for these years
Prices calculated to the nearest £100

fluctuation of 1882-3 was as severe in curtailing Moulton's sales as any of the commercial and industrial crises that preceded it. The fact that the rubber trade did not show the tendency to depression which affected most trades adversely in 1893 is attributed—in particular for the Moulton company—to the extraordinary demands for railway mechanicals, and for the industry as a whole to the cycling craze of the late Victorian era. Turning to the special circumstances affecting the market for rubber commodities in the period 1850-60, the sharp fall in sales experienced by the Bradford mill in 1856 not only resulted from the general recession but also from the aggressive sales policy of the Macintosh company, which by this time had reacted strongly to Moulton's invasion of the English market. With the appearance of the American company in Edinburgh in 1855 the struggle for markets was intensified.

The pricing of Moulton's first products was done by the general merchants, who not only priced and distributed the finished goods but also provided the working capital to make them : " At your express wish ", wrote Moulton's chief distributor in 1850,[1] "it was arranged that the prices should be fixed as soon as the market value could be ascertained", and it was in these circumstances that the level of prices was influenced more by what the market would bear (in the light of what Macintosh was already charging for similar goods) than by the Bradford manufacturer's costs. It was for the merchant and the manufacturer to arrive at a compromise on price ; one that met both their points of view as well as the conditions of a market supplied by no more that two or three manufacturers. At the outset for Moulton to be able to undersell Macintosh's goods by " the smallest trifle " was to secure " large orders for C.O.D." ; but to cast them above the Manchester company's prices " effectually stopped the sale of the article."[2]

The circumstances by which the Bradford manufacturer achieved financial independence of these ' pettyfogging ' merchants have been related above. The decline of the merchant's influence was

---

[1] Price Coker & Co. London, /SM, 12 August 1850, and 9 September 1850 : " We have all along advanced more than the amount of goods sold . . . We have advanced you £5,000 for the purpose of being laid out and expended in the manufacturing and production of such goods as you can make . . . "

[2] Price Coker & Co. London, /SM, 9 September 1850, and 8 January 1852. On 23 October 1850 Braithwaites had written : " In looking over Hancock's [Macintosh's] prices for vulcanized piping I find that he charges considerably less than you do . . . He charges for piping 1″ internal diameter 2 /- per foot, and for 1½″ diameter 2 /8d., while you charge 2 /6d. and for 1¾″ 3 /6d. . . . "

H

accompanied by a shift in the focal point of the manufacturer's interest from competitors' prices to the elements of his own manufacturing costs.   Moulton was never tired of reiterating to his correspondents that price was an extension of costs and that any change in price without a prior change in costs (primarily in the cost of crude rubber) was asking for trouble.   Similarly, the most convincing demands for price reductions made by the dealers were those based on evidence of falling costs.   Replying to such a demand in December, 1860 Moulton wrote :

> In answer to your letter of the 15th inst., I am equally interested with you on the proper adjustment of the price of our Goods, and I am attentively watching the market for the raw materials.   The *actual* fall has been on Para 4d. to 6d. per lb., on Java only 2d. or 3d.—the stock of the latter *very* small indeed.   I do not know of any Lot in London at present.   Purchases, *for arrival*, are speculations, and consequently not a proper basis upon which to reduce or raise, the price of Manufactured Goods.
>
> I think, on, reflection, from the prices of the raw material I have above quoted, you will see that the *actual* decline (especially in Java of which we use the greatest quantity) is as yet comparatively trifling, but should it return to its former price, or even tend towards it, I should of course in this case make a corresponding reduction.
>
> I do not notice the reduction you quote as made *again* by Mac., my 10%s are not so many as to bear such repetitions.   If you will favour me with a little consideration, comparing my Goods, and prices, with those of any of my competitors, and also consider the present *actual* fall in the raw gum (throwing aside the high price of the gum on hand and which ought not to be overlooked), I trust you will be satisfied that I cannot as yet in justice to myself make any reduction in our Lists to you, and the rest of my customers.
>
> Assuring you that I am fully sensible of the impolicy of high charges.
>
> I am &c.[1]

---

[1] As with Moulton so with the larger North British Company : " The state of the rubber market was then considered and in view of the very high prices being paid for raw material, the meeting unanimously resolved to advance the prices of manufactured goods, and instructed the Manager accordingly, leaving the details to be carried out by him." Extract from Minute of meeting of Directors of the North British Rubber Company, Limited, 9 August 1871.

It might be well to remark here that it was not so much the number of contestants that sharpened the struggle for markets as the circumstances under which the goods were produced and marketed. As regards production, once the vulcanisation process had been generally adopted there were no radical changes in technique to give any manufacturer a major advantage in costs. Moreover there is no evidence in the early days of this industry, certainly not as regards rubber mechanicals, that the larger were able to undercut the smaller firms because of the economies of scale. It is reasonable to think that the larger houses must have enjoyed some advantages of size, but if economies of scale enabled the Macintosh and North British Companies to produce a wider range of qualities at lower prices it was a fact never stressed either by the manufacturer or his agents in the field. As for marketing, by the 'fifties the manufactured article, as with the raw material, was bought and sold in a well-informed market ; and the absence of product differentiation, coupled with the relatively unimportant part played by transport costs, made price and the terms of sale the all-important factors for most consumers. In these circumstances either Moulton followed the price lead of the larger houses or his sales suffered the consequences :

> You know that our effort has been to keep Macintosh's agents out of the market [wrote a Birmingham house in 1856] both as to quality and as much as possible as to price, tho' in this we have failed as they reduced their washers in the same propor-tion as their buffers. If we cannot get your goods comfort-ably to ourselves we must sell out and replenish with Mac's goods which if not so satisfactory in some respects will be more profitable.

Moulton's dilemma, caught up as he was in the struggle between his two much larger rivals, is well brought out in the correspondence of the time :

> I don't know what the India Rubber trade is going to come to [wrote one of his agents from Gateshead in April, 1861] Macintosh have reduced their prices again. I apprehend it is with a view of trying to break up the Edinboro Coy who are sending out a washer at 1/6d. lb. which looks well, and I hear is good and answers well. It appears that they (Mac

& Co.) are allowing 20% nett off to all Engineers . . . which brings their goods lower than yours . . .[1]

By 1868, although total sales within the industry had increased, Stephen Moulton's share of the market (his prices still ranging above those of either Macintosh or North British) had declined, and he was faced with the necessity for the most stringent economy in the conduct of his business :

> The very great falling off in my business [he told his London manager in 1868][2] with every prospect of its continuance and the desperate, I may call it, competition amongst the manufacturers in reducing prices below cost and charges, renders it imperative upon me to reduce expenses as much as possible. I have therefore resolved to give up our London establishment . . .

This letter is important because like others written in the same vein it throws light on the manufacturer's pricing policy. The essential point is that when Moulton felt the squeeze of his larger competitors he did not turn to prices—at least not immediately—but costs ; particularly to the reduction of those overhead costs, as when he closed his London sales establishment in 1868, which would leave his manufacturing capacity unimpaired. To those who complained of his relatively high prices his answer was invariably the same: " that a good article in rubber cannot be made at a low price . . ."[3] and that whilst trying to " keep to the general level of the market " he did not " profess to compete in price with every kind of trash that is made by other parties . . . "[4] For Moulton to try to beat his competitors at price cutting, as he had done at the outset when the Macintosh Company was enjoying wide gross profit margins, quite apart from being in his eyes (without corresponding reductions having already been felt from the market for raw materials) an unfair practice, could only worsen his general position; particularly if in cheapening his goods he jeopardised the high quality market in rubber mechanicals he had striven to establish. The North British Company, as a price leader, could afford to forego profits to drive

---

[1] W. Clayton/SM, 18 April 1861. In view of the diversity of rubber manufactures and of their varying qualities it is not possible to plot wholesale and retail price curves. The graph on page 101 (Fig. 3) traces the wholesale price changes of Moulton's best grade rubber throughout the period 1855-90.

[2] SM/T. Goodwin, 13 April 1868.

[3] SM/Spencers, London, 3 September 1861.

[4] SM/J. A. Eaton, 13 June 1868.

invading Frenchmen out of the London rubber shoe market ;[1] Moulton could not do so.   As long as he was unable to seek refuge in product differentiation or the patent law, price changes were to be justified only on grounds of changing costs.   To make a price concession regardless of costs was fundamentally unsound :   " There is one satisfaction in declining competition [he wrote to a customer in 1861], and that is you leave your competitor in the enjoyment of a profitless business . . ." which meant the loss of customers, but for Moulton kept the core of his business sound.   Far better as he saw it to try to maintain his established price and surrender part of the market; and at the same time cut down his standing expenses. There was always a group of customers—even when his prices were well above the general level of the market—who either from conservatism or because they balanced quality with price, continued to do business with him;[2] and where engineering products were concerned dealers could not remove their moulds from the Bradford mill with every change in price.[3]   It needs to be remembered however (as in part the accompanying charts show) that it was one thing for the Bradford manufacturer to declare his allegiance to a costing and pricing procedure—to denounce those who, selling their goods " below costs and charges," brought distress to the trade— and another thing, as the price and discount concessions of the time reveal, to adhere to it and survive.

Two further points remain to be dealt with.   The first concerns the terms of sale; the other point concerns the movement towards price regulation in the closing years of the century.   As regards the

[1] Extract from a Minute of meeting of Directors of the North British Company Limited, on 8 August 1866.

[2] Had this not been so Moulton would have been driven out of the market in the struggle between The North British and Macintosh.   The net prices for best quality rubber (allowing for the trade discount) of several of the leading manufacturers in December 1860, was as follows :

Macintosh & Co.   ...   3s.1d.   lb.
Hooper & Co.   ...   3s.4½d.   lb.
Silver & Co.   ...   3s.9d.   lb.
Moulton & Co.   ...   4s.5d.   lb.

Source : W. Clayton/SM, 14 December 1860.   On 26 April 1861 the same writer gave Macintosh's price as " 3/7d., 20% off, your price is 3/3d. nett or 2½% off for cash ".

[3] Spencer/SM, 2 September 1861 :   " If we are compelled to move the greater part of our moulds we shall not be able to remove them again from Mac & Co. . . . "

terms of sale, a change in published mill prices normally affected all consumers, but in the adjustment of the rates of trade discount—published and secret—the manufacturer could avoid general price concessions, and might hope to retain or increase his share of a particular section of the market.   It is in this respect that any analysis of the price structure alone in this industry is an insufficient explanation of changing market conditions.   The normal terms allowed by Moulton at the outset were nett, 3 months bill; 1½% (raised in 1855 to 2½%) for cash.   The cash discount (together with the standard trade discount of 10%) was given on monthly accounts, and by the 'eighties the monthly account settled by cheque rather than by bill predominated.[1] But there were many exceptions to these so-called standard rates, the chief criterion determining the manufacturer's action being one of expediency.[2]   Indeed, the manufacturer's discount policy reflects most clearly his attempts to assess the competitive element in different parts of the market for rubber products; and the manner in which discount rates grew throughout this period from the 10–20% of the 'fifties to the 30% of the 'seventies (where they appear to have stabilised, see Fig. 3) throws an interesting light on the degree of competition met with.   As far as the Moulton papers are concerned there can be no doubt that it was not the small- or medium-sized manufacturer but the larger firms who were responsible for this upward trend.[3]

By 1860, as a result of the doubling of trade discounts by the two largest manufacturers in the trade—the Macintosh and

[1] SM/Fordred & Atkin, London, 20 August 1861 : " . . . Although we should be happy to extend our Business in garments, or any other branch as much as possible, yet we are not desirous of doing so on credit, especially long credit, the extent of credit allowed by us not exceeding 3 months, and even then we at all times give the preference to cash business . . . "

[2] Braithwaites/SM, 16 June 1851. When for instance in June, 1851, Moulton's London agent wrote : " The more I think of our customers and other retailers being allowed 10% discount off your Mill prices the more I am convinced of the ruinous injury it must inflict upon me and my brothers who with myself incurred serious expenses to enable you to weather a storm . . . " they were silenced by having their own discount raised from 10% to 15%.

[3] J. Cooper/SM, 18 May 1857, referring to a Lancashire company " who buy all their hose from Mac ", commented that they had no fault to find with the Bradford products " but get a larger discount, about 10% more".   In December 1860 Macintosh doubled his discount (from 10% to 20%) on " A " quality India-rubber at the same time reducing his price from 4s.6d. to 3s.10d. lb.

INDIA-RUBBER SPRINGS AND RINGS
AVERAGE PRICE PER LB.

and general rate of Trade Discount allowed by the
Moulton Company, 1855-90

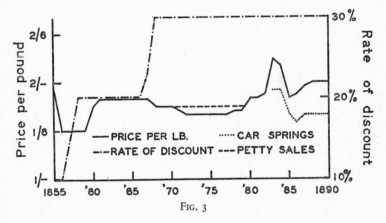

FIG. 3

Source : Moulton's Sales Ledgers

This chart (drawn to illustrate price and discount trends) needs to be studied in conjunction with Figs. 1 and 2. The price line is based on a quarterly average of the selling price to five of Moulton's largest customers, namely, the G.W. Railway, the Ebbw Vale Ironworks, G. Spencer & Co., Mechanical Engineers, Pumphrey & Co., a Birmingham wholesaler, and the Bristol & Exeter Railway. The Petty Sales curve for Springs and Rings (which except for the seventies follows the course of the general price line throughout) has been charted because it illustrates an interesting aspect of sales policy. When prices were at a low ebb in the seventies Moulton discriminated against small orders by charging a slightly higher price, yet when the price per pound of Springs and Rings rose again in the eighties the practice was discontinued. The price movements of American Car Springs—manufactured from a cheaper composition for the American market, and charted only for the years of most violent price changes—illustrates the tendency for the prices of different quality products to move together.

Edinburgh houses—a correspondent writing to Bradford[1] could " take it for granted that *all* your goods are subject to 20% and 2¼% monthly accounts", and in 1864 Moulton's London manager

---

[1] Bakewell, Crawley & Co., London,/SM, 17 February 1860.

informed him[1] "that the North British Company have travellers and agents in every part and principal town of Great Britain, and will allow 25% on even 5/- worth of goods". Just over a decade later in 1877 a London customer told Moulton that "No other firm has waited to be asked for a discount of 33⅓",[2] but by this time the movement which had raised discounts from the normal 10–20% in the 'fifties to the 30% of the 'seventies had almost spent itself, and in the case of the Bradford mill only rarely were the largest customers allowed a discount as high as 35%, which was first given by Moulton in 1879.

The second point concerns the movement towards price regulation in the closing years of the century. Unremunerative business, encroachment in the home market by the foreigner, the uncertainty of the supply of raw rubber, and the lowering of standards resulting from price warfare encouraged this development. On the other hand, while manufacturers were neither too numerous nor too scattered to exclude agreement between them, the traditionally secretive and competitive nature of the industry kept it divided against itself on price regulation. In any case :

> Not by these paltry devices [wrote the trade journal in 1887][3] did the pioneers of the Rubber trade rise to their proud position amongst British manufacturers . . . By ceaseless striving after

[1] W. Goodwin/SM, 10 April 1866. On 7 November 1860 Spencers had reported to Bradford that ". . . the North British company are doing us harm in certain quarters, and their prices all under ours . . ." and on 30 March 1863, G. P. Dodge & Co. of London confirmed the generally accepted opinion in the trade that ". . . the North British company are forcing the pace on prices. . ." Twelve years later, on 2 January 1875, W. Clayton of Gateshead wrote ". . . the North British are indefatigable to sell their goods . . ."

[2] W. Rogers & Co. London, 10 August 1877. James Syme, Moulton's Scottish agent, set out on 1 January 1870 the terms offered by several other rubber houses :

I.R., G.P. & Tele. Works Co. Ltd. ...	32½%	and 2½%
Foster & Williams	35%	and 2½%
Liverpool Rubber Co....	33½%	and 2½%

"don't imagine", the writer concluded, "that the dealer gets all that profit; in some cases customers have 25% and 2½% off LIST—others 20%, and many more 15% and so on."

[3] IRJ, 8 July 1887. The Moulton papers contain but one reference to price manipulation by concerted action of the manufacturers : Bunn/SM, 2 August 1854 : "I suppose that it would be useless (could it be brought about) for you, Silver and McIntosh to pull together and lower the market, or can you work together and raise the prices of the manufactured articles ?"

excellence, and allowing prices to be regulated by natural laws, by neglecting no opportunity for pushing goods in the markets of the world, and . . . by continuous and " bold advertisement " are the triumphs of trade realised.

Besides, the instability of prices arose in part from foreign competition over which the British manufacturer had no control; and there was the problem of issuing uniform price lists for goods whose quality differed greatly.[1]   Whatever the difficulties barring the way towards concerted action, the industry found itself drawn irresistibly towards it.   It only took a further decade for the *India Rubber Journal* to suggest (and here was the thin end of the wedge) that competition should be abolished in the cheap and retained in the higher grade good :[2]

> The greatest competition, the sorest and most annoying of all lies, or nearly all, in the very cheap goods and in the race to be in at the lowest . . . Let there be free competition in the higher grade goods. We do not wish to interfere with enterprise or liberty, but let there be a strong boycott upon the manufacturer who sells below a certain figure in any article.

In 1898 the first Rubber Manufacturers' Association of Great Britain was formed in Manchester.[3]   The interesting feature of this conference was that the oldest firms (such as Moultons and the North British) refused to have anything to do with it, but there were many less well-established houses who found the running hard and to whom self-preservation was the most compelling argument for uniform price policy within the trade.

A study of the Moulton papers (as for those of other early companies) permits one to suggest certain tentative conclusions. Firstly, as regards price determination. Save at the outset, when the merchants tested the market for him, and then allowed the manufacturer to adjust his costs to what they thought the market

---

[1] " The Rubber trade is a very peculiar one", wrote the *India Rubber Journal* on 4 March 1898, " . . . different to nearly all other trades ; when one buys cotton or silk goods they can estimate pretty nearly the actual value of the material they are buying but with rubber goods it is a very different matter . . . [the buyer] is just as likely to choose the one which has cost the least, even though the selling price is the same."

[2] *IRJ*, 13 May 1898.

[3] At a conference of seventeen firms at the Albion Hotel on 10 February 1898.

would bear, Moulton's price was determined on the average cost of a single batch or a day's working. The paramount factor in his pricing procedure was his adherence to the average cost principle, and it is interesting that he should have been prepared to work his plant in the long as well as the short run on an average cost basis. He could hardly have believed that the average costs of supplies and the finished products would remain the same over a period— for the price of crude rubber was constantly changing—but the costing margin (the percentage added to direct costs for ' Standing Expenses ') and the anticipated profit return on sales were thought to be large enough to allow for any marginal changes. Fundamentally, Moulton behaved as if his marginal and average costs were identical. A false assumption on his part, perhaps, but not sufficiently inaccurate to warrant the preparation of special cost data, which for the small manufacturer would have been difficult to obtain and of little practical value. As long as price covered direct and indirect costs (Moulton's " cost and charges "), plus a profit margin on sales (not for all products or for all circumstances the same profit margin, which would be to attribute to the manufacturer's calculations a greater degree of exactness and constancy than they actually possessed), he was happy to expand production to the point where plant and labour were fully employed; and in boom periods— by readapting his manufacturing organisation—beyond that point. In other words Moulton's prices were determined not so much by movement to and from a point of equilibrium in the scale of operations, as by changes in the cost of raw materials; particularly movements in the crude rubber market that affected from 20-40% of his total manufacturing costs. Over a period, and this point needs to be stressed, no other factor could so easily spell prosperity or disaster for the producer as changes in the value of his rubber stocks. Alongside this, changes in unit cost dependent on variations in the scale of operations were of little consequence. When Moulton's profits declined, either through internal or external forces (internal in a less intensive use of his working capital, external in the increased competition in the market for his products or because of changes in the costs of raw rubber), or perhaps from a combination of these factors, his immediate reaction was not to reduce prices but costs, particularly his overhead costs. He did not expect the market to be indifferent to his prices, but his attitude towards a market that would not yield a profit when his costs and prices had been reduced to a minimum was straightforward: abandon it, as he did in the case of rubber footwear. Or if a product was " light of profit", such as the easily constructed rubber hose, he produced only sufficient of the article to satisfy the needs of his chief customers. It would be pedantic as well as inaccurate to suggest that either Moulton or the other companies always worked on the full-cost principle (there are too many instances of " weak selling ", particularly in the trade war of the 'sixties and the early 'seventies, for this to be so), but over a period either the price covered " costs and charges " (as well as a reasonable degree of profit) or the manufacturer declined competition; especially where it involved out-of-pocket loss. The phrase " a reasonable degree of profit " has been employed because it is the term used by the manufacturer himself. The possibility of earning a 5% profit on an order in 1861 was " working against the bone", as against his generally accepted 20% margin; and the 20-30 (and even 40%) profits of the 'fifties were far removed from the 10-20% of the 'nineties, though in the light of the closing years of the century no less " reasonable".[1] In any event, total profits of the firm over a period depended not only on the addition to costs of a profit margin, or variations in output, but also on windfall gains and losses arising out of price changes in the supply of crude rubber, and in the constituent elements of costs themselves, as for instance in the changing amounts allowed for depreciation of fixed equipment and other contingencies.

Until the late 'fifties, as the figures in Appendix IV and those given in the table below illustrate, American manufactured rubber imports into the United Kingdom outweighed total British manufactured rubber exports. " . . . I can walk from here [wrote a London merchant in 1854] in 10 minutes into the warehouses filled with your articles from America . . . " Hancock's triumph over the Americans in the English courts in the 'fifties, however,

[1] " Reasonable", that is, from the manufacturer's point of view. At the meeting of shareholders of the North British Company on 29 January 1866 for example: "... The weaving department for the manufacture of elastic fabric has shown a fair profit and it is the intention of the Directors to extend this branch of the works . . . " Writing to Spencers on 3 September 1861 on Macintosh's ability to undersell the Bradford house, Moulton wrote : " . . . If they (Macintosh & Co.) possess a large capital they have also a large expenditure, and in one way or another, rely upon it they will have a good profit, i.e., a reasonable one . . . "

Some idea of the profitability of the Edinburgh and Bradford houses can be gained from the figures given in Appendix VII.

coupled with the domestic expansion of the United States, and the
establishment of branch factories in Europe, resulted in the decline
of American exports. Thenceforth, until the reappearance of
American sellers in the United Kingdom in the 'eighties, the
Germans dominated the British import trade in manufactured
rubber products. The growing volume of German imports into
the United Kingdom was an important contributory factor in the
collapse of the British market in 1868.

UNITED STATES EXPORTS OF MANUFACTURED RUBBER
PRODUCTS TO THE UNITED KINGDOM 1855-1900

	Boots & Shoes Quantity (1,000 prs.)	(Value ($1,000))	Other Articles Value ($1,000)
1855	472	318	282
1856	138	83	166
1857	86	40	106
1858	61	28	65
1859	8	3	24
1860	3	2	45
1870	1	1	12
1875	—	—	24
1880	*	†	6
1885	17	14	198
1890	49	35	290
1891	94	52	310
1892	84	40	348
1895	240	109	454
1900	306	167	791

* Less than 500 pairs.   † Less than 500 dollars.

Source : *Foreign Commerce and Navigation Returns of the United States*, U.S.
Dept. of Commerce. See Edgar M. Hoover, *Location Theory and the Shoe and
Leather Industries*, (Cambridge, Mass., 1937) 184-5.

Britain's largest market in rubber manufactures in the second half
of the nineteenth century was Western Europe . With the spread of
industrialisation the market extended to Eastern Europe, South and
North America, and the Far East.[1]   In the last quarter of the century
the value of Empire trade amounted to approximately one-fifth of
the whole. The rate of increase in the export trade was at its

[1] Moulton sent clothing and rubber mechanicals all over the world. The
first orders from Swedish and Spanish railways were received in 1856, from
Eastern Europe and Russia in 1861, and from Australia in 1862.

greatest in the 'sixties, and from 1879 until 1884, when American competitors re-entered the overseas market. The general depressed tone of business, common to most branches of trade and industry in the mid-'seventies and 'eighties, is reflected in the downward swing of the British export curve.

The problems confronting the early manufacturer in the export market encouraged Moulton to seek the superior experience and judgment of the commercial houses :

> I am happy to inform you [wrote Chas. Braithwaites in October 1850] that Mr. Windeler has at last succeeded in inducing Messrs. Huth to take up the business of exporting your goods and he has received instructions to proceed immediately. He is very anxious to see you and my father to make arrangements for sending samples to Paris, Hambro' and Amsterdam and Russia.

It was the task of these export and foreign commission merchants (the latter looked to the manufacturer for remuneration[1] as well as to their customers overseas), to find a market abroad and also to smooth out the numerous difficulties which arose.

> The first parcel of your goods for Russia has met with such difficulties, [wrote Windeler in the following month, November 1850] high duties, a fine of 20% upon the duties for not having specified the weights upon the Bills of Lading that we hardly know how the affair will end. In Prussia the duty upon all garments and made up goods are almost prohibitory, and the different reports are anything but satisfactory. It becomes necessary to become better informed and to look before we leap any further ; particularly with regard to France where with proper and good management I hope to find a stronghold as I keep Algiers in view. According to our last information from Paris there is no chance to obtain Government orders or contracts unless our goods are Patented in France. To obtain this specimens of each article

---

[1] I. N. Blumenthal & Sons, London, /SM, 10 January 1860 : " In the last two settlements we have abstained from deducting the 1¼% regularly allowed here by all the Houses to foreign Commission Merchants. As a new year begins now we hope you will do the same, as we render just your own account with all discounts thereon to our constituents and have no more than a bare commission of 2% which includes the responsibility of several months credit." Messrs. Huth & Co., London export merchants, received 3% " remuneration for a year's very disagreeable labour".

must be submitted to a Committee of the Academy of Science, who will no doubt examine and test close enough ; their report is the best advertisement for the public.

As long as Moulton was dependent on these houses for working capital,[1] his activities overseas were restricted.[2] Yet beyond the short advertisements which appeared in the French and Belgian technical Press the Bradford Company never took the trouble to develop its foreign markets. Moulton concentrated on the home trade, relying on the quality of his goods and the recommendation of British contractors and engineers to make his wares known abroad.[3]

In addition to American competition on the continent of Europe ("Those terrible Americans are again in the field", wrote a merchant to Bradford in 1852), the earliest letters provide evidence of a vigorous native manufacture, especially in the German States. A Viennese house asked Moulton in 1856 to :

consent to such a reduction in price as would enable me to compete with the resident manufacturer here (Reithoffer) and with the Berlin people, who sell here now at very low prices compared to those formerly obtained.

The Germans were not only able to compete with the British in

[1] Moulton's first cash book shows that between 22 October 1850 and 20 June 1853, F. Huth & Co. had advanced between £7-8,000 which Windeler argued on 19 May 1851 saved Moulton "from utter ruin".

[2] Braithwaites/SM, 14 November 1850, warned Moulton : "not to allow one of your coats to find their way into France, Spain or Portugal, because Huth & Co. have so many agents that if they were to hear of such a thing they would at once give up exporting your goods . . . " The Bradford manufacturer chose to ignore many of these instructions. Muller of Hamburg wrote on 16 July 1852 : "Pray do not mention that I have written to you direct . . . If you execute my small order it will prove to me that you are not tyrannized by Huth & Co. . . . " ; and Windeler/SM, 19 October 1852 : "Our Berlin Agent will prove that you have been supplying the Zollverein while our orders were standing still . . . " The almost constant dispute over terms brought the export agreement with Huth's to an end on 18 July 1853.

[3] Windeler/SM, 28 August 1851 : "Can we get a certificate from Brunel which will clinch the French Railway deal." Writing to Bradford on 17 May 1855 : "I mentioned to you in a previous letter that Mr. Brassey is contractor for the rolling plant of the Frankfort and Hamburg Railway. I am now in communication with a friend of Mr. B. and have asked him to endeavour to induce him (Brassey) to apply our springs, but, of course the most persuasive argument is always self interest. Will you authorise me to offer a commission of 5% to this party should he succeed in getting our springs adopted."

European markets,[1] where at least the tariffs were in their favour, but also in the British Empire. Their challenge came from superior marketing methods, better commercial and technical education, fierce energy, and an ability to exercise their ingenuity and skill to the full. "The superior quality does not exist [wrote the *India Rubber Journal* in May 1898], . . . the Germans send out men capable of finding out what is desired and of intelligibly reporting it to the factory."[2]

The greatest market for British rubber goods outside Europe was North America. Although a certain amount of trade was done there in articles of dress, Moulton's progress in the market for rubber mechanicals was barred by the restrictive effect of the American patent law. His exports to Canada, however, were probably the first of their kind to reach that Dominion from the United Kingdom.[3]

Regarding the terms of sale for foreign trade, little needs to be added to what has already been said. Until the 'eighties there was the same upward tendency in discounts as in the home trade, though the rates for foreign trade were greater than those given at home,[4]

---

[1] Steffelaard and Schulstkamp, Rotterdam,/SM, 2 March 1873 : " The German manufacturers are very serious competitors ; our friends have now ordered in Dresden the pipes of embedded suction hose at 2/5d. per foot franco here . . . German and Belgium manufacturers offer here 30-40% cheaper. Your prices are so very high in comparison that unless you reduce &c. . . . " ; and J. Samson, Vienna,/SM, 6 December 1875 : " It is very difficult to take any orders just now, as the manufacturers here sell goods at a loss, only to get orders . . . "

[2] See the articles *IRJ*, 27 May 1898, and 4 March 1898 : " . . . It is not a question of price or of cheap labour but is mainly the result of the good finish put upon the goods . . . When looked at carefully it will be seen that the better education and better taste of the German rubber workers is accountable for it . . . "

[3] Only by working through a Montreal firm of importers was Moulton able to enter the market and meet the competition of the price leaders in that country, the Canadian Rubber Corporation.

[4] Normally 5-10% in advance of home discounts. Paget, Vienna,/SM, 16 June 1856 : " The price charged me by Hooper and Fry for Buffer Rings was 2/- with 17½% off . . . but I have learned that they allowed Mr. Windeler 25% and he in consequence undersold me here. If you could supply me at 1/6d. f.o.b., the steamer in London river I might do a good business. Anything higher than that now will neither compete with Windeler, with the Berlin people, nor with Reithoffer of this place . . . "

and in addition to more favourable discounts, longer terms of credit were granted.[1]

Before leaving the subject of marketing a word should be said about the rise of the specialised distributor. As long as rubber products were few and simple in construction the general merchant remained an important intermediary between factory and consumer. From the 'fifties onwards, however, the growing complexity of the rubber trade made the carrying of large and varied stocks increasingly difficult, and the merchant was forced to give ground to the clothier, the shoe dealer, the engineer, and other specialised distributors. This trend is most clearly reflected in the experience of the Bradford mill, culminating in the amalgamation of the houses of Spencer and Moulton in 1891.

The firm of George Spencer & Company was founded in London in 1853. Primarily concerned with the designing of rubber mechanicals for the growing railway network, it was not long before they began to place orders with Moulton. The friendly relations between the two families fostered closer business cooperation until eventually the Spencers became the most important distributor of Moulton's products. By the late 'sixties almost half the total output of the Kingston Mill was being distributed by them. A decade later it was 98%, and the situation remained unchanged until the union of the two businesses in 1891. If either firm saw the dangers involved in such a degree of interdependence they never chose to mention it in their letters. An arrangement whereby the Spencers could concentrate on design and distribution whilst the Moultons concentrated on manufacture was acceptable to both parties. They found it pleasant and profitable to work together, and it was not until October 1889, nine years after the death of Stephen Moulton, that the Spencers made the first move towards amalgamation. The reasons given may be summarised: firstly, " the natural desire on the part of Spencers for the purpose of their business to say with truth that they are Partners and therefore manufacturers of the articles they sell";[2] secondly, to be assured against any sudden interruption in the supply of the manufactured article on the death or resignation of Horatio Moulton; and lastly,

---

[1] Englefield/SM, 22 March 1856 : " We allow our client 5% and six months credit . . . " SM/Goodwin, 20 October 1862 : " You may offer Short & Co., our packing &c. with a discount of 10% and brokerage of 5% f.o.b. London, six months approved bill . . . "

[2] John Moulton/Horatio Moulton, 20 January 1890.

so that they could become acquainted with the manufacturing process. Little more than a year later the two houses were completely merged, the Spencers becoming the dominant influence in the Bradford concern;[1] and to meet the growing capital needs of the expanding business a joint-stock corporation was formed.

[1] On the 25 August 1893 the capital of the new company was distributed as follows :

Shareholders	£10 Shares	
Moulton, H.	4,280	
Moulton, J.	4,281	
Stidolph, A.	3,392	*
Spencer, A. G.	3,392	
Spencer, Alex	3,457	
Spencer, F.	1,583	
Spencer, A. G. & Alex ...	2,748	
Popham, Henry	1	
Spencer, Jem	33	
Spencer, Emily Sarah... ...	81	
Clarke, Amy	33	
Spencer, Sydney	32	

* An associate of the Spencers and operating with them from their Cannon Street headquarters.

I

Chapter VI

WORK AND WAGES

ONE of the major problems entailed in locating a branch of the rubber industry in Britain a century ago was the recruiting of experienced rubber workers :

> The cheapest and most sure way to begin [William Rider had cautioned Moulton from New York in October 1848], is to have the best and most experienced workmen, particularly for a new concern. You will find it very easy to spoil more than three times the amount of the wages of such workmen and still continue in the dark. Had Goodyear the advantage of his present means of obtaining skill, five years ago, he could have saved at least one hundred thousand dollars . . .

It is an interesting fact that all the American rubber pioneers took it for granted that when the time came to establish a rubber manufactory in Europe skilled labour would be available from the United States: " Give us the man ", Rider told his English partner in the spring of 1848, " who will . . . furnish the funds . . . and we will put hands enough into the factory to start it and learn others. . ."; a promise that took no account of other American manufacturers " . . . being in the field for a sett of hands to go to France . . . ", or of the reluctance of the American artisan to work in Europe. By early July only two skilled workers had been secured for the Bradford factory. "We have had great trouble in getting hands for you ", William Rider wrote to Moulton. But four days later he wrote again, " . . . we have at last engaged the best callender man[1] in the country . . . and have engaged a first rate girl who Emory thinks will be better than a man to learn other girls . . . Emory says he (Abbot) can learn a man to tend the heater with very little trouble, and therefore thinks it better not to send one from here . . ." A few weeks later the first two American rubber workers arrived in

---

[1] The ' callender hand ' was the key man in the manufacturing process. His ability to control the heat and speed of the callender was crucial. The evidence shows that in the early days it was Americans (or Britons who had spent many years training in the United States) who took charge of calendering work in the United Kingdom : Abbot in the West Country, Cassidy in Manchester, and Henry in Edinburgh. (Moulton, Birley and North British MSS.)

Bradford-on-Avon "to teach and instruct . . . in the art and secret of working India Rubber . . ."[1] In bringing to Bradford a new technique they followed the example set by Flemish spinners and French weavers in earlier centuries.[2]

Apart from the essential nucleus of trained personnel drawn from the United States and the pioneering factories in London and Manchester[3] (a procedure not without special hazards), Moulton was able to meet all his needs for unskilled labour from local sources—the decay of the Bradford cloth industry having thrown many woollen workers out of employment. Whereas, according to Leland,[4] in the reign of Henry VIII " All the town of Bradford stondith by cloth making . . . ", by the mid-nineteenth century the decline of the Bradford cloth trade was manifest. Between 1841-51 the population of the town and the immediate neighbourhood declined by approximately 25 per cent, and the number of woollen factories at work was less than a fifth of those in operation fifty years earlier.[5]

Although the statistics given below are imperfect for several years[6] there is sufficient evidence to show the conditions of employment at Bradford in the period 1850-1900. Much of the extraordinary fluctuation in the employment figures during Moulton's first year, from October 1848 to September 1849, when the number rose from 22 to 42 and then fell away to 10, can be accounted for by the

[1] Letter of introduction from E. Rider /SM, 6 July 1850.

[2] See W. H. Jones, *History of Bradford-on-Avon*, revised J. Beddoe, (1907), 55.

[3] Kirkman Brown & Co., London /SM, 7 September 1851 : " Upon consideration you had better keep the man from Macintosh in the dark until we hear something more of him." J. A. Jacques /SM, 31 December 1849 : ". . . I have seen the proofer ", wrote one of his intermediaries from London, " he has been accustomed to callendering for the last 20 years—he has worked at Hancock's London establishment, at the Tottenham Mills, and is now at the Gutta Percha works . . . He wants 35 /- a week. I told him I considered he was asking high wages. He said that he could not take less and that he had a few years since received as much as 40 /- . . ." Dealing with another worker recruited from the Manchester area the writer continued : " Foxwell will be already to start next Sunday . . . he needs a sub. of £5 to be repaid by weekly instalments . . . "

[4] Leland's *Itin.*, ed Toulmin Smith (1907-10), I., 135.

[5] Jones, *op. cit.* 66-8.

[6] For 1858, 1887-90 and 1894-7. It is thought that there was little change in the first period ; the latter periods (1887-90 and 1894-7) covered years of rapid growth in the numbers employed.

temporary employment of workers engaged in converting the mill from woollen to rubber manufacture. Throughout 1850, however, when production was under way, the labour force increased rapidly until by December 1851 it had reached a record figure of 106—a total not reached again until the closing years of the century. The composition of the early labour force can be seen from the following table :

HANDS EMPLOYED IN THE MILL

4 Weeks January–February 1851 :

Average :	1 man	@ 6/8d each day	Foreman
	2 men	@ 4/6d ,, ,,	}Mechanics
	5 ,,	@ 3/6d ,, ,,	
	4 ,,	@ 2/6d ,, ,,	}Proofing hands
	5 ,,	@ 2/-d ,, ,,	
	17 ,,	@ 1/9d ,, ,,	Labourers and boys
	1 woman	@ 14/7d per week and board	}Forewoman
	2 woman	@ 1/8d per day	
	57 ,,	@ 1/-d ,, ,,	Ordinary women

March :	Jan. 4 week Factory Labour averaged £38.	
Averages : 40 men	Feb. 4 week Factory Labour averaged £43.	
60 women	Mar. 5 week Factory Labour averaged £44.	

During 1852-3 the number of workers declined, ranging between 55 and 78; but the upward turn of trade, and in particular the stimulus of the Crimean War, prevented any serious fall in employment between 1854-6. The growing demand for railway mechanicals assured the Bradford mill of a widening market in the post-war period. Whilst total employment between the early 'sixties and the mid-'eighties was notably steady, the number employed had fallen to a much lower level than during the 'fifties. It was during the 'sixties and the 'seventies that the Bradford business achieved stability in its employment of labour. The absence of wage records makes it difficult to say what happened between 1887-90, although it is evident that the number of operatives grew rapidly. In the first pay-week of December 1886 the total stood at 55, whereas by December 1891 it had reached 78 ; by December 1895 it was 135 ; at the end of 1900 it was 164. In less than a decade and a half the Bradford mill had increased its labour force threefold ; and by 6

January 1905 the number had risen again to a total of 184, which was made up as follows :

		Young Persons Male	Female	Above 18 yrs	Total Male and Female
1.	Mixers, Washers and Cutting Shop ...	2		49	51
2.	Hose Room	1	14	21	36
3.	Heater	2		37	39
4.	Fitters, Smiths, Joiners, Pattern Makers and Enginemen ...	1		28	29
5.	Trimming Shops ...	1		20	21
6.	Messenger and Watchman			2	2
7.	Stores			6	6
		7	14	163	184

By comparing these figures with those of the entire British rubber industry given on page 118, it will be apparent that the Bradford manufactory did not follow the general pattern of continuous expansion. The explanation for this is to be found in Moulton's financial and marketing difficulties rather than in the absence of a suitable labour force. It is also well to distinguish Bradford's rapid expansion in its working force in the 'nineties from that of the industry in general. The large increase in the figures for the whole of England, from 10,612 in 1891 to 18,516 in 1901 was due to the growing needs of the bicycle and electrical industries ; whereas the increase at Bradford in the same years is to be ascribed almost entirely to the demands of the railway industry.

It says something for the attractiveness of rubber working, and for the availability of labour supply in the West Country, that the Bradford mill could double its number of workers in less than a decade at the end of the century, as well as make innumerable shifts and adjustments in its labour force in the earlier years. The fact that it could absorb such a large increase in numbers in the later period without any corresponding additions to plant and machinery suggests (if the possibility of working extra shifts is ruled out) that some part of the existing plant was not already fully used ; or it demonstrates an extraordinary flexibility on the part of a small rubber manufactory to readapt its manufacturing organisation.

Table A — Employment Tables of the Bradford Manufactory 1850–1900

Year	Week Ending	Men	Boys	Women	Total Empl.	Total Hours Men and Boys	Total Hours Women	Av. Week Men and Boys	Av. Week Women	Weekly Wage Bill—Men	Weekly Wage Bill—Women	Men Av. Hrly. Rate d.	Women Av. Hrly. Rate d.	Men Av. Weekly Wage	Women Av. Weekly Wage	Total Yearly Wage Bill
1850	7/12/50	31	–	47	78	1682½	2347½	54¼	50	£17. 2. 3	£13.17. 7	2½	1½	11/0½	5/11	£770. 5. 0
51	6/12/51	49	–	57	106	3287½	3367½	67	59	37.17. 7	17.11.11	2¾	1¼	15/6	6/2	2515.16. 1
52	4/12/52	38	–	32	70	2677½	2170	70½	67¾	26.16. 3	10.18. 4	2½	1¼	14/1¼	6/10	1832.11. 5
53	3/12/53	42	–	36	78	3115	2117½	74¼	58¾	35.14.11½	13. 9.10½	2¾	1½	17/0¼	7/6	2047.16. 1
54	2/12/54	44	–	36	80	3175	2080	72¼	57¾	35.14. 7½	14. 9. 4	2¾	1¾	16/3	8/0½	2623.11.10
55	1/ 9/55	44	1	31	76	2680	1525	59½	49¼	31. 4. 8	10.10. 4	2¾	1¾	13/11	6/9½	2698. 5. 6
56	6/12/56	45	3	32	80	3190	1845	66½	57¾	37.14. 2½	12.13. 0	2¾	1¾	15/8½	7/11	2423. 8. 4
57	6/ 6/57	44	4	31	79	3130	1800	65¼	58	35.16. 8	12. 4. 4	2¾	1¾	14/11¼	7/10½	2471.17. 8
58																
59	3/12/59	43	6	22	71	3147½	1207½	64¼	55	35.12. 0½	8. 8. 0	2¾	1¾	14/6½	7/7¾	2462. 7. 9
1860	1/12/60	43	5	23	71	3615	1532½	75¼	66¾	42. 6. 0	10. 9. 0	2¾	1¾	17/7½	9/1	2453. 8.10
61	7/12/61	45	4	21	70	3252½	1220	66½	58	37. 9. 3	8. 9. 8	2¾	1¾	15/3½	8/1	2452. 3. 7
62	6/12/62	43	4	17	64	3007½	1012½	64	59½	36. 2. 8	7. 2. 0	3	1¾	15/4½	8/4¼	2361.11. 5
63	5/12/63	41	4	15	60	3050	885	67¾	59	37. 7. 9	6. 5. 0	3	1¾	16/7½	8/4	2222.19. 3
64	3/12/64	39	3	13	55	3110	775	74	59½	39. 4. 2	5.10. 4	3	1¾	18/8	8/6	2258. 4. 8
65	2/12/65	39	3	12	54	3092½	717½	73¾	59¾	39.15. 3½	5. 2. 8	3	1¾	18/11¼	8/6¾	2195.17. 3
66	1/12/66	40	2	11	53	2677½	652½	63¾	59¼	35.12. 3	4.14. 8	3¼	1¾	16/11½	8/7¼	2154.10. 0
67	7/12/67	37	2	11	50	2350	642½	60¼	58½	32. 0.11	4.12. 8	3¼	1¾	16/5¼	8/5	2040. 3. 8
68	5/12/68	39	2	10	51	3170	582½	77¼	58¼	43. 9. 9½	4. 4. 8	3¼	1¾	21/2½	8/5½	2031. 8. 5
69	4/12/69	38	2	10	50	2737½	587½	68½	58¾	37. 0. 3	4. 5. 4	3¼	1¾	18/6	8/6¼	2165. 3. 3
1870	3/12/70	36	1	8	45	2547½	480	68¾	60	34. 8. 0	3.11. 0	3¼	1¾	18/7	8/10½	2098. 9. 9
71	2/12/71	35	3	11	49	2787½	657½	73¼	59¾	41.16. 1½	4.13. 8	3½	1¾	22/–	8/6¼	2091. 9. 4
72	7/12/72	37	2	11	50	2807½	652½	72	59¼	37.12. 3½	5. 4.10½	3¼	2d	19/3½	9/6½	2263. 3. 0
73	6/12/73	40	2	11	53	3025	635	72	57¾	36. 4.10½	5. 2. 3	3	2d	17/3	9/3½	2392. 8. 5
74	5/12/74	39	2	11	52	2922½	655	71¼	59½	41. 9. 2½	5. 5. 3	3½	2d	20/2¾	9/6¾	2472.15. 7
1875	4/12/75	41	1	10	52	2950	577½	70¼	57¾	41.15. 9½	4.16. 1½	3½	2d	19/11	9/7½	2408. 2. 1

TABLE A EMPLOYMENT TABLES OF THE BRADFORD MANUFACTORY 1850-1900—*Continued*

Year	Week Ending	Men	Boys	Women	Total Empl.	Total Hours Men and Boys	Total Hours Women	Av. Week Men and Boys	Av. Week Women	Weekly Wage Bill—Men	Weekly Wage Bill—Women	Men Av. Hrly. Rate d.	Women Av. Hrly. Rate d.	Men Av. Weekly Wage	Women Av. Weekly Wage	Total Yearly Wage Bill
1876	2/12/76	42	1	10	53	3115	575	72½	57½	£43.17.10	£4.15. 8	3½	2d	20/5	9/6¾	£2479. 6. 8
77	1/12/77	42	1	10	53	3015	545	70	54½	44. 1. 1	4.15.11	3½	2d	20/6	9/7	2534. 2. 0
78	7/12/78	43	1	9	53	3250	515	73¾	57¼	46. 9. 7	4.11. 7	3½	2d	21/1½	10/2	2545. 5. 1
79	6/12/79	43	2	9	54	3260	515	72½	57¼	45.11.11½	4.11. 4½	3½	2d	20/3¼	10/2	2514. 0. 6
1880	4/12/80	43	1	7	51	3232½	397½	73½	56¾	46. 0. 1½	3.12.10	3½	2¼	20/11	10/5	2552.11. 2
81	3/12/81	46	1	7	54	3110	410	66¼	58½	44.15. 7	3.14.11	3½	2¼	19/0¾	10/8½	2687.12. 7
82	2/12/82	48	1	6	55	3667½	345	74¾	57½	53. 9. 9	3. 4. 3	3½	2¼	21/10	10/8½	2725. 6. 1
83	1/12/83	48	–	4	52	3440	237½	71¾	59¼	50.13. 9½	2. 7. 1	3½	2½	21/1½	11/9¼	2713.12.10
84	6/12/84	46	–	4	50	3602½	235	78¼	58¾	52. 0. 5	2. 6. 8	3½	2½	22/7½	11/8	2650. 4. 7
85	5/12/85	49	–	4	53	2525	187½	51½	47	38. 2. 4	2. 1. 3	3½	2½	15/6¾	10/3¾	2872. 4. 8
86	4/12/86	51	–	4	55	3775	237½	74	59½	55.13. 8½	2. 9. 7	3½	2½	21/10	12/4¾	2783.15. 9
87	4/ 6/87	54	–	5	59	2847½	227½	52¾	45½	42.16. 5	2. 7.11	3½	2½	15/10¼	9/7	2910. 7. 8
88																
89																
1890																
91	5/12/91	72	–	6	78	5300	337½	73½	56¼	82. 2. 3	3. 6. 3	3¾	2½	22/10	11/0½	4215.0 . 0
92	3/12/92	72	–	6	78	5427½	347½	75½	58	84. 5. 2	3. 7.11	3¾	2½	23/5	11/4	4355.10. 0
93	2/12/93	80	–	8	88	6095	477½	76¼	59¾	93. 7. 0	4. 9. 7	3¾	2¼	23/4	11/2½	4646. 4. 2
94																
95																
96																
97																
98	3/12/98	127	–	14	141	8612½	762½	67¾	54½	194. 1. 4½	7. 9. 0	5½	2½	30/6¾	10/8	11348. 0. 8
99	2/12/99	131	–	15	146	9165	847½	70	56½	238. 8. 0	8. 7. 3	6¼	2½	36/4¾	11/2	11080.14. 7
1900	1/12/00	148	–	16	164	10402½	940	70¼	58¾	269. 3. 2	9. 1. 6	6¼	2½	36/4½	11/4	13836.18.10

Growth and Distribution of India-Rubber Workers in Great Britain according to the Census Returns of 1861-1901

	1861		1871		1881		1891		1901	
	M.	F.	M.	F.	M.	F.	M.	F.	M.	F.
Eastern	Concentrated in the North-west, the North Midlands and the London Areas		231	16	171	15	453	136	1435	851
South Eastern			44	8	83	9	114	16	183	69
South Midland			71	33	236	163	403	252	448	311
North-west			622	233	1137	426	2297	1369	4131	2769
South-west			40	9	75	12	130	15	270	57
London			410	98	791	343	1036	1034	1372	1113
West Midland			390	97	659	201	539	348	1464	1074
North Midland			1924	383	1409	609	1185	887	1423	991
Yorkshire			38	9	123	15	210	67	243	98
Northern Counties			6	2	42	3	59	13	88	10
Wales and Monmouth			6	4	24	2	40	9	90	27
Total for England and Wales	947	343	3782	892	4750	1798	6466	4146	11,147	7370
Scotland	358	192	425	255	617	307	2010	1162	2698	2340
Total ...	1305	535	4207	1147	5367	2105	8476	5308	13,845	9,710

As regards general conditions in the industry, it is noteworthy that as a result of the Factory Acts Extension Act and the Workshop Act passed by Parliament in 1867[1] the rubber industry, as well as certain other trades, was brought within the scope of the factory and workshop legislation. Henceforth no child could be employed in a rubber mill below the age of 8 years—in 1874 the age was raised to 9, and in 1876 to 10—and the working hours of women and young persons[2] were limited to 10½ hours per day.[3]

For the Bradford mill it meant little change; 10½ hours—exclusive of the 1½ hours for meals—was the normal daily employment throughout the period 1850-1900. Mill hours were from 6 a.m. until 6 p.m. and on Saturdays work finished at 2 p.m. Yet it becomes clear from a glance at columns 9 and 10 of Table A that, taking the average number of hours worked by males, the 10½-hour day and 60-hour week were more the exception than the rule. In this industry, as in so many others in the nineteenth century, the working day finished when the work was done—even if it entailed working far into the night. Slack trade was met by short-time working; busy periods by working harder and longer—some men working an incredible number of hours. Indeed, it would not be an exaggeration to say that, on occasions, the number of hours worked by some men was well-nigh the equivalent of a normal day and night shift combined.[4] Even when the average number of hours worked was low, as for instance the 52 hours worked in the pay-week 7 February 1850, a more detailed study reveals that one worker did 85 hrs.; 4 : 70 hrs.; 13 : 60 hrs.; 50 : 50 hrs.; 6 :

[1] *A History of Factory Legislation*, by B. L. Hutchins and A. Harrison, Ch.XIII.

[2] A young person is defined to be a person of the age of 13 and under the age of 18 (3 & 4 William IV, c. 103, ss. 1, 14). From 1 January 1876 (under the Act of 1874), the age of a " young person " was raised from 13 to 14.

[3] The rise in the proportion of female workers during the second half of the nineteenth century is explained largely by the growth of those branches of the industry (such as footwear and clothing) where female labour predominated. The sharp fall in the number of female workers at the Bradford mill in the 'fifties was undoubtedly caused by the switch to the heavier work on rubber mechanicals, for which female labour was unsuitable.

[4] A practice not confined to Bradford. In the pay-week 17 January 1891, fifteen of the male workers of the neighbouring Avon India Rubber Co. Ltd., (founded at Melksham in 1890) worked on average 2⅓rd nights as well as days. See *The Chairman's Memories etc.* The Avon India Rubber Co. Ltd., (privately printed, 1935).

40 hrs. ; 2 : 30 hrs. ; 2 : 20 hrs. ; and in a week of high average such
as the pay-week 4 December 1852, when fewer operatives (70 as
against 78) worked a greater number of hours than in the corresponding week in 1850, two workers did 110 hrs. each; 1 : 105 hrs. ;
2 : 95 hrs.; 6 : 65 hrs. ; 5 : 62½ hrs.; 19 : 60 hrs.; 1 : 55 hrs. ; 1 : 32½ hrs.
In the pay week 4 December 1869 the average working week was
73¼ hrs. The greatest number of hours worked in this period was
92½ ; the lowest 45. The figures for the corresponding week in
1884, 1892 and 1893—all years of high average—were :

| | | Hours Worked | | |
Year	Total Employed	Average	Maximum	Minimum
1884	50	74 hrs.	102¼ hrs.	55 hrs.
1892	78	74 hrs.	105 hrs.	40 hrs.
1893	88	77¼ hrs.	97¼ hrs.	47¼ hrs.

But these figures represent periods of intensive activity at the mill,
and it would be unwise to generalise from them. Long hours were
not confined to the rubber industry ; and certainly, within the
industry, the longest were by no means confined to the West
Country. Instances of relay working and all-night shifts, even
of young boys, are met with in the London and Manchester
areas.[1] It was the considered opinion of one of the largest employers
in the industry at the time of the inquiry into working conditions in
1863—Mr. Herbert Birley, senior partner in the firm of Charles
Macintosh and Co., Manchester—that the trade ought to be brought
within the scope of the Factory Acts: " I should prefer for several
reasons to be under regulations . . . Most of our hands are
piece workers, and are excessively jealous of new comers; they would
at any time rather work several hours overtime than have fresh hands
introduced. For us limitation of the hours would be more convenient, and more advantageous. We should save the gas in the
first place, and besides that the effect of late work over night often
is that they do not come till after breakfast on the following morning.
Be that as it may, for the younger ones at all events, staying at work
till 8 and 9 p.m. is bad and I should be glad to see it stopped, but I

[1] From the *Report upon India-Rubber Works*, by H. W. Lord, 103 *et seq.* ;
Fourth Report of the Children's Employment Commission (1862), an inquiry into
the employment of children in trades and manufactures.

cannot effectually stop it myself; the interests, pecuniary, that is, and the habits of the work-people are both against me."[1]

It was the opinion of other witnesses[2] that overtime was very common in the trade because: " . . . there are still secrets in the manufacture which would lead an employer to keep the hands he might have on overtime in preference to getting fresh ones, whom he must discharge when the pressure is over, while the hands themselves are pleased with the opportunity of earning extra wages, and therefore ready to work longer." For these reasons, as well as the fact that the employer paid no more for overtime than for a normal days' labour (the chief source of the workers' objection to it),[3] late working remained a marked characteristic of this industry in the nineteenth century. Some manufacturers, however, refused to work overtime because it did not pay them " . . . as the workers used to loiter over their work in order to get paid for overtime ", but they were in a minority. The majority of them thought it more practical to vary working hours with the state of trade—an attitude shared by the workers themselves. In the negotiations in 1890 it was the workers who pressed for more overtime and the employers who tried to limit it ; and in 1896 when the legislature reduced the maximum period of overtime to be worked by women in any one year from 48 to 30 nights, it was the employees who made the loudest protest.[4]

In these matters the Bradford mill seems to have followed its own course. Neither the Royal Commission on Children's Employment in the 'sixties, nor the legislation that followed it, affecting the

---

[1] *Ibid.* 105. Birley also said : " I . . . have repeatedly forbidden any of the very young ones being allowed to stay after 6 p.m. But they and their parents like the extra earnings . . . and those whom they help of course like to keep them so long as they are working themselves . . . "

[2] *Ibid.* 107. Mr. Hall, the manager, and Mr. Elston, the foreman of the London India Rubber Company, West Ham. (December 1864).

[3] Extra payment for overtime (usually time and a quarter was mentioned) was invariably one of the workers' demands in the strikes of the later period. As far as the West Country is concerned the growing consciousness on the part of labour that late working should have an extra reward (other than the privilege of carrying buckets of ale into the workshop, which in Bradford's case were normally paid for by the employer) is a relatively recent development. The evidence of some of the oldest rubber workers in the West Country (octogenarians Tom Davies, Henry Wiltshire, and the late Henry Vennell) is that overtime, and the prospect of more pay, was an opportunity to be seized—not a favour to be done for the employer on payment of extra reward.

[4] See a letter on this subject from " A Worker ", *IRJ*, 12 June 1896.

employment of women and young persons, caused much change. Child labour was not a problem at the Kingston Mill as only one or two boys were employed, and the number of women workers was reduced as Moulton's share of the clothing trade declined. The Employment Table given above demonstrates that there was little difference in the length of the average working week for males or females at the beginning and end of this period.[1]

On the question of labour turnover and absenteeism at Bradford it is noteworthy that in 1851, when Moulton was struggling with what correspondents had termed "green hands", fourteen workers were discharged as unsuitable, (four left of their own choice) ; whereas ten years later, in 1861, only one worker was dismissed. Thenceforth very few were dismissed or took up employment elsewhere. The chief cause of labour turnover from the 'sixties was retirement or misadventure. As for temporary absenteeism, the figures show that the nineteenth-century Bradford worker was regular in his habits. In the year 1863, for example, less than one male worker per week was absent out of a total of over 40 men. Conversely, female workers were absent for 101 weeks during the same year, that is almost two per week out of just over a dozen women. The lowest female rates of absenteeism were never less than twice as great as those for the male worker.

The course of money wages at Bradford is shown on the accompanying tables and by Fig. 4. As outwork was almost unknown in the industry, the whole of these amounts is concerned with payment for work done in the mill itself. For purposes of wage calculations the week ended on Friday ; pay being distributed the following day. Unlike the cost of raw rubber, money wages showed no marked fluctuations. There was an upward tendency throughout the period, the average hourly rate for men growing from approximately 2½d in 1850 to 6¼d in 1900, and that for women from approximately 1½d to 2½d. Wages advanced with general

---

[1] These figures need to be compared with the Board of Trade Returns C. 375 and C. 5172, showing the average number of hours worked as a week's work in certain principal industries in the years 1850, 1860, 1870, 1880 and 1890. With the exception of railway employees most of the trades listed had reduced their hours below 60 by 1890. At the time of the publication of the *Report of an Enquiry by the Board of Trade into the Earnings and Hours of Labour of Workpeople of the United Kingdom in 1906* (Cd. 6556), however, the average hours in a full working week in the rubber industry were 55 ; a figure which compares favourably with those given for other trades.

prices, particularly during the 'fifties, 'seventies and the late 'nineties. They showed no inclination to follow the rapid decline in prices in the period 1874-96. Under these conditions the average daily rate for men rose one and a half times, whilst the rate for female

AVERAGE HOURLY RATES OF PAY
AT THE BRADFORD MANUFACTORY, 1850-1900

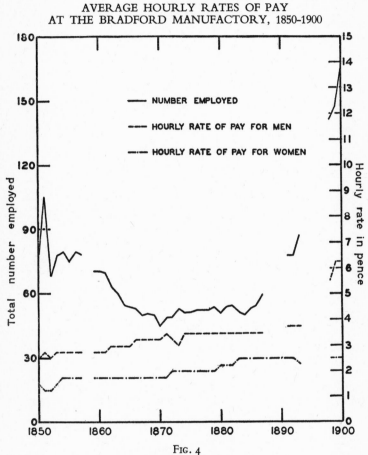

FIG. 4
Source : Moulton's Wages Book

workers, as Fig. 4 shows, was almost doubled. In 1850 only one-third of the men received more than 2s. per day; by 1891 only 4 out of 70 received less. With the exception of the peculiarly difficult years between 1850-2, and 1871-3, Bradford workers either

	1850		1855		1860		1865		1870		1875		1880		1885		1891		1900		Rates paid per 10 hr. day s. d.		Possible Weekly Earnings for a standard week: 6 10-hr. days.
	M.	F.	M.	F.	M.	F.	M.	F.	M.	F.	M.	F.	M.	F.	M.	F.	M.	F.	M.	F.			
																					9	2	£2 15 0
																	1		1		8	4	2 10 0
																	1				8	0	2 8 0
															1				1		7	6	2 5 0
	1		1		1		1		1		1		1						1		6	8	2 0 0
							1		1								1		2		6	0	1 16 6
											1		1		2				6		5	5	1 12 0
	1		1		1		1		1		1		1		1				2		5	4	1 12 0
	2		1		1		2		1				1				2				5	0	1 10 0
					1				1		1		1		1		1		3		4	8	1 8 0
			2		1		1		1		1		1				1				4	6	1 7 0
			2								1		1		1				3		4	4	1 6 0
			1												1		2		1		4	2	1 5 0
	4																1		3		4	0	1 4 0
																	1		3		3	8	1 2 0
					1						2	1	2		2		3	1	4		3	6	1 1 0
											1		1	1	3		1		4	1	3	4	1 0 0
			3		2		3		5		2		3		2		11		10		3	2	19 0
															2	1	11		12		3	0	18 6
			1		1		2		2		3		3		6				22		2	11	17 6
																	7		14		2	10	17 0

TABLE B — EMPLOYMENT TABLES OF THE BRADFORD MANUFACTORY, 1850–1900—*Continued*

1850 M.	1850 F.	1855 M.	1855 F.	1860 M.	1860 F.	1865 M.	1865 F.	1870 M.	1870 F.	1875 M.	1875 F.	1880 M.	1880 F.	1885 M.	1885 F.	1891 M.	1891 F.	1900 M.	1900 F.	Rates paid per 10 hr. day s.	d.	Possible Weekly Earnings for a standard week: 6 10-hr. days s.	d.
		3		4		5		3		3		12		9		16		20		2	8	16	0
		1		5		2		7		15		9		10		14		11		2	6	15	0
		4		3		10		8		2		4		3		3		8		2	4	14	6
		5		2		5		2		5								2		2	3	13	6
		1		6		7		4		1		3		3						2	2	13	0
		1		11	1						1	1						5	2	2	1	12	6
6		12		1		2				1		1	5		3	1		5	2	2	0	12	0
8				1	20		11		7	1	8	1				1		4	5	1	10	11	6
		1	30	4	2													6	6	1	9	11	0
	1	2		1									5					1		1	8	10	6
		1											1							1	6	10	0
1		2						1										1		1	4	9	0
4		2																2		1	2	8	0
1																				1	0	7	6
3		1		1								1										6	6
	28																				10	5	0
	17																				8	4	6
																					7	3	6
																					4	2	0
Totals																							
31	47	45	31	48	23	42	12	37	8	42	10	44	7	49	4	70	6	148	16				

improved their lot or retained whatever gains they had made; and they profited from the boom conditions at the end of the century without the assistance of a powerful trades union. Yet the wage-bill expressed as a percentage of total costs or total sales declined throughout the half century. As a result of increased specialisation, and the rise in the costs of other factors (including increased capitalisa-tion), the wage-bill, which in the 'fifties was approximately one-fifth of total costs, had fallen to one-eighth by the 'nineties. Likewise labour costs as a proportion of total sales had declined from about one-tenth to one-sixteenth.

Daily wage-rates varied for children as they did for adults accord-ing to age and skill. The remarkable thing about these child workers is that, relative to their parents, they earned so much. In the first pay-week of December 1855, the only child employed was paid 7d. per day. In the corresponding week in 1860 the daily rates were: 1s., 1s.2d., 1s.4d., and for a ' beginner ' 4d.; in 1865: 10d. and 1s.2d.; in 1870: 1s.8d.; in 1875 one able lad earned 2s.6d. per day for five days, a rate greater than that paid to seven adult workers in the same week. In 1880 only one boy was employed at 1s.10d., and by 1883 the practice of employing children in the mill had ceased altogether.

Table A, unlike Table B which is concerned with the earnings for a sixty-hour week, shows the trend of average money wages including payment for any overtime worked. A sixty-hour week however, as it has already been observed, was the minimum for a male worker. Most weeks offered an opportunity to work longer and earn more ; which, if the evidence of the oldest retired rubber workers is to be relied upon, was probably one of the strongest attractions offered by the Kingston Mill. The workers' preference was heavily weighted in favour of income rather than leisure, and this was not because Bradford wage rates were lower than those paid elsewhere.[1]

---

[1] The references to money wages paid elsewhere in the industry are scattered and unsatisfactory. According to the *Board of Trade Returns of Wages* made in 1887 for the period 1830-86 (C. 5172), 307, the average daily wage rates in the Edinburgh area in 1858 were, Men : Time, 2s.8d. ; Piecework, 3s.8d. ; Women : Time, 1s.4d. ; Piecework, 1s.8d. These rates are on the high side compared with Bradford but like so many estimates they are of questionable value as they do not give the number of hours worked. Such is the case of the average women's earnings of 16s. or 17s. per week mentioned in the *Children's Employment Commission Report (Fourth Report, 1862), 107.* D. Bremner, however, in his *The Industries of Scotland* (1869), gives Edinburgh female wages as 10s. to 14s. for $57\frac{1}{2}$ hours work ; which accords with the average wage of 11s. recorded several years earlier by the *Children's Employment Commission, Second Report* (1864), C. 3414. In 1887 a Manchester correspon-

Piecework wages never played the same part in the Bradford mechanical trade as they did in the more seasonal Lancashire and Scottish waterproof clothing and footwear industry.[1] In an attempt to speed up the orders for the Crimea in 1855 Moulton paid for work by the piece, but as the demands of the War Department fell he quickly reverted to day-rates of pay. Piecework was only resorted to again in the boom period of the 'nineties. In the first pay-week in December 1898, piecework wages amounting to £55 15s. 3½d. were paid in addition to the normal weekly wages. In the corresponding week in 1900 the amount earned in piecework was over £90.

The closing years of this period were not only important for the reappearance of piecework but also for the growing number of workers paid on a weekly rather than a daily wage basis. Until the last decade of the century it was customary to pay a weekly wage only to the foreman and forewoman. By 1898 there were thirteen week-workers out of a total of 142 employed, and the proportion of week- to day-workers was increasing rapidly. In addition these years saw the emergence of a system of bonus payments calculated as a percentage of the weekly earnings. Incentive payments were not new to the Kingston Mill. From the earliest days Moulton had paid an "extra" ranging from 3d. to 1s. to the more productive workers. The new system differed from the old primarily in that the "extra" depended less on the whim of the employer and more on the productive capacity of the employee.

The practice of making a beer allowance to certain workers is

dent stated that women rubber workers earned an average of 12s., while men earned an average of 25s. per week in that area. (*IRJ*, 8 July 1887). London rubber workers, striking for increased pay two years later in 1889, argued that the average male worker in London received between 3¾d and 4¾d an hour. At the turn of the century the trade journal gave 21s. as the average weekly wage over the year for the Glasgow rubber and waterproof workers ; though it did not distinguish between male and female workers (*IRJ*, 24 July 1899). There is little difference between this estimate and that contained in the *Board of Trade Enquiry into Earnings and Hours* (C.D. 6556), (1906), 32, where average earnings for a full week (55 hours exclusive of meal times and overtime) are given as : Men, 26s.9d.; Lads and Boys, 9s.11d.; Women, 12s.8d.; Girls, 7s.9d. ; all workpeople : 19s.3d.

[1] See the *Children's Employment Commission* (1863), 105. The situation in the early years of the present century is stated clearly in the *Board of Trade Enquiry into Earnings and Hours* (C.D. 6556), (1906), 238, where the number of time and piece workers was 5,021 and 2,309 respectively.

K

worth mentioning. Whilst wages were paid weekly and in cash,[1] a beer allowance was made for overtime, as well as for a number of other tasks such as " Cleaning the Mill " (which in the absence of a week's holiday had to be fitted in with the rest of the work), " Repairs at Boiler ", " a broken waterwheel ", or " weighing rubber ". In addition an allowance was made to certain workers whose tasks occasioned much sweating. On Christmas Eve all the men were entitled to drink at the employer's expense ; and, if the quantity of beer consumed is anything to go by, they made the most of their opportunity.

It is difficult to say what the real wages, as distinct from the money wages, were at the Kingston Mill. As far as the chief price trends were concerned, the half century was divided fairly equally into a period of rising (1849-74) and falling (1874-96) general prices. From available statistics it is reasonable to suppose that the rising prices of the third quarter of the century (where they affected food and shelter at all) were offset in part by the increase in money wages ; while the price falls of the last quarter of the century (unaccompanied by general wage reductions) must have allowed for a greater degree of comfort. Whatever the effect of these movements on the family budget, no assessment of the workers' income would be complete without making an allowance for the relative stability of the wages paid,[2]

---

[1] There appears to have been no difficulty in obtaining the necessary small change to do this ; a state of affairs by no means universal. The abuses of wage payment are mentioned by the Manchester historian, Love, in 1842 : " The method of paying the wages of the workpeople in Messrs. Birley & Co's establishment, Chas. Macintosh & Co. is one that is worth of imitation, and ought to be made known. By procuring a large amount of silver and copper every week, each individual receives his or her wages separately before leaving the premises, thus obviating the necessity of going to the publichouse or beer-shop to seek change, a practice much too general on the Saturday evenings." B. Love, *The Handbook of Manchester,* (Manchester, 1842).

[2] For example, John Moulton writing from Bradford to George Spencer in London (23 October 1894) concerning the assistance which should be granted to a widow of a late employee : ". . . Her husband was employed at the factory and was there for 42 years at a salary of 17/- per week, not of course including overtime . . . " Yet in describing the waterproof garment trade of Glasgow in 1899 the trade journal wrote : " In the Rubber trade there are eight months of the year slack and four busy . . . " (*IRJ,* 24 July 1899) ; which is certainly not borne out by the statistics contained in the First Census of Pro-

and the low cost of living in Wiltshire compared with certain other areas.[1]

On the score of wages and hours there was no great disparity between the West Country and the other centres of the industry, certainly none that shows the Kingston Mill in an unfavourable light. Nor is there any evidence to suggest that Bradford lagged behind the great progress made during this period in general working conditions. In fact the town was especially fortunate as it did not experience the same enormous growth in population as some of the new urban areas of the North, with the consequent threat to sanitation and health.[2] In one other respect the Bradford rubber worker was fortunate. In 1897, following upon the investigation made by the Secretary of State in 1894 and 1896, rubber manufacture was declared to be a "Dangerous Trade", and the Home Office was empowered to issue "Special Rules" laying down precautions to be followed.[3] Of the necessity for these steps there was

duction in 1906. In that Report the variation in employment is given as follows :

TOTAL NUMBER OF PERSONS EMPLOYED
ON THE LAST WEDNESDAY IN

January	April	July	October
23,404	24,205	23,603	22,485

Final Report on the First Census of Production (1907), 670.

[1] Job Underwood, a Wiltshire carter befriended by Moulton, who in 1857 had moved to Kettering, wrote to Bradford on 13 August 1857 : " I shall be obliged to sell my goods to take us back . . . things are very dear hear than it is at Trowbridge. It cost us 4/6 per week moore to live hear than it did at Trowbridge . . . "

[2] The applications for employment show there were a number of rubber workers who preferred Bradford to the " impure air " of Manchester and London.

According to the Census Returns the population trends of Bradford, (Urban and Rural), for the period 1801-1901 are as follows :

1801	9,602	1851	11,607
1811	10,441	1861	10,474
1821	12,857	1871	10,646
1831	12,660	1881	10,860
1841	13,379	1891	10,351
		1901	9,583

[3] See the *Interim Report of the Departmental Committee appointed to inquire and report upon certain Miscellaneous Dangerous Trades*, C. 8149 (1896).

some difference of opinion,[1] although it was generally agreed that the dangers to be guarded against were lead poisoning, naphtha fumes, and the carbon disulphide used in the vulcanisation process.[2] Moulton's workers were fortunate, however, in that he neither used naphtha as a general solvent for rubber, nor carbon disulphide (used chiefly in the manufacture of waterproof garments) as a vulcanising agent.

Any account of life at the Kingston Mill which concerned itself solely with the State's influence on the worker's life would leave many interesting Bradford practices unmentioned, such as the practice of 'subbing' on Moulton by the workers in time of financial stringency,[3] the payments of non-contributory pensions since 1860,[4] and the relief given by the employer to a worker's dependants—often before the need for assistance had become apparent to the community. Indeed, the essential characteristic of the Moulton undertaking was not to look to the State at all but to itself. To a large degree conditions were what the employer in

---

[1] For instance between the members of the Departmental Committee (C. 8149) and Dr. J. T. Arlidge, who carried out the first inquiry into health hazards in this industry for the Secretary of State in 1894. Likewise in the *Children's Employment Commission* (1862) Mr. S. Hamer considered the occupation unhealthy whilst " Mr. Birley " (Chas. Macintosh & Co., Manchester), " whose sincerity and regard for his workpeople are undoubted, states that the hands, who have suffered from ill-health while working in the cotton mill owned by his firm, often change to the India-Rubber works, and do so with great benefit to their physical condition." *Fourth Report,* 1865, 103-8.

[2] The tendency for the Edinburgh rubber workers to contract serious diseases of the chest was investigated by the Departmental Committee in 1896. On this aspect see Appendix V of their report.

[3] Though most common in the 'fifties and 'sixties, examples are to be found in the last quarter of the century of small (5s. to £1) interest-free loans. Sometimes the " sub " only meant being paid a week or two in advance : 15 May 1854 : " Smith paid 10/- for next week " ; sometimes it was a loan to tide the person or his family through a difficult period—the money to be repaid at so much per week when the worker returned to the mill : 23 February 1856 " Stop 2/6 a/c Stephen Moulton", and on 18 April 1863 " John Simmons has paid his debt in full " and so on.

[4] Retirement usually took place at 65 years. The first pension paid was 7s. per week to John Simms in 1863. From then until the end of the century there were usually 2-4 pensioners receiving amounts from 2s.6d to 7s. according to length of service and position held in the firm.

particular and the men in general chose to make them.[1] Even as late as the 'eighties it was not "idle to talk of fraternity" at the Kingston Mill. A sense of awkwardness and patronage, where it existed, did not stop the employer and the workers coming together at the summer fête[2] held on the master's lawns, and at the annual works' supper. Both these events were landmarks in the worker's life. The more food and drink consumed, the more the master had to pay—which evidently in those days was as it should be.

To try to summarise conditions at Bradford in a few words is an almost impossible task. It would not be difficult to make of it all either a sombre or cheerful picture. There were the long hours of labour, the small earnings, the brief periods of leisure,[3] and, before the Welfare State had made its appearance, the utmost dependence of the worker upon himself, his fellow-workers, and, the good will of the employer. Conversely, if the hours were long, harshness and drive were absent from them. If there was trouble at home, which for the majority was no more than a few minutes' distance away. the worker could slip in and out of the mill without the master being any wiser. If the pay was small it was free from deductions,[4]

[1] Many firms organised their own contributory health schemes, control of the funds normally resting with the employees. In the 'fifties subscriptions of ½d, 1d or 1½d were normal. At the end of the century a weekly payment of 6d, 4d or 3d provided a sick benefit of 10s., 6s.8d and 5s. per week, the company adding 50% to these payments. There was also a funeral club to which members paid 1s., 8d or 6d, the company paying an equal sum.

[2] It was at such a fête that Herbert Birley (Macintosh & Co.), who gave evidence before the Children's Employment Commission in April, 1863, noticed the distressed condition of one of his girl workers and learnt that his order against late working for young persons had been disregarded. *Fourth Report* (C. 3548). It is evident from these early papers that some employers still adhered to a Puritan sense of obligation towards their workers. Against certain names in the early Moulton wage records Moulton has written "Immoral" and other remarks which leads one to think that he was concerned with the workers' conduct outside as well as during mill hours. From the late 'sixties it was the practice of the North British to set aside £100 per annum to be spent on benevolent works ; part of which went to "the Bible woman employed for the benefit of the employees . . ." (Moulton, Birley, North British MSS.)

[3] Under the Factory Act of 1874, no child, young person, or woman was allowed to be employed on Christmas Day or Good Friday ; and in addition they had to have eight half-holidays in the course of the year. It was customary at Bradford to pay for 2 days at Whitsuntide, August Bank Holiday, Good Friday and 2 days at Christmas.

[4] The Truck Act of 1895 (dealing with deductions from workers' pay) left the industry undisturbed.

it bought much, and needs were simple.   If the work was hard, it was neither monotonous nor degrading; and if the dependence of the worker on the employer was great, there is no evidence that it was ever abused.[1] Whilst " The Amalgamated Society of India-Rubber Workers ", formed in Manchester in 1890,[2] spread quickly to the Scottish and London branches of the industry, it made little impression on the West Country.   This situation might be explained by the absence of class consciousness[3] and the degree of loyalty existing between Bradford families and the house of Moulton.

---

[1] "Sweating" was confined to a small section of the waterproof garment trade. S.C. (1889), *Parliamentary Papers* Vol. XIV, 405-41.

[2] (Registered No. 545, T.U.) Comprising spreaders, mixers, packing and hose makers, calenderers, vulcanisers, thread cutters, mechanical hands, and garment makers. Membership was heavily concentrated in Manchester and its environs. William Broomhead, the Union's first General Secretary, in a letter to Sidney Webb on 27 February 1894, wrote : " . . . I should just like to say that our Trade is one . . . of the worst I think to Organise (which is not surprising in view of the diverse and scattered nature of the industry, and the large number of female workers). Our Membership is only about 500 where it ought to be many thousands . . . "   *Webb Papers,* Library of the London School of Economics and Political Science.   According to the *India Rubber Journal* for 1889-91 strikes broke out in London, Manchester and Glasgow. It is worth noting that the beginnings of the India-Rubber Union coincided with the new mass movement among the unskilled workers.

[3] Although there is abundant evidence of industrial unrest in Bradford at an earlier period. See Jones, *op. cit.* 65, 206 ;   *Wilts. Arch. Mag.,* XL, 444 ; XLII, 127 ; *Wilts. Notes and Queries,* VIII, 261.

Chapter VII

PATENTS

ONE of the most important aspects in the development of this industry is concerned with early patent rights. In 1847, in an attempt to determine these rights, the industry resorted to a legal contest that continued until January 1856, barely two years before Hancock's master patent had expired. These proceedings not only provide an insight into the character of the men concerned, but in certain respects they also illustrate the unsatisfactory state of the patent law.

Whilst Moulton's activities at Bradford in 1849 challenged the virtual monopoly of Thomas Hancock and the Macintosh Company, it was not until May 1852 that proceedings for infringement of patent were commenced against him. This delay is explained by the much more formidable challenge of the rapidly growing American industry operating under the rival Goodyear patent. By 1847, with the arrival of the first important consignments of American rubber products (particularly footwear) in Britain, it became imperative for the English combine to test the validity of its own (Hancock's) patent. The outcome of this litigation was an arrangement between Macintosh & Company and the Hayward Rubber Company of Colchester, Connecticut, whereby, in consideration of a royalty paid to the Manchester company, the American company was granted the sole right of selling rubber footwear in the British market.

Hancock's reluctance to take up the shoe trade himself might be ascribed to the initial inertia shown by the British in contrast to the American manufacturer in this particular field. A more direct reason, as Goodyear and Moulton were to argue in the courts at a later date, might have been that, in the absence of lead compounds —declared as a necessary ingredient in the Goodyear patent—it was not technically possible to make merchantable footwear by means of Hancock's specification.[1] Hancock's belief that he could limit the supply of American rubber products in Britain to those manufactured by the Hayward Company was incredible. On both sides of the Atlantic there was a growing number of people interested in the sale

[1] A strange state of affairs, for the English court had granted Hancock exclusive rights to manufacture rubber footwear which—in the light of his patent—he was technically incapable of doing.

of American products of all kinds—indeed some branches of the early American industry were largely dependent on foreign demand —and no sooner was the agreement between the Hayward and Macintosh companies made known than the British and American manufacturers and dealers set themselves to undo it.[1] Hancock was left to lament—strangely enough in the age of individualism— " the competition which followed . . . "[2]

Goodyear's agents having failed[3] to dissuade Hancock from going

---

[1] From *The Times,* 4 November 1848 :

> *Hancock's Patent.* At a meeting of Dealers in American Overshoes, and parties connected with the Boot and Shoe trade in London, held at the Guildhall Coffeehouse, on Friday, November 30th 1848 the following resolutions were unanimously agreed to viz. :
> 1. " That in the opinion of this Meeting there is not the slightest grounds for the actions commenced against several parties for alleged infringement of Mr. Thomas Hancock's Patent ; that this meeting is perfectly satisfied that the American Metallic India Rubber shoes are utterly unlike, as they are infinitely superior, to the articles made under the English Patent, and that to allow the establishment of a monopoly in an article of the sort and in favour of so inferior a production, would be as injurious to the trade and the public, as the means taken to that end are discreditable to the parties attempting it.
> 2. " That a Committee consisting of six gentlemen, with power to add to their number, having been appointed to watch over the interests of the trade, and take such measures as they may deem advisable, more particularly to obtain the best legal and other opinions on the subject, and to procure the consolidation of the various actions with a view to a fair and just trial of the question at issue, the appointment of the Committee is hereby confirmed.
> 3. " That with a view more particularly to protect the smaller dealers who seem specially selected for the proceedings and threats of the parties referred to, it is advisable that a union be effected and subscriptions made in terms of an agreement submitted to the meeting, and that the Committee do appoint someone to receive and keep account of such subscriptions . . . "

[2] Hancock, *op. cit.* 142 : " . . . Whatever might have been the feeling amongst rival manufacturers elsewhere, it is not easy to imagine why the shoe-dealers in this country should not have been content to have taken their shoes from our licensees (who paid only a very moderate royalty) ; they would then have all been served on equal terms, and the competition which followed, arising from an opposite course, would not have occurred, nor an excellent and profitable trade spoiled by it, as it since has been . . . "

[3] J. A. Jacques/SM, 17 January 1850 :

> " . . . Mr Judson has had an interview with Mr. Brockedon for the purpose if possible of persuading him of his folly in endeavouring to establish the validity of his Patent to the prejudice of Mr. Goodyear. He will hear of no reason and is determined to bring it into court. As

to law, an action was begun by the Manchester combine in the Court of Common Pleas in the spring of 1849[1] against a British importer of Goodyear products. It took three years to bring this legal contest to an end. In it Moulton testified how he had brought the first vulcanised rubber to England, and how these samples had passed into Hancock's hands. This was not denied by Hancock. His claim was that his English patent preceded that of Charles Goodyear, and that he had discovered the vulcanisation process independently of Goodyear's samples—a claim upheld by the court.

In all this the Bradford manufacturer's position was unenviable. His customers were under a threat of litigation by Macintosh & Company, his time and energy were being consumed in the Law Courts, and if Hancock's claim was vindicated the Kingston Mill could be shut down altogether.[2]

It will not surprise the reader to be told that no sooner had Hancock established the validity of his patent in this action to the prejudice of Goodyear than he filed a bill in Chancery to obtain an injunction against the Bradford company.[3] Moulton had been a thorn in the side of the Manchester combine for some

for you I don't know what he is not going to do—suffice it is to say he . . . will put a stop to your manufacturing . . . "
The Moulton Papers show that negotiations between the Americans and the British went on throughout the Somervell trial. W. Long (Moulton's lawyer)/SM, 3 April 1850 : "Judson starts for America Saturday morning. Proposed arrangement with Hancock and Goodyear is this, viz. : Both their patents be sustained, you to become a licensee at a small tariff to be employed jointly with other contributions in supporting the validity of the patents . . . "

[1] Hancock v. Somervell & Burr, Newton's *London Journal*, Vol. XXXIX, 158 *et seq.*

[2] Compulsory licences were introduced by the Patent Act of 1883. Until then a patentee could refuse to license his process absolutely. Support for compulsory licences had been given in Government Reports in 1829 and 1851, by the British Association for the Advancement of Science in 1860, and the House of Commons Select Committee in 1872. In the international field the principle had been accepted by the Patent Congress at Vienna in 1873. One of the most influential English bodies opposed to compulsory licences was the Royal Society of Arts. On this see the discussion in *The Times* of 9 March 1877, also papers by A. T. Wood, *R.S.A. Journal*, Vol. XXV, 339 and Vol. XXXI, 558.

[3] Hancock v. Moulton. Action commenced in the Vice-Chancellor's Court, Monday, 31 May 1852. *Mechanics' Magazine*, 1852, Vol. LVI, Nos. 1504 and 1506, 456-7 and 491-2.

time. He had never changed his belief that they had taken the credit for Goodyear's discovery of vulcanisation; he had been a principal witness against Hancock in the courts ; and his manufactory had eaten into Hancock's markets for rubber mechanicals. At least one member of the Manchester company would have been glad to see Moulton driven from the trade altogether. Yet it was more than embittered personal relations that took Hancock back into the courts. Moulton's patent represented an alternative system of vulcanisation. Hence the favourable decision secured against Somervell and others who had been selling American shoes did not invalidate Moulton's patent of 1847. Before Hancock could claim a monopoly of English vulcanisation rights he had to dispose of Moulton's claim. If he could prove that his own vulcanisation patent of 1843 and Moulton's patent of 1847 were alike, then (having disposed of Goodyear's claim and having purchased Parke's invention)[1] no vulcanised rubber product could be sold on the British market without paying royalty to the Macintosh Company. If Moulton's claim went unchallenged it was possible for the Kingston Mill to become the centre of American activities in Britain.

The trial between Moulton and Hancock was heard in the spring of 1852 in the Vice-Chancellor's court. The evidence—presented in extremely scientific and complicated language—eventually resolved itself around three chief points. Was Hancock's patent valid ? If so, could an infringement be proven against Moulton ? Did not the delay which had been allowed to take place between the time Moulton took out his patent and the present application preclude the court from interfering by injunction ?

As to the first point, Hancock submitted that his patent had been taken out almost a decade previously. No one had successfully challenged it, and when it had been tested in the Somervell action his claim to prior rights of vulcanisation had been upheld. As to the second point, it might be argued that Moulton's patent differed essentially from Hancock's. The best answer to this was the scientific evidence given on Hancock's behalf, which showed that lead in the hyposulphite (the basis of Moulton's patent) was merely a vehicle for the sulphur, and that sulphur, and not hyposulphite of lead, was the vulcanising agent. Lastly, as to the delay in bringing the action against Moulton, Hancock submitted that this had been

[1] Alexander Parkes' invention of cold vulcanisation was purchased by Macintosh & Co. shortly after its discovery in 1846 for £5,000.

occasioned by the Somervell action having taken so long to resolve.

Moulton's case was put at great length and with considerable skill.[1] Counsel first argued that Hancock's patent of 1843 was invalid because the title of Hancock's deposit paper did not fore-shadow the specification.   If the law was that the one must be in conformity with the other—otherwise of what use was the deposit paper or the title—then Hancock's patent of 1843 could not be sustained. In other words, what Hancock had proposed to do and what he had subsequently done were entirely and essentially different. In fact Hancock had not discovered vulcanisation at the time of his application for a patent in November 1843 at all.   Could anyone imagine for a moment, counsel for the defence argued, that :

> Rendering leather, cloth and other fabrics waterproof, and the various other purposes for which caoutchouc is employed [which Hancock had stated as the object of his patent in November 1843] could also by the ordinary rules of common sense be supposed to include the entirely new substance contained in his specification in May 1844, namely that of imparting to caoutchouc properties it was never before known to possess?

Not only was there a fundamental difference between the title of November 1843 and the specification of May 1844, but the degree of heat prescribed in Hancock's specification was declared by the defence to be impracticable.   Furthermore how could the charge that Moulton was infringing Hancock's patent be substantiated? Moulton was manufacturing under a patent taken out in 1847 for using the hyposulphite of lead and the artificial sulphuret of lead, instead of the crude sulphur of commerce patented by Hancock.   As Moulton achieved vulcanisation by an entirely different process from either Goodyear or Hancock it could not be argued that Hancock's patent had been established against Moulton by the Somervell decision.   Moreover Hancock's charge that the Moulton process was merely an improvement upon his own was rebutted by counsel.   Even if it were an improvement the court could not rightly grant an unconditional injunction, be-cause this would give the plaintiff the power to stop the Bradford manufactory altogether and thus secure to himself a monopoly and

---

[1] For this I have drawn largely upon the notes prepared by Moulton for Sir W. P. Wood, Mr. Hindmarch (who figures in the Hancock v. Somervell trial) and Mr. Southgate, who opposed the motion for injunction, and the reports contained in the *Mechanics' Magazine*.

not merely a patent. In any event Hancock's patent could not be sustained because Moulton had exhibited vulcanised goods in England prior to November 1843. Let it be assumed, in accordance with the scientific evidence submitted, that there was no essential difference between the Hancock, Goodyear and Moulton patents ; then how could the court deprive Moulton of the right to manufacture the goods he brought over from America in 1842, by a patent granted in 1843 to the party to whom he had exhibited these goods? If Moulton knew the details of Goodyear's process—as he claimed he did—before the date of Hancock's patent then to deprive him of the right to manufacture according to the Goodyear process would be to deny him " a freedom or liberty he had before " Hancock applied for his patent in 1843. It would be a denial of Moulton's rights as a British subject, either to import the goods as the produce of a foreign country under the treaty of commerce existing between it and Great Britain, or to manufacture the goods at home. One last plea was made on Moulton's behalf. Counsel for the plaintiff had argued that Hancock had used due diligence in maintaining his patent against Moulton by commencing an action against the importers of Goodyear's products the moment they appeared in Britain. Was it seriously suggested that the Bradford mill should have stood idle for three years whilst the Hancock v. Somervell action was decided?

The decision of the court—which was to have its repercussions throughout the trade—is best given in the judge's own words. In summing up he held that there was little doubt concerning the validity of Hancock's master patent. Whether Moulton had infringed that patent was a technical question turning upon the scientific evidence submitted at the trial. On this score His Honour " was of the opinion that the evidence preponderated very considerably in favour of Hancock", and if he were " bound to decide the case upon scientific evidence which had been given he should decide it in favour of the plaintiffs". Yet "weighing all these considerations, and admitting the strength of the plaintiff's evidence he was of opinion that he should not be warranted in committing the defendant without a trial at law of the question of the infringement". Even if an unanswerable case had been made out for infringement " the plaintiffs had not proceeded with that promptitude[1] which the course of the court required and he had come to

[1] Hancock submitted that as he had been given to understand by Moulton in 1849 that he was working to Goodyear's patent, his action against Somervell was intended to include the Moulton Company. Moulton strongly denied this, asserting that he had let it be known in 1849 that he was working according to his own patent of 1847.

the conclusion that he must refuse the injunction". The motion was ordered to stand over, with liberty to the plaintiffs to bring further action.

Thus one unsatisfactory situation had been exchanged for another. The Kingston Mill could still carry on but Moulton was only buying time. Hancock was free to take him to law again whenever it pleased him, and the exhausting procedure would begin all over again. Whilst Moulton had no appetite for these things—his only desire being to remain absorbed in his business—the Bradford sales chart makes it clear that sales, despite the course of litigation, continued to expand throughout the years 1850-5.

Meanwhile, the contempt in which sections of the trade held Hancock's patent is well summarised in the letter given below :[1]

3 Falcon Square, London.

12 September, 1853.

I feel it due to myself, and my customers, and the trade generally, to set Hancock & Macintosh in their proper position . . . The Firm who would be guilty of threatening . . . Merchants with proceedings at law, under *Mr. Thos. Hancock's alleged Patent,* when they themselves are liable to be proceeded against for infringing *Mr. Chas. Goodyear's patent,* would do or say anything that would advance their own pecuniary interest.

The origin and history of Mr. Thos. Hancock's alleged patent is known only to a few. That he obtained whatever knowledge he possesses of Vulcanising India Rubber from *American* Vulcanised goods . . . has been uncontestably proved ; this fact alone would be fatal to said alleged patent in any court of law either in America or England. Messrs. Macintosh & Co. has succeeded so well by intimidating and coercing the public, that some two years since they adopted another experiment and filed a bill in Chancery to obtain an injunction against Messrs. Stephen Moulton & Co., of Bradford, Wilts. (who by the way are large manufacturers of all sorts of Vulcanised goods which are precisely like the American goods, and far superior to any ever made by Messrs. Macintosh & Co.), but Messrs. Moulton & Co., like true and independent men resisted this aggression on their rights, and the result was that the Chancellor dismissed said bill on its merits. After this one would think Messrs. Macintosh

[1] Moulton MSS.

& Co. ought to have ceased to intimidate and coerce the trade, but it appears although defeated again and again, they return to the charge and persevere in it . . .

That it is impossible to make merchantable goods by Mr. Thos. Hancock's Specification every manufacturer of Rubber can prove, and the fact that Messrs. Macintosh & Co. have abandoned the manufacture of their miserable rags or goloshes falsely so called (which were made in imitation of the American overshoes), and now advertise to supply the public with American goods made under *Mr. Chas. Goodyear's patent,* puts the fact beyond all controversy. However in a few days a Scire facias will be brought to set aside Mr. Thos. Hancock's claim to a patent as by it the Queen's subjects are put to a great loss and inconvenience . . .

The American Rubber Companies as well as Mr. Chas. Goodyear are determined to stop Messrs. Macintoshes' invasion on their rights and if ever Macintosh & Co. proceed at law against me, they will sustain me. And the trade may rest assured that no privileges Messrs. Macintosh & Co. can bestow nor all the money they can offer will ever purchase a verdict in their favor.

I am,

Your obedient servant,

George Ross.

This letter reveals contempt and open hostility to Hancock and the Somervell judgment which sustained him. It was a declaration of war, and behind it stood powerful British and American interests.[1] Hanock did not wait until the threatened writ of *scire facias* was issued against him. He chose to make the first move and in the Court of Exchequer at Westminster in June 1854, before the Lord Chief Baron, he charged Ross—as he had charged Somervell, Burr and Moulton—with infringing his patent of 1843; the infringe-

---

[1] The trade had been preparing for the conflict during the past six months or more. For example : E. Spencer & Co., London/SM, 1 October 1853 :

Dear Sir,

It is intended to hold a meeting of a few of the leading parties interested in the sale of American overshoes at the London Tavern, Bishopsgate St., on Wednesday next the 5th inst., at 2 o.c., for the purpose of discussing the present aspect of affairs with reference to proceedings adopted by Mr. Hancock against certain dealers in Town, and the best mode of checking the same, and creating confidence by taking counter proceedings . . . " (Moulton MSS.)

ment consisting of the sale of American overshoes " not the produce of the Hayward Company."[1]

As can be expected, many of the old arguments were heard again: Hancock's invention was not new; the use of sulphur alone had been anticipated in Fanshawe's English patent (No. 9189) in 1841; at the time Hancock applied for a patent he had neither understood nor effected vulcanisation, and he had unfairly obtained a knowledge of the invention from Goodyear's samples. The case for the defence—supported by American shoe manufacturers[2] who resented Hayward's exclusive licence as much as the London shoe dealers themselves—was that the Goodyear triple compound of rubber, sulphur, and white lead was essentially different from that described in Hancock's specification. Without the lead a good article could not be made. Hancock's case, conversely, was that whilst it was admitted that the overshoes sold by Ross were composed of rubber, sulphur and oxide of lead, the vulcanisation was attributed entirely to the agency of the sulphur, and the shoes were therefore an infringement of his patent. In spite of an able summing-up for the jury by the Lord Chief Baron, who recapitulated the chief points concerning the invention and the question of infringement by Ross, the jury failed to agree on a verdict and was discharged. The trial had proved to be little more than a speculation on the ignorance of both judge and jury ; and the trade now proceeded to submit Hancock's master patent to the most exhaustive test of legality known to the English law: to issue the writ of *scire facias*[3] mentioned in Ross's letter above.

[1] Hancock v. Ross and others, *Mechanics' Magazine*, 1854, Vol. LXI, 37 *et seq.*

[2] This opposition was organised from the signing of the Macintosh-Hayward agreement. WR/SM, 20 December 1848 : ". . . The Newark Co. and others, as you are probably aware, are determined to break up Hayward's monopoly in the English market for shoes—they have an agent in London for that purpose . . ."

[3] The writ of *scire facias* was a most severe test of any patent. John Horatio Lloyd, a barrister, giving evidence before the House of Lords Committee on the Patent Law Amendment Bills, 1851, had this to say :
" The greatest satire I have ever known passed upon the patent laws, I found the other day in a pamphlet published by one of the most eminent practitioners in that branch. He says, that as a general rule, where men are plaintiffs, and sue for an infringement, they succeed ; where they are defendants, being sued under a writ of *scire facias,* they fail . . . " S.C. 1851. *Parliamentary Papers,* Vol. XVIII, 605.
It was the opinion of Alfred Vincent Newton, a patent agent, before the Royal Commission of 1863 " . . . that patents are not subjected to the ordeal of *scire facias* proceedings unless of great commercial value . . ." *Parliamentary Papers,* Vol. XXIX, 458.

In June 1855 the action Reg. v. Hancock was heard in the Court of Queen's Bench.[1] Essentially there is very little to add to what has gone before, except perhaps that Hancock now appeared in the unusual role of defendant, and that it was in this trial that Goodyear made a great struggle to regain what he considered to be his patent rights. Had he done so he would have been able to exact a royalty from every mill using the Hancock process. The case against Hancock was based on the same allegations as had been made in the Courts of Chancery and Exchequer, namely, that Hancock only effected vulcanisation in the interval between the taking out of his patent in November 1843 and the filing of his complete specification in May 1844. The whole issue turned on whether or not Hancock had effected vulcanisation when he took out his patent in November 1843. If he had discovered the vulcanisation process in the interval between his preliminary specification (November 1843) and his final specification (May 1844)—and that only by working on Goodyear's samples—then his case fell to the ground. In his summing up Lord Campbell had this to say :

> If Goodyear's invention was prior in point of time, it was not handsome in Hancock to look at his specimens and try and find out his discovery ; and if Goodyear was the inventor it was to be regretted that he should not have the benefit of the invention. The question, however, was whether before his patent Hancock was the inventor of this process, for if he was, the objection failed and the defendant was entitled to a verdict. But if he did not know it then, but by a subsequent discovery was enabled to insert it in his Specification, he was not entitled to the patent and the jury ought to find their verdict for the prosecutors . . .

In returning a verdict in Hancock's favour the jury put an end to this prolonged litigation.[2] Moulton was granted a restrictive licence[3]—an arrangement which certainly did not please him—to continue to manufacture at Bradford on payment of £600 per annum. There was nothing further Charles Goodyear could do except hasten to France to salvage what remained of his patent rights

---

[1] Reg. v. Hancock and others. *Mechanics' Magazine*, Vol. LXIII, 80.

[2] *London Daily News*, dated 15 January 1856.

[3] The licence granted to Moulton excluded clothing and medical goods. See copy correspondence Whitaker/Karslake for 6,7,8 March 1856. (Moulton MSS.)

there.[1] His own countrymen, however, were of a different mind. In fact one of the most interesting sequels to the story told above was the founding of an American rubber manufactory in Edinburgh simultaneously with Hancock's triumph in the English courts. The latter had barely time to congratulate himself on the outcome of his struggle with Goodyear and Moulton when there sailed up the Clyde the American ship *Harmonia* bringing machinery and workers to found Scotland's first vulcanised rubber manufactory.[2] Unhampered by outmoded traditions, and with a rising demand for its products, the British rubber industry offered chances of the greatest profits, which the Americans were determined to secure. The patent law is too complicated a matter to invite sweeping generalisations, but the available evidence shows that Hancock's delay in protecting his discovery in Scotland, (in this instance curiously enough Goodyear's Scottish patent preceded Hancock's), had revealed a weakness which the Americans were quick to exploit.[3]

[1] The question will be asked: why did Goodyear allow Hancock to forestall him ? Of the several explanations the most important are Goodyear's extreme poverty at the time, his desire to perfect his invention before making it public, and the necessity to announce his discovery simultaneously in America, Britain and France. Rider's description of Goodyear in his letters to Moulton, as well as Goodyear's own letters to Bradford, give ample evidence of a genius, but it was a genius who almost drove the bustling Riders and Moultons of his day to distraction. In 1848 Rider described his friend " Charley " as " still that same uncertain Charles Goodyear and to all appearances he will continue to be so for all time . . . " And to Rider's forecast that Goodyear would make up his mind to come to England soon, Moulton replied in July 1848 : " Goodyear is coming, of course so is the year 46732009, the latter will arrive first—I opine . . . "

[2] Appendix V.

[3] Bannatynes & Kirkwood/Henry Lee Norris, 8 January 1856 : " . . . In reference to Hancock's Scotch Patent we are of opinion, therefore, that there are two good objections to it. The first founded on the long interval which was allowed to elapse between the dates of his English and Scottish Patents and English and Scotch specifications. And the second on the circumstance of Newton (for Mr. Goodyear) having anticipated in date Hancock's Scotch Patent and Specification by his own . . . " (North British MSS.)

The dates of the English and Scottish Vulcanisation Patents are as follows :

DATES OF PATENTS AND ENROLMENT OF SPECIFICATIONS

	Dated	Spec. enrolled
Hancock's English Patent	21 Nov. 1843	21 May 1844
Newton's (Goodyear's) English Patent	20 Jan. 1844	30 July 1844
Newton's (Goodyear's) Scottish Patent	12 March 1844	11 Sept. 1844
Hancock's Scottish Patent	25 June 1844	19 Oct. 1844

If further evidence is required to support the contention that the foundations of the rubber industry were laid in the first half of the nineteenth century by pioneers such as Goodyear, Hancock, Hayward, Chaffee and Parkes, it can readily be gleaned from the records of the British Patent Office. Refinements, adaptations, extensions, improvements in the processes devised in the first half of the century are there by the score; unimportant innovations— particularly as changes in the law facilitated the growth of the patent system in Britain—can be counted by the hundred.[1]   Yet with the exception of the discovery of the acid and alkali processes of reclaiming rubber by Hall in 1856[2] and Marks in 1899,[3] and Waddington's[4] dry heat process of vulcanisation in 1887, there are no major developments in the period 1850-1900 worth recording. At the end of the century all the separate stages of manufacture: preparing, cleansing, cutting, masticating, compounding, milling, vulcanising, hardening, moulding and finishing were fundamentally what Goodyear, Hancock and the others had made them.   As with processes so with markets.   Until the tyre boom of the 'nineties opened a new era in the history of the industry, footwear, waterproof clothing, mechanicals, electrical appliances[5] and medical supplies remained the chief branches of rubber manufacture.

Whilst the Kingston Mill played only a minor role in the develop-

---

[1] For the period 1867-1900 there are 146 abridgments each containing many thousands of specifications.   Those relating to the treatment, process, recovery and manipulation of rubber, etc. (Class No. 70) were few in number until the Act of 1852.   In 1859 the figure was 43 ; but on the eve of the Patents Act of 1883 patents granted in this class had fallen to 9.   A marked increase followed the Act of 1883, and in 1899 the figure had risen to 44.   A wider class of patents such as the old abridgment No. 16 (1791-1866) relating to India-rubber, etc., including air, fire- and water-proofing, gives evidence of a much larger number of inventors making use of rubber.   Under this heading many more patents were granted.   For instance the 21 patents granted in 1851 increased to 138 in 1852, and 275 in 1853.

[2] Patent No. 141, 18 January 1856.

[3] Patent No. 11,159, 29 May 1899.   Patents dealing with waste, substitute, and devulcanising rubber were few in number until the scarcity prices of the late 'nineties.   For instance there were 8 such patents granted in 1855 ; 3 in 1865 ; 3 in 1875 ; 3 in 1885 ; 7 in 1895, and 18 in 1898 and 1899.

[4] Patent No. 15,680, 16 November 1887.

[5] As the abridgments (Nos. 36-41) dealing with electricity show, the manifold demands of this growing industry in the closing years of the century provided a vast new market for rubber products, particularly for the use of hard rubber or vulcanite.

ment of the pneumatic tyre industry there are one or two points concerning tyre patents which should be mentioned in passing. The first of these is that like so many other successful inventions Dunlop's discovery of the pneumatic tyre in 1888 had been anticipated[1] by Thomson in 1845, and on these grounds Dunlop's master patent was set aside shortly afterwards.[2]   Dunlop's invention was the natural outcome of a need which is clearly reflected in the patent lists.[3] Thomson's invention was a generation before its time and remained neglected and undeveloped.   The former's success was due to the growing mobility of society, and the changing attitude towards outdoor life of the late Victorian era.   Added to this was the growing availability of capital—particularly the "cheap money" of the mid-'nineties, the increasing activity of the company promoter,[4] and the development of the internal combustion engine after 1895.[5]   The Dunlop organisation did not come to play a major role in this vast new enterprise because they possessed Dunlop's patents—these were of little consequence

---

[1] See " The Patents for Inventions Bill ", *R.S.A. Journal*, Vol. XXV, 339.

[2] Arthur Du Cros, *op. cit.* 48–50.   As with all other valuable rubber patents (such as those of Goodyear and Hancock) the trade lost no time in joining together to overthrow it.

[3] From the late 'sixties onwards the search for an improved rubber tyre had been intensified.   Prior to Dunlop's patent in 1888, English patents concerned with the pneumatic principle were as follows : R. W. Thomson, No. 10990, 1845 ; J. E. Croce-Spinelli, No. 3380, 1869 ; in 1870 provisional protection was granted to the patents of V. Pendred, No. 3219, and T. Wilkinson, No. 3287. With the publication of Dunlop's patent in 1888 the number of would-be pneumatic tyre inventors grew rapidly.   Restricting the search to those patents granted in the post-Dunlop era for improved pneumatic air tubes and chambers, the number had increased from 1 in 1888 to 173 in 1896.

The same feverish activity of the mid-'nineties is reflected in the growing number of patent applications for solid rubber tyres. In 1868 the number had been 4 ; in 1869 it was 8 ; in 1870 : 18. Throughout the 'eighties (and this is the " felt want " that Dunlop set himself out to meet) the number of patents ran at a high level.   By 1890 the figure stood at 70 ; in 1892 it was 80 ; 1893 : 86 ; 1896 : 184 ; 1897 : 175 ; 1898 : 110 ; 1899 : 87 ; and 1900 : 95.   In searching for an improved bicycle tyre Dunlop was merely doing what many other men were doing at the same time ; the peculiar fact about his discovery is that, unlike the others, he chose to concentrate his efforts on an air-filled tyre.

[4] J. H. Clapham *op. cit.* III, 236–7.

[5] In 1895 the first motor-car to use pneumatic tyres appeared in the Paris-Bordeaux races.

compared with others[1]—but because they took the precaution of buying up important patent rights as they appeared and so assured themselves of a degree of control unequalled elsewhere. Long before the patents owned by the company were due to expire they had begun to manufacture their own tyres. From their original assembly plant in Coventry—in the early days they had been quite prepared to leave the manufacturing of tyres to others[2]—they extended their control over the English Midlands.[3]   In the Coventry and Birmingham area, the centre of the bicycle and later the motor-car industry, the Dunlop Company extended its activities from one branch of rubber manufacture to another until eventually it sat astride a great part of the British rubber industry.[4]

Although the Patent Law Amendment Act of 1852[5] and the Patents Act of 1883 did much to improve the patent system in Great Britain—the increase in the number of patents following upon the

---

[1] Unfortunately for Dunlop, Thomson had patented his tyre in England in 1845, in France in 1846, and in the United States in 1847.   The English courts declared Dunlop's master patent invalid in 1892, the French courts in 1896. In the period 1889-1900 Dunlop took out thirteen patents, none of which were of any great consequence.   Of far greater importance in the history of the Dunlop Company were the Welch (14,563, 16 September 1890) and the Bartlett (16,783, 21 October 1890) patents, which—along with several other major inventions—the Dunlop corporation had the good fortune to purchase outright.   Arthur Du Cros, op. cit. 48-50, 133-4.

[2] *IRW*, 1 September 1938.

[3] On 1 July 1896 the Dunlop Company purchased the rubber factory of Byrne Bros. at Aston, Birmingham.   *The Stock Exchange Official Intelligence,* 1927, XXXXV, 689 ;   *IRW*, 1 March 1899, 149 ;   1 July 1901, 290.

[4] The activities of the Dunlop Company account in part for the formation of the Rubber Manufacturers' Association in 1898. *IRW*, 1 March 1899, 149; 1 January 1900, 91 ;   1 December 1902, 78.

[5] Introduced as a result of considerable agitation for reform, it greatly simplified procedure and reduced the costs of the patentee.   It centralised the control of patents of invention under the newly created Commissioners of Patents.   Henceforth one patent (instead of the customary three under the old patent laws) was sufficient for the whole of the United Kingdom.   The Act of 1883 further simplified procedure and reduced the fees.   The Commissioners of Patents were replaced by the Patent Office as a department of the Board of Trade.   On this see A. A. Gomme, *Patents of Invention,* (London 1946), 39 *et seq.*   Also H. G. Fox, *Monopolies and Patents* (University of Toronto, 1947).

GENERAL PATENT OFFICE,

ESTABLISHED IN 1830.

10, RUE DE LA FIDÉLITÉ, PARIS.   21, RUE DE L'ÉVÈQUE, BRUXELLES.

London, March, 1863.
4, South Street, Finsbury.

I BEG to submit to your notice the following statement of charges, and information with regard to obtaining Patents for Inventions in the United Kingdom of Great Britain, in the principal States of Europe and in America. A long and extensive practice and numerous connexions enable me to offer considerable facilities for procuring and disposing of Patents, as can be attested by the numerous Patents sold by my agency both in England and abroad.

ENGLISH PATENTS.

The Government tax, inclusive of Agency fees, is as follows :—

Application for Letters Patent (by which Provisional Protection for Six Months is obtained), inclusive of Provisional Specification	£7 0 0
Notice to Proceed	7 0 0
Warrant and Great Seal (Letters Patent)	11 0 0
Average cost of Final or Complete Specification	12 0 0

To apply for a Patent, it is necessary to fix upon a title, and to draw up a short description of the Invention, styled the " Provisional Specification." It is optional to lodge with the application a Complete Specification. In the first case (most generally adopted), the proper documents being lodged, a certificate of " Provisional Protection" for Six Months is granted, which dates from the day of leaving the application. Directly after the Certificate of Provisional Protection is granted, the Inventor is at liberty to take the next step, give " Notice to Proceed," which must be done, at latest, eight weeks before the expiration of Provisional Protection. When given, the name of the applicant and title of the invention are advertised in the " London Gazette," with a notice that objections (an opposition) may be made to the grant during twenty-one days from the date of the publication. If no opposition is entered within the specified time, or if the objections raised at the " Hearing" appointed are overruled, the Petitioner can forthwith apply for the Warrant and Great Seal, which must be paid for, at the latest, fourteen days before the " Provisional Protection" expires.

If a " Provisional Specification" has been lodged with application, a Complete Specification must be filed after obtaining Letters Patent, before the Six Months expire.

When a " Complete Specification " has been deposited at first, the course for obtaining the Patent is the same, except that no second Specification has to be made.

Letters Patent extend to England, Scotland, Ireland, and the Channel Islands, and are granted for the term of Fourteen Years, subject to the payment of £50 before the expiration of Three Years, and £100 before the expiration of Seven Years from the date of the grant.

Registers are kept in this office of all Protections, Notices to Proceed, and Letters Patent, from the earliest period, which may be consulted without charge,

Specifications drawn, Translations and Drawings made or copied, and all other Patent business transacted on moderate terms.

COPY OF A CIRCULAR OF MESSRS. DE FONTAINMOREAU
Showing patents charges and conditions

FOREIGN PATENTS.

The application for most Foreign Patents should be made before lodging Complete or Final Specification in England.

The following average prices are inclusive of the charge for Translation, Copies of Description, Drawings, and all other expenses necessary for passing the Patents.

FRANCE.—Patents are granted for 15 years, at an annual tax of £4.
    The average cost of a French Patent, including all expenses and tax for the first year, is £6 12s.
    A Certificate is delivered on depositing papers at the proper office, and the legal rights of the Patentee date from that time. The Patent is generally issued in about two months from application. Improvements may be secured at a small cost.

BELGIUM.—The Government tax is 10 francs for the first, and 20 francs for the second year, proportionally increasing every year. The average cost of a Patent is £2 12s.

HOLLAND.—The average cost of application for a Patent is £4 0 0
The tax for a Patent for . . . . 5 years is about 14 0 0
    ,,   ,, ... 10 ,,   ,,   27 0 0
    ,,   ,, ... 15 ,,   ,,   55 0 0
The payment of tax may be delayed about eighteen months from date of grant.

AUSTRIA AND BAVARIA.—The average cost of a Patent for either country for one year, is £12 to £15. The Patent may be extended from year to year by paying an annual tax, at first about £4 10s.

ITALY.—Average cost of Patent, £14, including the yearly and part of the proportionate tax for time specified in the petition. It may be extended by paying an annual tax, commencing at about £2.

PRUSSIA.—Average cost of a Patent for Ten Years £10 0 0

SAXONY, WURTEMBURG, AND HANOVER.—Average cost of
a Patent in each country for . . . . 5 Years £10 to £15 0 0

NORWAY, SWEDEN, AND DENMARK.—Average cost of a
Patent in each country for . . . . 5 Years £20 0 0

RUSSIA.—Average cost of a Patent for . . . . 3 ,,   35 0 0
    ,,   ,, ... 6 ,,   50 0 0
    ,,   ,, ... 10 ,,   95 0 0

SPAIN.— ,,   ,, ... 5 ,,   30 0 0
    ,,   ,, ... 10 ,,   50 0 0
    ,,   ,, ... 15 ,,   85 0 0

PORTUGAL ,,   ,, ... 5 ,   25 0 0
    ,,   ,, ... 10 ,,   45 0 0
    ,,   ,, ... 15 ,,   60 0 0

AMERICA ,,   ,, ... 17 ,,   25 0 0

In the above countries the Invention should be worked within specified terms from date of grant, and in the United States, the application must be besides accompanied by a model or specimen.

COPYRIGHT OF DESIGNS.

ENGLAND.

Copyright for the form of the whole, or part of any article of manufacture, having for object some useful result may be secured for Three Years at an average expense of £15.
    Copyright for ornamental designs for articles of manufactures, &c., may be secured at a cost of 10s. to £3.
    Provisional Registration for both classes for One Year may be effected at an average cost of 10s. to £5.
The Designs Act extends protection to England, Ireland and Scotland.

FRANCE.

Protection in English Trade Marks and Designs may be secured through this office at a small cost.
    Inventors desirous of obtaining information relating to British or Foreign Patents, can have, on application at my Office, any particulars or assistance gratuitously afforded to them.
    References to be had of my Bankers in—

    LONDON.—Sir Charles Price, Bart., & Co. | PARIS.—Charles Noel & Co.
            BRUSSELS.—Delloye & Tibergien.

                         I am, your obedient Servant,

                              DE FONTAINMOREAU.

N. B.—Cheques to be crossed SIR CHARLES PRICE, BART., & Co.

passing of these Acts is sufficient evidence that this was so[1]—the services of the British Patent Office remained largely nugatory. Indeed, so unsatisfactory had the situation become at the turn of the century that the *India Rubber Journal* was constrained to refer to the Patent Office as " Muddledom "—a registration office for " every bit of idiocy."[2]   In contrast to German and American practices, which required the inventor to show that his patent was novel and deserving,[3] it was enough for the British authorities that the patent should be properly described and the fees paid.   Furthermore, in the absence of a system of preliminary investigation carried on elsewhere,[4] it was up to the patentee to ensure that his patent had not been anticipated; either that or, as the trade journal put it, take out the patent and calmly wait " until the day of reckoning." When that day arrived—normally at the instigation of a prior claimant—the " reckoning " was done in such highly technical language as to make the legal outcome entirely fortuitous.

To help the inventor to secure a patent (the necessary stages are set out in the circular of Messrs. de Fontainmoreau which is repro-duced here facing pp. 146 and 147) there had arisen in the early years of the century a new kind of professional worker: the patent agent, combining the services of lawyer and engineer.[5]   In the case of the Bradford company it was the patent agent who investigated the validity of Moulton's inventions, advised him on the choice of title,[6] drew up and lodged the provisional and final specifications

[1] The number of patents rose from an average of 468 a year for the decade 1842-51, to 2187 in 1853, and to 2047 in the decade 1853-62.   In 1882, 4337 patents were granted ; by 1884 this figure had risen to 9118.

[2] *IRJ*, 10 December 1900 : " . . . The capacious maw of the Patent Office knows no bounds.   It accepts your fee without demur, but in return gives no guarantee of the validity—that is, novelty—of your patent . . . "

[3] Moulton discovered, as did Bessemer and Siemen, that " it is a settled policy on the part of Prussia . . . not to grant patents . . . "   Commons' Committee on Letters Patent, (1872), *Parliamentary Papers,* Vol. XXI, 464.

[4] The system of preliminary investigation was first introduced by Prussia and the United States.   It was finally incorporated into British patent law by the Act of 1902.

[5] *The Professions,* A. M. Carr-Saunders and P. A. Wilson (Oxford, 1933), 58-64.

[6] Tongue and Birkbeck/SM, 23 February 1861 : " . . . We do not approve of your title.   Your invention is not an Improvement in the Manufacture of India Rubber but in the mode of confining India Rubber used in the manu-facture of Springs, valves, &c. . . . "

(upon which the validity of the patent was almost entirely dependent),[1] and undertook, if necessary, to negotiate the sale of the patent either at home or abroad. Perhaps the most striking evidence of the growing demand for these services in Britain lies in the fact that the handful of patent agents listed in the London Directory for 1840 by 1891 had become more than two hundred strong, most of them members of the Institute of Patent Agents, incorporated by Royal Charter in that year.

Aided by a London house of patent agents (whose account is given below) the Bradford manufacturer obtained five English patents, some of which were also taken out in other parts of Europe and the United States. These were the master vulcanisation patent of 1847 which was the occasion of so much litigation ; the further patent for the improvement in the preparation of rubber in 1851 ;[2] the patent for rubber-embedded steel springs in January, 1861 ;[3] the patent to lessen the recoil of cannon by rubber springs[4] in 1863 ; and the patent for porous or sponge rubber in 1868.[5] In addition, on 31 January 1861, Moulton obtained provisional protection for a patent embracing certain improvements in the construction of telegraph cable ; but this invention was not developed.

With the exception of the patent for vulcanisation, Moulton's inventions were never attacked by other members of the trade— a sure sign that they were not of major importance in the industry. His attempts to obtain or to dispose of patent rights in other countries were unsuccessful. For instance, his application in 1861 for a Prussian patent for his rubber-embedded spring was refused because particulars of the invention had already been published by a London

---

[1] Tongue and Birkbeck/SM, 28 January 1861 : " . . . We will attend to your instructions as to a provisional Protection for Telegraph Cables. Tongue will look over some of the latest Patents for cables, and prepare you a draft specification for your approval, which, together with a declaration form properly filled in we will forward you by tomorrow's post . . . We will draw the claim as broadly as possible and you can cut out any parts of it you may think in excess of your ideas . . . " The greatest care was required in drawing up the title, provisional and final specifications, as any fault in them could easily invalidate the patent later on. Lord's Committee, Parliamentary Papers (1851), Vol. XVIII, 602.

[2] Patent No. 13,721, dated 14 August 1851.

[3] Patent No. 62, dated 10 January 1861.

[4] Patent No. 958, dated 16 April 1863.

[5] Patent No. 1522, dated 9 May 1868.

journal;[1] and his efforts to dispose of the same invention in the United States were completely frustrated by a New England spring company,[2] who held the Goodyear rights of manufacture. They would neither purchase the invention outright nor manufacture it under licence. Moulton fared no better in France or Belgium. He obtained patent rights in these countries without any great difficulty, but he never succeeded in disposing of them at a profit to a native manufacturer as he had hoped to do. In fact the most important observation to be made here is that it is doubtful if Moulton ever made a penny out of his foreign ventures as a patentee. If his vulcanisation patent of 1847 is excluded, he probably lost more than he gained through the Patent Office. It is a most significant and telling fact that with the recovery of the mechanical trade in the late 'sixties " Patented Improvements " were not heard of again at the Bradford mill.

In resolving the origins of the major rubber patents in the nineteenth century it would do well to begin by excluding the possibility of accidental cause, for the available evidence shows the major inventions to have been the result of prolonged and arduous investigation.[3] Whilst the inventions of the early rubber pioneers may seem to have revolutionised the rubber industry almost overnight, closer inquiry reveals that their work was part of a broad evolutionary movement whose progress was largely independent of the discovery of any single person. In the last analysis it is extremely difficult—if not impossible—to say to what extent Goodyear's discovery of vulcanisation evolved from the sulphur-dusted sheets of Nathaniel Hayward; or how far Moulton's or Hancock's discovery of vulcanisation issued directly from Goodyear's work. As far as this industry is concerned, it is in the interests of historical exactitude

---

[1] Fonrobert & Reimann of Berlin informed Moulton on 24 September 1861 that the application was refused on the grounds that the invention had appeared in the *Mechanics' Magazine*, London, in May 1861.

[2] Henry Moulton to his father 26 October 1861 : " . . . I have had three meetings with the New England Car Spring Company and they insist that the Patent is not worth a shilling without you purchase from them the right to use Goodyear's Patent Rubber, for without the Rubber the Spring is nothing, and they have the right exclusively to use Rubber for a Spring of any kind that is appertaining to vehicles . . . "

[3] In this respect a letter to *The Times* on 11 May 1939 written by Lt.-Col. Karslake is of interest.

S. Moulton Esq.,
Kingston House, Bradford on Avon.

to Tongue & Birkbeck,
Patent Agents, Engineers &c.

34, Southampton Buildings,
Chancery Lane, W.C.
July 12, 1861.

S. MOULTON ESQ., BRADFORD—IN ACCOUNT WITH TONGUE & BIRKBECK.

Dr. 1861			£	s.	d.
January	11	To obtaining Provisional Protection for your invention of improvements in India rubber springs, valves &c. No. 62...	8	8	0
„	25	To giving "notice to Proceed" and to obtaining "Letters Patent" for the above invention	18	18	0
„	25	To 2 specifications S. Moulton, & W. E. Newton		10	
„	31	To obtaining Provisional Protection for your invention of Improvements in Telegraph cables No. 260	8	8	0
February	9	To obtaining Patent for France for the invention of Improvements in springs and valves (No. 62) including the 1st years annuity tax and two copies of the drawings ...	12	12	0
„	9	To obtaining Patent for Belgium for the same invention including the payment of the 1st years annuity tax and the drawings	10	10	0
		Carried forward ...	£58	16	10

Cr. 1861			£	s.	d
January	11	By cash received Messrs. Moulton & Son	8	8	0
„	31	By draft from Mr. S. Moulton on account of expenses of Patent	50	0	0
May	28	By cash received draft on L. & W. Bank fm Mr. Moulton	110	0	0
		Carried forward ...	£168	8	0

		£	s.	d.
	Amount brought forward ...	58	16	10
February 18	To printing 250 copies of patent valves on extra bank post paper at 25/- Lithographing amt charged	3	2	6
March 1	To obtaining Patent for United States of America including all charges	31	10	0
April	To specifications supplied to order		1	0
,, 27	To cash sent to you by cheque Baring Bros. on account of excess on American Patent...	80	0	0
July 8	To drawing up and preparing the Complete Specification of your invention No. 62 "Impt. in India rubber valves &c.", ...	3	3	0
	To engrossing the same on Parchment and preparing fair copy of same, to file with the Commissioner of Patents, and attending filing the same, and paid Stamp on final Specification	7	7	0
	To preparing original drawing of the valves to illustrate the invention	2	2	0
	To preparing 2 copies of the drawing on Parchment to file with the Complete Spec. ...	2	10	0
	Paid for leather covered box for warrant and Great seal		4	6
	Letters, Parcels, &c.			
		£188	16	10

		£	s.	d.
	Amount brought forward ...	168	8	0
	To Balance due July 12 ...	20	8	10
	balance paid 11/9/61			
		£188	16	10

to discount the "heroic" and the "accident" explanations of technical progress.

One does not have to read very much of the Rider-Moulton correspondence to understand that the "necessity" felt by the inventor James Thomas was a very different thing to the "necessity" felt by the entrepreneur Stephen Moulton; for whilst the former "like all inventors" thought "more of the honour of being an inventor than the money to be made"[1] the latter was concerned primarily with the commercial value of the invention. It would be foolish to argue that the industry owes more to one side than to the other, as it would be to contend that most inventors were unaffected by the prospect of commercial gain, or that most of their financial backers thought of nothing else. In any case, men like Thomas Hancock and Stephen Moulton possessed both inventive skill and business capacity, and the line between inventor and entrepreneur becomes extremely difficult to determine. It is not the purpose here to stress the contribution made by either the inventor or the business man to the exclusion of the other, but to remark that the history of this industry shows the progress of invention as arising out of a much closer union of inventive skill and business capacity than might generally be supposed. It waited upon Goodyear and the others to solve the problem of vulcanisation by means of sulphur, lead and heat; likewise, it waited upon Thomson, and later Dunlop, to perceive the idea of an air-filled tyre. But the history of the Bradford company—as that of the other branches of the industry— shows that it rested with men like William Rider and Stephen Moulton to pass judgment on the discoveries[2]; to reject or accept them, and, of those that were accepted, to put them to use in a practicable commercial manner.[3] In this connection, the entrepreneurial function of Rider and Moulton in their relations with Goodyear and Thomas was duplicated elsewhere in the industry by Birley and Du Cros with Hancock and Dunlop respectively.

[1] W. Rider/SM, 28 January 1846. And 9 May 1848 : " . . . I must say he is the most queer fellow I have ever met with in a business way . . . "

[2] Dodge/SM, 27 January 1861 : " . . . The principle of embedding steel springs in rubber may have been tried by some stupid fellow without the wit enough to see its value, and thus have occupied the field without cropping the ground . . . "

[3] WR/SM, 19 July 1848 : " . . . and I will venture to guess again that without the aid of W.R. & B. [Wm. Rider & Bros.] in more ways than one, Thomas would not have been able to get along as well as he did . . . " WR/SM, 15 August 1848 shows that the Riders had spent approximately $3,000 in financing the Thomas patent.

A study of the early records of this industry shows that only on the points of multiple paternity and the interdependence of the entrepreneur and the inventor can the investigator feel any degree of assurance; beyond that it is unwise to dogmatise. Likewise, whilst the Bradford manufacturer's inventiveness was at its greatest in times of shrinking markets, such as during the 'sixties, it would be wrong to generalise from a single example.

A further point to be considered is whether the British patent system was conducive to the growth and practice of inventive talent. The verdict of many authoritative Victorians, such as the famous engineer (and friend of Moulton) Isambard Kingdom Brunel,[1] was that the system did the precise opposite: it discouraged invention, stultified the progress of industry, left the inventor unprotected in his patent rights, and often confirmed monopoly rights of invention in the person least entitled to them.

One of the most serious abuses of the patent system in its effect upon the rubber industry was that it permitted Thomas Hancock to seek a monopolist's position; not because he had invented the vulcanisation process first, but simply because he applied for a patent before Goodyear and Moulton. Having anticipated Goodyear's English patent by a few weeks he was able to exclude the superior American process from the United Kingdom except on his own terms. A still greater evil was the fact that the Hancock patent extended to the manufacture of footwear as well, to which Macintosh & Company did not apply it effectively for many years.[2]

---

[1] Isambard Brunel, *The Life of Isambard Kingdom Brunel,* (London, 1870), 450, 451, 454, 485, 489, 490-8. See also his evidence before the Select Committee of the House of Lords on the Patent Laws, 1851, 246. Other eminent Victorians who joined with Brunel in opposing the patent system were the distinguished civil engineers Sir William Armstrong and Sir William Cubitt. The Royal Commissions of 1862-4 were supported in their opposition to the patent system by such influential organs as *The Times* and *The Economist.*

[2] See the evidence of Paul Rapsey Hodge, Patent Agent, given before the Select Committee of the House of Lords on 12 May 1851 :

"A great evil arises from patentees being allowed to make their specifications too general ; we have evidence of that in all our shoe-shops in London. The American India-rubber shoes, and many other of their articles, are superior to ours. It is in consequence of the patent which is held by a wealthy company in Manchester, claiming in their patent the use of India-rubber generally for braces, coats, gloves, shoes and other articles. But where there is such a general specification it shuts out almost everybody else . . . "

S.C (1851), *Parliamentary Papers,* Vol. XVIII, 333.

More than any other factor it was this patent which later placed the British rubber footwear manufacturer at a disadvantage with American and Canadian competitors; and it is not to be wondered at that the Americans were quick to seize upon Newton's (Goodyear) Scottish patent to establish themselves in Edinburgh.[1]

Stephen Moulton had good reason to know the pitfalls of the patent system. His royalty payment of £600 per annum put him at a temporary disadvantage in competing with the Manchester company ; and (whilst evidence on this point is lacking), if the rates charged the Macintosh licensees differed, it is possible that the Kingston Mill also faced unequal competition elsewhere.

Other abuses of the patent system were that specifications were drawn up as widely as possible in order to gain control over the different branches of the industry, as Hancock did with rubber footwear; inventors were allowed to patent one process and to develop another which bore only faint resemblance to their original ideas, as was done with rubber cable;[2] and there was the abuse— easier in the case of a chemical than a mechanical process—of concealing the true patented improvement by muffling up the specification,[3] as Thomas did with the Riders and Moulton, and

---

[1] The stages by which the North British Company of Edinburgh was able to make use of Goodyear's Scottish patent can be traced through the following indentures in the company's possession : indenture dated 2 November 1852, between Newton and Goodyear, whereby Goodyear obtained full rights over the Scottish vulcanisation patent ; indenture dated 4 August 1856, between Goodyear and Judson, which transferred these rights to the latter, who, on 9 August 1856, vested them in the Directors of the North British Company.

[2] See a paper by T. P. Bruce Warren (at that time analytical chemist to the India Rubber, Gutta Percha and Telegraph Company, Silvertown) "The Manufacture of India Rubber and its application to Telegraphic Purposes", R.S.A. Journal, Vol. XXVI, 129, 18 January 1878 : " . . . I am confident that the Patent Laws have done but little to forward the development of India Rubber in this important branch of its manufacture. Improvements have been stultified to so glaring an extent that whereas, some few years ago, it was impossible to commend India Rubber too highly, it is now in the opinion of many completing the ebb of an ephemeral existence . . . "

[3] See the evidence of Arthur Aiken, before the Commons' Committee of 1829 : Q. " Are you aware that specifications are frequently, especially in chemical processes, made imperfect, with the view of concealing the process ? " A. " Yes, I am certain of it, and it was with the view of preventing the fraud which runs through the whole system of patenting, that I think examiners ought to be appointed . . . "

S.C. (1829), Parliamentary Papers, Vol. III, 558.

(it is possible) Hancock did with the rubber trade generally. On the strength of an alleged incomplete and inaccurate patent Hancock prevented others from manufacturing according to his own or to Goodyear's patent. The same is largely true of Moulton's patent of 1847. He had not used hyposulphite of lead as a vulcanising agent when his patent was granted. In fact, as his letters make clear, he knew very little about the process at that date, but by taking out a patent he could—like Hancock—exclude others from using it. It is incidents such as these which throw light on one of the more serious weaknesses of the system: the fact that the British authorities were concerned neither in proving the originality nor the validity of the patent. They were content to register claims, not to guarantee them. Whilst the British were probably wise in refusing to deal with the question of originality, for the whole history of the industry is the story of the evolution of a manufacturing process in which it becomes extremely difficult to decide what is new and what is old, it cannot be doubted that if they had kept a closer watch on these things, as they were to do with the introduction of preliminary examination in 1902, much vexatious litigation might have been avoided. Preliminary examination, for instance, would certainly have made it unnecessary for the Dunlop Company to learn with surprise of Thomson's pneumatic tyre patent in the courts in 1890. It would also have reduced the number of frivolous and—worse than this—fraudulent patents which deliberately infringed upon every major invention.

Yet it is all too easy to trace abuses to the absence of preliminary investigation in Britain, and to overlook what was going on elsewhere; it is well to remember that the supposed thoroughness of the American authorities, who with the Germans followed an opposite course to the British and the French, did not prevent Charles Goodyear from being reduced at times almost to beggary by endless trials at law. Regardless of the country of origin, or the principles under which they were issued, all major rubber patents gave rise to prolonged litigation. The more important the patent, the more certain that the inventor and those who stood with him would be hounded through the courts.

The experience of Macintosh, Goodyear, Hancock, Moulton, Dunlop and the rest shows that in the last resort the inventor had no more than a hypothetical monopoly to support his claims. On this score the patent system offered almost the same facilities to the usurper and the infringer as it did to the genuine inventor; the initiative resting with the "more rapid projector".[1]   When the inventor was not forestalled, (as Goodyear claimed he had been by Hancock), it was not unknown for him to buy up the more troublesome claims against his patent rather than contest them at law.[2] It is not surprising that certain sections of the rubber industry became convinced that it was hazardous to patent anything worthwhile.[3]

Finally, it is a disputable point whether or not the patent system can be charged with raising the price of commodities and injuring trade.   There are so many factors to be taken into account—such as the changing cost of crude rubber, the varying qualities of the manufactured product, and the general commercial and financial position—that it would be rash to generalise.   Nevertheless, the experience of these early companies points to the conclusion that patents helped to sustain if they did not actually raise prices.   It was in the 'sixties—when the essential processes of the industry were common property—that price trends showed a downward turn ; but by then the open defiance of Hancock by a large part of the rubber trade, and the competition offered first by Moulton, and then by the Edinburgh house, had already lowered the price levels and reduced the profit margins of Chas. Macintosh & Company.

It would not be difficult to conclude from this account that the

---

[1] For instance Brunel before the Lords' Committee of 1851 :

Q.   Speaking of concurrent inventions, you would say that that was by no means the best invention which wins the race ?

A.   I believe it is rarely so ; the chances are entirely against it.   I believe it is rare that the man most able to work it out, and who really has arrived at the best collection of ideas upon the subject, is the patentee.

Q.   He generally finds himself anticipated by some more rapid projector ?

A.   Yes.

S.C. (1851), *Parliamentary Papers*, Vol. XVIII, 492.

[2] Take for example the statement made by J. L. Ricardo, M.P., before the Lords' Committee of 1851 : " . . . In the case of the Electric Telegraph Company, the company hold a very large number of patents, because they make it a rule, if a man offers reasonable terms, to buy any invention, however bad it may be, sooner than litigate it.   They find it much cheaper to pay blackmail than to litigate an invention which may be set up against them.   S.C. (1851), *Parliamentary Papers*, Vol. XVIII, 615.

[3] *IRJ*, 24 December 1900 : " . . . One cannot fail to be struck by the fact that very few of the really best rubber firms appear . . . in our patent pages.   Is it because they have absolutely no faith whatever in the office ? . . . it is generally the less experienced firms that indulge in the luxury of patents . . . "

patent system provided a barrier rather than a stimulus to the development of the early British rubber industry. Yet such a conclusion would be unfortunate, and in the light of nineteenth-century experience, unjustified ; for in combining the necessary inventive talent, entrepreneurship, and capital resources to carry an invention forward to commercial success, the patent system played a vital role in the progress of this industry. It was the prospect of future economic gain—offered by a patent monopoly—which joined the Riders and Moulton to Goodyear and Thomas, the Birleys to Macintosh and Hancock, and Du Cros to Dunlop. It is not disputed that the vulcanisation process might well have been evolved for its own sake rather than for the possession of patent rights. The only argument here is that with the help of the patent system the process was in fact evolved much more rapidly than it would have been. However uncertain these patent rights proved to be they were better than nothing;[1] and their existence provided a mainspring of joint action between the entrepreneur and the inventor.

[1] For instance the evidence given by Thomas Webster before the Lords' Committee on the 15 April 1851 : " . . . my observation was rather directed to the creation of certain new trades and manufactures ; as for instance the caoutchouc [India-rubber], the gutta percha and the composite candle trade, and some other instances which have been more prominently before me, in which new trades have been built up, created and established within a very short period . . . by reason of the protection for a limited time which the patent gave during what may be called the infancy of the manufacture . . . " S.C. (1851) *Parliamentary Papers*, Vol. XVIII, 249. See also the evidence of William Carpmael given on 5 May 1851.

Chapter VIII

THE MEDIUM OF EXCHANGE

THE principal instruments of trade credit for domestic as well as overseas payments at Bradford in 1848 were the bill of exchange, the promissory note and the bank-note—there being few references to the use of barter.[1] If the foundrymen who made the rubber machinery and the merchants who supplied the crude rubber had been unwilling to accept Moulton's commercial paper for three, four, and even six months, it is difficult to see how the venture could have got under way at all.[2] Whilst the bill of exchange (variously termed in these early papers: the acceptance, draft or bill), helped the young firm to its feet, at the time of Moulton's death in 1880 the technical defects of the bill had caused it to be largely superseded by the cheque. The last bill entry to be made in Moulton's records was during the spring of 1884; and two years later in 1886 the Bradford company told a London firm of importers:[3] ". . . We never have any bill transactions and do not wish to go in for them . . ."

As regards the financing of the crude rubber trade, unless Moulton was obliged to pay cash (as in the case of East Indian supplies[4] and of

---

[1] There are scattered references in the 'fifties and 'sixties to the barter of finished goods and rubber scrap for crude rubber and cloth, but the last mention of this subject appears on 21 April 1876. Radstock Coal & Wagon Co./SM.

[2] True of the Bilston Foundry, who accepted Moulton's paper at four and six months, as well as the foundrymen Thomas and Edward Bush of Bristol. Accounts 1848-50. On the discounting of Moulton's commercial paper for the supply of crude rubber, see L. Bunn/SM, 14 June 1854 : ". . . The first [parcel of rubber] you said you would take if I would Discount your paper to the extent of £3,000 & etc . . ." For chemicals it was customary either to pay cash within seven days and receive a discount, or to be given credit for one month ; for textiles until the late 'seventies the system varied, one house accepting a two months' bill of exchange, the other preferring a monthly cash settlement. With the decline of a real economic need for the bill of exchange in the last two decades of the century textile supplies—as with crude rubber—came to be purchased on a monthly or bimonthly credit account.

[3] Hecht, Levis & Kahn/SM, 9 July 1886.

[4] L. Bunn /SM, 16 August 1856 : ". . . East India rubber is C.O.D. all over the world. . ." Brown /SM, 19 October 1870 : ". . . E. I. rubber. . . the only terms I could obtain were usual conditions : cash . . ."

rubber sold at public auction), or where he preferred to make a cash settlement and obtain a discount, the three and four months' bill remained the chief means of payment until the 'seventies. Until the last quarter of the nineteenth century the Dutch terms for cash settlements (for what the British regarded as superior East Indian supplies), were not as attractive as those offered by the English houses, being $1\frac{1}{4}\%$ at 14 days as against $2\frac{1}{2}\%$; and in June 1867 this was reduced temporarily to 1%. Likewise, Moulton's bill transactions with Dutch houses were for a shorter period (two as against the more customary three months), than those of the home trade.[1]

Moulton appears to have had little difficulty in arranging credit terms either with his broker—who was ever ready to offer, or to obtain for him, the most favourable terms of payment:[2]

I will endeavour to make any arrangement you suggest. I can arrange to draw at 3 months adding Interest at the Bank Rate, or, if preferable, half in cash at the end of the month and half at 2 mos. date . . .

or directly with the importers one of whom had " no hesitation in acceding to your [Moulton's] request as other houses have allowed it [3 months' draft] to you . . ."[3]

Where accommodation was given it was customary to charge a rate of interest on the value of the bill which followed closely the bank rate. This interest was of considerable importance to brokers and merchants. When a bill or, later in the century, an open credit account was not met on the due date these men looked for the interest as well as the principal.

The over-all picture in the case of crude rubber supplies throughout the period 1850-1900, shows the decline of the bill and the rise of the cheque. But to regard the bill as supplanted by the cheque in the rubber trade in the 'seventies would be to antedate its decline. Rubber bought on a three months' bill in 1881 was still a penny a

---

[1] Correspondence with Matthes & Bormeester, and Goll & Co., Amsterdam, and Dunlop & Mees, Rotterdam. (Moulton Papers).

The Dutch draft for acceptance, accompanied by the bill of lading, enabled Moulton to claim the goods at the port. Insurance of the cargo (paid in Holland and " effected till Bradford" at $\frac{3}{8}$ or $\frac{1}{2}$ %), and freight charges, were the responsibility of the buyer.

[2] Brown & Co./SM, 14 January 1879 : " . . . Messrs. Heilbut & Co. could not allow discount $2\frac{1}{2}\%$ (on this parcel) but I have induced them to concede $1\frac{1}{4}\%$ for cash ; being equivalent to 5% per annum, this since the value of money here is $3\frac{1}{2}$-4% may not be considered an unfair offer . . . "

[3] Heilbut Symonds & Co./SM, 28 July 1856.

M

pound cheaper than on a three months' prompt[1] settled by cheque. In June 1883 when Moulton's broker announced that he had secured a three months' bill on a parcel of Assam rubber instead of paying cash, he added: " I frequently see heaps of Bills taken out of the Bill case [that is of Hecht, Levis & Kahn] and sent to the Bank of England for discount . . ."; and although the same house of importers had insisted in their letter to Moulton at the beginning of 1884 that:[2] " All rubber, Assam also, is now invariably sold here at reweight, 14 days prompt, 2½% discount, instead of 3 months, no discount . . .", six months later in an attempt to meet Moulton's request for longer credit they were quick to suggest the use of bills again.   This suggestion was not received kindly at Bradford:[3]

> We have nothing to do with Bill transactions of any kind, and if we did, we should certainly object to paying interest . . .
> With regard to the terms that suit us to buy, we like a credit of 2 to 3 months—preferring the latter . . .

So far as the Bradford house was concerned it was cheaper and more convenient to operate in this manner.   There was not the bother of bill transactions ; the increasing stamp duty on new bills could be avoided (a cause associated with the decline of the rival bankers' draft) ; and more important, Moulton did not have to pay for accommodation.   So far as the importers were concerned the explanation offered[4] for the decline of the bill during the 'seventies and 'eighties was that the growing willingness of the London and Liverpool banks to facilitate the crude rubber trade made it more economical for the import houses to finance their business by secured overdraft rather than by the bill of exchange.

While the total amount of payments in the last quarter of the century made by cheque cannot be determined precisely, the Moulton papers show an unmistakable shift during the 'seventies from rather long credits (3-4 months) supported by bills, to the fairly short prompt settlements (14 days) made by cheque.   In 1886, when

---

[1] Meiers/SM, 26 February 1881.   A prompt was an agreement between the importer and the manufacturer, by which the latter undertook to buy specified goods at a fixed price, the goods to be taken and paid for at a named date. It was not a negotiable instrument and could not be discounted.

[2] H.L. & K./SM, 15 January 1884.   Also G. Le Doux & Co. London/SM, 26 May 1886.

[3] SM/H.L. & K., 9 July 1884.

[4] I am indebted for this explanation to Charles Fletcher, who spent his working life as a rubber importer.   Until his retirement he was the senior member of the house of Hecht, Levis & Kahn, founded by his grandfather.

the Bradford company obtained both long credit and a discount on their purchases, the importers felt constrained to remind them—particularly as regards the long credit—that buying rubber " . . . at reweights, discount 2½%, no commission, three months open credit" were terms " more favourable than those allowed to any other firm . . ."[1]

In contrast to its steady employment in the crude rubber market the decline of the bill of exchange in the inland trade in manufactured goods (hastened by the charges made for stamp duty), was well underway in the 'sixties. One of the chief reasons given for refusing to accept a bill, even in the early 'fifties, was the smallness of the amount.[2] In 1861 Moulton's paid cheques had " become numerous and troublesome to keep"; and by the 'seventies, assisted by the growth in the habit of banking, and the improvement in communications, the more easily available and more readily acceptable cheque, together with bank-notes, postal orders, stamps and specie, had ousted the small bill of say £20 or less (which had been common half a century before) altogether.

Some houses, however, were reluctant to accept Moulton's country cheques on the grounds of expense, delay and possible insecurity.[3] With reference to expense, it is evident that the charges made by the country banks were not always uniform. Whereas, in December 1856 the Wilts. and Dorset Bank charged one of Moulton's suppliers 3s.9d. commission on a cheque for £75.17s.11d, cheques to other country banks were " seldom charged a fraction and if at all not more than 6d. or 1s."[4] Whether this disparity in charges was as marked as some correspondents would have Moulton believe is not known. In the absence of statistical proof many of these statements can only be accepted with reservation. What is certain is that the objection against country cheques on the grounds of expense continued to be received at Bradford during the next decade and a half: " . . . a cheque except on London [wrote a Liverpool house in January 1864], costs bank commission and three

---

[1] H.L. & K./SM, 2 August 1886.

[2] Stothert, Slaughter & Co., Bristol, SM, 11 April 1854 : " . . . We do not accept for less than £200 . . . "

[3] J. Warner & Sons/SM, 22 September 1860 : " . . . There are grave objections to sending cheques by post—it is not the custom of our firm, and we are not disposed to do so. Therefore we pay to the London & Westminster Bank £279.13.9 . . . "

[4] J. Englefield & Co., London/SM, 8 December 1856.

days interest—and half notes would be preferable ".[1]   The complaints made on the grounds of delay (" a country cheque only being put to credit three days afterwards "), were heard until the 'eighties. Where the need for cash was urgent traders preferred a banker's order or sight draft, but the charges incurred for stamp duty made Moulton reluctant to use this medium from the very beginning. His suppliers either had to accept a bill (preferably a reissued bill which did not occasion the same expense), or a country cheque, which, once the practice of crossing them had become customary from the 'sixties onwards, no longer offered the same temptation to theft.

By the 'seventies the cheque had become the normal means of exchange, and the banker's draft, the bill, and the promissory note, increasingly inconvenient exceptions:

> A country cheque [wrote a London house in 1878][2] is, as you are aware, not put to credit for three days, in London.   Still, if it be of any inconvenience to you to obtain a draft, we shall of course be happy to conform, in future, to your usual custom . . .

On the rise of the cheque and the decline of the bill in the inland trade it is worth noting that those who objected to the bill of exchange were normally to be found in the larger cities.   They were not necessarily the smallest dealers in the trade, and were not confined to any particular part of the country.

The manner in which the bill was used in times of credit stringency, such as during the late 'fifties and 'sixties, is illustrated by a letter written to Bradford in December 1857 : [3]

> Permit us to ask whether you cannot use some of our trade Bills in payment of the balance we owe you up to December 31st. We are really ashamed to bother you about so trivial a matter, but you can have no idea of the difficulty in collecting money . . . We can give you our draft Nov. 16th, 3 months accepted by John Mosley, one of our customers, for £87. 10. 0, and another Nov. 10th, 3 months for £66. 17. 0, accepted by Mr. G. Thomas, both good ; and we will pay you the balance in cash, or we will send you our cheque on Monday for another £100 on account . . .

[1] Refers to the practice in the 'fifties and 'sixties of sending the two halves of a bank-note by separate posts.

[2] Thos. Stiff & Co./SM, 25 May 1878.

[3] Dodge & Grandonati, London,/SM, 17 December 1857.

Conversely, whilst some dealers regarded the substitution of a bill for cash as a favour granted by the manufacturer (and this applied to renewals and extensions of bills), there were many others during the 'fifties and 'sixties who regarded it as a purely normal commercial undertaking :

> We are surprised [wrote a Sheffield firm in 1854][1] you object to take our bill. We only send it because it happens to be rather inconvenient to pay cash this month. We have done a large business with Messrs. Mac & Co., and have occasionally sent them a bill at the same date which they never for a moment objected to . . .

And as late as 1868 a Banbury house[2] pointed out that they asked for accommodation " commercially " and not as a favour. Much, of course, depended on the quality of the paper offered and the circumstances of the time.[3] Moulton's credit was limited like any other manufacturer's, and he protected himself from the consequences of an over-extension of credit by taking paper for short date only or refusing accommodation altogether; and in certain instances where it was given, by charging the highest discount rate for the bill:

> We enclose your bill accepted [wrote a Liverpool house in 1862][4] but we do not like paying on the scale of ten per cent, while the Bankers are only allowing the under [signed] 2% for money deposited. Most of our friends, when they do draw upon us, act upon the principle we named, taking off the $2\frac{1}{2}$% and charging interest—and you have done the same by us on more than one occasion . . .

[1] Ibbotson Bros. Sheffield,/SM, 13 April 1854.

[2] Kirby & Barrows, Banbury,/SM, 5 September 1868.

[3] SM/J. Fearns, London, 17 March 1868 : " we are much obliged to you for your favour of the 16th instant rendering us a bill upon a first rate house for £150 @ 4 months which we willingly accept in these bad times, and we are very sorry that you feel them in common with us all . . . "

[4] D. H. & S. Johnson, Liverpool,/SM, 17 April 1862. Yet in the disturbed mid-'fifties Dodge&Grandonati, London,/SM, 17 December 1857 (and others) had been prepared to pay this high rate for accommodation :—

> " . . . acceptances of

G. Thomas	...	£66	17	0
J. Mosley	...	87	10	0
Cheque	...	34	0	8
		188	7	8 to balance your account

to October 31st : £185.14.6.
Discount on Notes 21.3.2 @ 10% £188.7.8."

In all these negotiations the manufacturer had to tread warily. There were many considerations to take into account in accepting or declining another's bill ; and in these matters it was easy to give offence, and just as easy to jeopardise one's own position by an over-extension of credit. It says something for Moulton's powers of discrimination that he had few dishonoured bills—or other bad debts—to worry about ; in any event no house dishonoured its bill—and so stamped its character in the commercial world—without grave cause.

In turning from inland trade bills to promissory notes, which though little used by Moulton's customers[1] represented an important source of working capital for the Kingston Mill in the early 'fifties, a word or two ought to be said about the accommodation bill. Like the promissory note, but unlike the trade bill, which was self-liquidating commercial paper based upon the exchange of goods, it was used for the borrowing and lending of money. One example worth mentioning was the bill drawn by Stephen Moulton upon himself in 1851, when an adverse court judgment placed him in a precarious financial position. The best commentary perhaps on this particular transaction is contained in a letter written by Moulton's solicitors in 1857, which for convenience, is set out as a footnote below.[2] Other than this bill—and the bank

[1] J. Marshall, engineers, London, /SM, 28 February 1862 : " Enclosed here with I hand you my Promissory Note for the amount of Xmas account. I would have sent you a cheque but have had some large contracts going on which keep me short of cash until settled for . . ."

[2] Sewell, Fox & Sewell, London, /SM, 9 October 1857 : " . . . in case you have forgot the facts we will briefly explain them : In March 1851 Kirkman & Brown obtained a Judgment against you for £1,979 and which Judgment was registered by them so as to affect Real Estate . . . On the 26 May 1851 you drew a Bill for £5,000 upon Moulton & Co. which they accepted, and you indorsed to Kirkman & Brown who indorsed it to Mr. Foster. On the 27 May 1851 a Mortgage Deed between yourself of the 1st part, Kirkman & Brown of the 2nd part and Mr. Foster of the 3rd part was executed to the latter and by this Deed Kirkman & Brown assign their Judgment, and you convey certain real Estate and Machinery to Mr. Foster to secure the payment by Moulton & Co.—yourself or Kirkman & Brown—at maturity of the Bill for £5,000 and also of such further sums of money as Mr. Foster should at any time thereafter pay or advance to yourself or to Kirkman & Brown with Interest. And such Deed provides that on such payment Mr. Foster shall reassign the Judgment to Kirkman & Brown their Executors, Admins. or Assigns and convey the real Estate to you. Kirkman & Brown subsequently became Bankrupts whereupon their Interest in the Judgment (subsequent to the payment by Moulton & Co. of the Bill of £5,000, and also subject to the payment of any other monies which Mr. Foster had advanced) passed to their

overdrafts and trade credits discussed above—Moulton obtained all
other temporary loans in the 'fifties (he does not appear to have given
his notes after this date though other houses in the trade were using
them until the 'seventies), by the use of promissory notes. The
bulk of the loans were made by men who were fully aware of his
difficult financial circumstances. Moulton's own bank manager for
instance, Samuel Provis, knew the extent of his client's indebtedness,
the difficulties Moulton had in meeting his commitments, and that
the Kingston Mill was fully mortgaged. Yet Provis and others were
prepared to finance the Bradford undertaking at a most critical time
in its history; a fact which certainly throws an interesting light on the
activities of some of the early country banking officials,[1] and
emphasises the confidence which these men had in Moulton's
personal obligation to repay the money he had borrowed from
them.[2] Whatever private opinion the manufacturer had formed
of Samuel Provis, and his extraordinary colleague " Cannister "

assigns. This statement will then we think pretty clearly shew you that if
Moulton & Co. or yourself have paid the Bill (for we assume the Company
and yourself to be one and the same) Kirkman & Brown's assignees can also
claim from Mr. Foster an assignment of the Judgment, and that no Assignment
to yourself would be of any avail . . . "

[1] Provis/SM, 17 May 1854, shows £530 outstanding (" with Interest
to the 18th instant @ 5% £18.16.5."). Similarly there were sums owing
to Bracher (Bracher/SM, 29-30 May 1854) for £150 and £517. When
on 17 May Provis asked for the repayment of £550 Moulton (18 May)
replied : " With respect to the immediate repayment of the amounts you
were so good as to advance me, allow me to observe to you that I am but
badly off for cash just now, and that the taking out at the present conjuncture
of so large a sum comparatively as £550 in the face of the probability of a like
demand from Mr. Bracher would place me in a very impoverished and unsatisfactory condition towards my three principal creditors, if compelled to
meet them at once and single handed. I am anxious therefore at once to know
whether I can rely upon your bank (through your recommendation, based
upon its own proper interest, as shown by the result of what it has hitherto
done for me) assisting me as heretofore to discharge my obligations to your
Directors and the other two Creditors ; if this can be effected, as I hope it will
be through the Wilts & Dorset Bank I can then instantly and with the greatest
pleasure send you a cheque for the money I borrowed off you . . . " In
fairness to Provis it is as well to add that he replied at once (20 May 1854) that
he was " . . . particularly careful not to mix up my own affairs with those of
the Bank therefore I must decline to enter now upon the question raised in
your letter . . . "

[2] Apart from the officers of the Wilts. & Dorset Bank, the merchants
Coleman (£150), Evans (£200), Windeler (£100) and Bunn were all making
temporary loans to Moulton in the 'fifties on the strength of Moulton's
promise to pay.

Bracher—the ex-tinker banker of New Sarum[1]—their willingness to take up his notes meant the difference to him between failure and success. The price they charged for their money (5%) was no more than the rate of interest demanded by their own bank, or that paid to Moulton's chief creditor Henry Foster. Unlike Foster and the Wilts. & Dorset Bank they neither had a possessory lien on the Kingston Mill, nor did they require of Moulton that his notes should be endorsed before they accepted them. It is not surprising therefore that on the dissolution of the Moulton-Rider partnership in 1854, Moulton should have made a determined effort to get these men to join forces with him.

Stephen Moulton to Samuel Provis, 28 April 1854 :

> Since I last met you our connexion has been the subject of my daily thoughts, and of frequent conference with my friends, Mr. Bush and Mr. Thompson, and with a view of not deferring it beyond the time proposed viz. 11 May next I have sketched the enclosed which I submit for your consideration—not as my definite conclusion. I find it varies essentially from Mr. Bracher's ideas, and that it will do so likewise from yours, as the terms Mr. Bracher considered to be settled upon were :
>
> 1. An equal contribution of capital by us three—pro rata—,
> 2. ½ profits between you and Mr. Bracher,
> 3. Term of Partnership : 14 years.
>
> To this I will only observe that I have been most unintentionally misunderstood with regard to the 1 and 3 conditions. But I do not think this at all material, or as rendering our union the less easy to be effected—resting, as I do, on the belief that each one of us is honestly desirous of forming a co-partnership upon just and fair principles. On my part I acknowledge now my great obligations, both to you and Mr. Bracher, and thus it is I am both anxious, and have the power, liberally to remunerate you for it . . .

---

[1] " For where may I ask," wrote an embittered Thomas Cavendish in a broadsheet of the period, " did he get his knowledge of banking ? Was it whilst making and mending the tin kettles of the good housewives of New Sarum ? or in selling soft soap, pack thread and brick dust in Wincanton . . . Was it as a local preacher of the Wesleyan Connexion ?—or as a little Farmer at King Weston ? or did the light of the New Moral World and of the Science of Banking burst upon his capacious mind instantaneously " . . . causing him " . . . to be promoted over the heads of really able, experienced, and meritorious officers . . ." February 24, 1842. Thorndick & Co., Printers, St. Andrew's, Norwich. (Moulton MSS.)

Proposals :

(1) ⅓rd of the Nett Profits to be divided between Bracher and Provis—on condition of their investing immediately £15,000 Cash in the business.

(2) 5% p.ann. Interest on the amount to be charted against Trade a/c.

(3) ⅔rds of the Nett profits to belong to Stephen Moulton. The disposition of his Stock & Book debts to be arranged.

(4) Rent at £500 per ann. to be charged against Trade a/c for the use of the Mill and machinery.

(5) The entire management of the manufacturing department to remain under the sole control of Stephen Moulton.

(6) Each partner's private drawings to be limited to a certain sum per annum.

(7) Term of partnership 5 years from 11 May 1854.

S. Moulton to Bracher, 5 May 1854 :

. . . I am disposed to make other propositions—and as Mr. Provis has declined the proposal above alluded to, I will, to simplify our negotiation, withdraw it.

I now submit other propositions for your consideration and for Mr. Provis's also :

1. Capital to be arranged—that is not to require more than the exigencies of the business demand, instead of fixing it at any particular sum, and the proportion to be furnished pro rata.

2. ⅓rd of the profit between you and Mr. Provis and ⅔rds to myself.

3. Period of Partnership 5 years.

4. The position of Mr. Provis as regards the Bank to be so considered as not to prevent him from joining the partnership.

OR

In lieu of partnership 15% to be paid by me to you and Mr. Provis for any sum of money advanced to me for the purposes of the business, the period of loan 5 years . . .

A last point here concerns the promissory note set out below :

> Bradford, Wilts.
> 30th Oct., 1849.

£325 0. 0.

> Twelve months after date I promise to pay to the Order of the Wilts, Somerset & Weymouth Railway

Company, Three hundred and twenty five pounds value received.

Signed : Stephen Moulton.

Payable at the North Wilts Banking Co., Bradford.

> *Reverse indorsed as follows :*
>
> Pay to the Order of the Great Western Railway Co.
>
> For the Wilts, Somerset & Weymouth Railway Co.
>
> (Signed by two of the Directors of the said Co.)
>
> Received payment of the within mentioned sum by a renewed acceptance payable three months after date with interest added together £329 1. 3. Bill due 5th Feb. 1851.
>
> (Signed, Secretary of the Great Western Railway Co.)

Against the advice of a friend ". . . pray keep the Kingston Mill and get out of debt . . ." Moulton had set himself to secure the neighbouring Middle Mill. To do so he required £325 which at that moment he did not possess. He therefore secured the property by means of the promissory note shown above, the Wilts, Somerset & Weymouth Railway Co. having subsequently indorsed the note to the Great Western Company ; and then, having had to renew his note, mortgaged the mill to Foster at the purchase price of £325. Four years later the debt was discharged with interest.

For several reasons there are few foreign bills covering the purchase and sale of manufactured rubber products to be found among the Moulton papers. The Bradford manufacturer (like most of the early British but unlike some American companies) concentrated his efforts on the home market. In addition, from the 'seventies, the Spencer Company was handling almost the whole of Bradford's foreign trade ; and also because almost the entire quantity of bills received by Moulton from overseas had been drawn and made payable within the British Isles, and thus, technically speaking, were not foreign bills at all. In fact the trickle of foreign remittances being made to Bradford in the 'eighties was made up chiefly of small sight drafts on London. Yet in the period 1850-75 Stephen Moulton had many foreign connections and it is these which help to throw light on the medium of exchange of the time.

The first point which emerges from a study of these transactions is the supremacy of the bill of exchange over all other forms of payment. Sterling bills—the vast majority of them from sixty to ninety days' duration drawn on London—were received at Bradford from all parts of Europe, as well as from the eastern seaboard of North America. Unlike the procedure followed with inland bills it was sometimes left to the foreigner—because of possible fluctuations in the rate of exchange—to decide (within limits) when the time was opportune to buy bills on London.[1] A Hamburg customer invariably paid with the more common two and three months' bills ; a Viennese house,[2] by short sight (one month) bills drawn on various London houses, or long sight (three months') bills drawn on Barings, whichever Moulton preferred. Conversely, a Berlin merchant always paid with sight or 10-14 day drafts on a London house,[3] and thus earned a cash discount.

---

[1] Witness the letter sent to Bradford from E. Samson, Vienna, 5 December 1856 : ". . . I shall be very happy to accept the proposition you make me . . . @ 80 days from the date of shipment, but with the following alteration, You not to draw on me, but I promise to send you within those 80 days a bill payable in London for the amount of money due. This modification is very important for me, and perfectly immaterial, I suppose, to you, as in this way I can choose my own time when the exchange is low for remitting you the money, whilst if you were to draw on me I should have to pay on a fixed day whatever the exchange might be at that time."

[2] Emile Samson, Vienna, /SM, 10 September 1866 : " I enclose two bills on London : viz.

per 28 September on Bankley & Co. (original ref. G. A. Worms)	£200
per 28 September on Vyse, Sons & Co. (original ref. C. G. Hambro & Sons)	£100
and I add, for 2 months, 3% interest per anno.	£1.10.

making £301.10. for which please give me credit. I think you will find no objection to allowing me 3% p.a. for the difference for short sight, but if you do, I can send you long sights on Baring Bros. & Co. who allow me 4% p.a. on my balance . . . "

[3] Schwanitz & Co., Berlin, /SM, 31 August 1864. " We always pay cash and will send you bills, i.e. our drafts on Messrs. Robinson & Fleming, 21 Austin Friars, London . . . "

Whilst the most common procedure in the third quarter of the nineteenth century was for Moulton's foreign customers to settle their accounts with a sixty or a ninety day bill on London— although there are instances of bills on Liverpool and Manchester houses as well in these early papers—there were many interesting exceptions. Samuel Guppy, for instance, " better known as the builder of the ' Great Britain ' ", writing from Naples in 1852, told Moulton that " for small amounts " his practice was to " send a cheque on my bankers in London " ; another Italian house made their remittances to Bradford in precisely the same way as a Newcastle-on-Tyne firm had been doing for some time : with a 7-day draft on the Bank of England.   There were many such drafts used on London banks, and a small sum like £5 was settled with a bank-note.   It would be difficult to list all the alternatives to a bill of exchange (certainly any such list would have to include foreign dividend warrants)[1], as it would be to explain the peculiar practices employed by certain foreign houses in settling their English accounts. One Hamburg dealer had no compunction in using the Moulton Company as a clearing house for his sundry English debtors[2]—a practice which cannot have been as troublesome or as unusual as it might appear at first sight, or Moulton would have quickly brought it to an end.

Companies like Moultons and the North British had manifold financial relations with North America.   In the 'forties and 'fifties Moulton had bill transactions with the Rider Brothers and Charles

---

[1] M. B. Bonfort, Hamburg,/SM, 27 February 1856 : " I beg to hand inclosed :

£21.4.6.	14 days date. L. & W. Bk.
£12.10.0.	Dividend Warrant B. 271. Danish 5% loan of 1850.
£7.10.	ditto. C. 6928./3(1219) £210. each, Sardinian 5% Loan.

Which please to place to the credit of my account . . . "

[2] Gebrüder Reye, Hamburg,/SM, 3 August 1867 :

" Enclosed we beg to hand you no. 153. no. 2788—a bill of exchange for £26.15.2. on demand on the L. & W. Bank, London from the Royal Bank of Liverpool, of which sum we beg of you as a great favor to pay for our account against receipts at once with cheques or postal orders the following five amounts, and charge the receivers for the cost if there are any. The receipts please send together with your own to Messrs. Coleman & Co. London . . . "

Goodyear.[1] The reliance of the North British Company on American finance—facilitated by bill transactions between leading American and British houses[2]—is evident from the list of capital subscribers and the statement of account of a New York commission agent for 1855-6 given in Appendix V. Whilst most of these transactions on the American exchanges do not warrant special comment, there is however one aspect which might more appropriately be incorporated here than in Chapter IX. This refers to the triangular financial arrangement which grew up in the early days of the American Civil War between Stephen Moulton in Bradford, one of his sons, Henry (a commission and shipping agent in New York), and the persons for whom Henry Moulton was acting in his shipments from New York to the Cape Province and Natal. In this three-cornered arrangement Stephen Moulton's role was twofold : first and foremost, to give financial support to his son's company in New York by accepting and meeting their bills drawn upon him—" bills on London being as good as bullion "—and thus meeting the New York house's need for that " cash in hand which sometimes puts us to the wall . . . in loading a vessel as in purchasing cargoes".

Moulton not only made available to the New York house an overdraft of several hundred pounds sterling, he also acted as a clearing house for their bill transactions. Some of these bills on London originated from the Cape or Natal ; others (where shipments were made from New York to South Africa on " English

---

[1] Who discharged a good deal of his indebtedness to Moulton with bills on American companies, for instance on the 1 August 1857 C.G./SM : " . . . as they [Goodyear's London house] have not sent you a cheque as requested I have some drafts of Judson's, of short date, on the New York Packing & Belting Co., one of which for £100 will I think suit you equally as well as a cheque for a less amount . . . "

On 18 January 1858 Charles Goodyear having sent a second-class bill to Bradford wrote : " . . . I supposed you would prefer it to one on America, not having the cash or anyone in London on whom I could draw. If you wish a bill on America, you will let me know by bearer. . . " In the following month on 16 February Goodyear paid his Bradford account with an American draft at four months for £200.

[2] James Bishop & Co., New York, and Brown, Shipley & Co., Liverpool. Parmelee writing to Bishop & Co. on 10 January 1856 : " . . . we drew on 7th instant, 4 months date on Messrs. B. Shipley & Co. for £1000 . . . ", and on 1 September 1857 Bishop & Co's account was settled by drawing on the North British Co. for £400 sterling in favour of B. Shipley & Co. at 60 days' sight payable in London.

account ") originated with English houses in London, and were met there. In the latter case Moulton acted as an intermediary. He presented his son's sixty-and ninety-day bills for acceptance, and then held this paper until maturity against bills drawn upon him by the New York house.[1] If the New York house suffered disappointments in the Cape Mail and required sterling urgently—over and above the balance held on their account at Bradford—then the rubber manufacturer entered the market prior to maturity and sold the bill or bills for whatever they would fetch.[2]

The most striking thing about these foreign remittances—whether to or from Europe or America—was the smoothness and efficiency of the mechanism by which they were effected. The fact that in 1871 a Viennese merchant could write to Bradford that " during the 25 years of doing business with Barings we never had a difference of one half-penny ", is eloquent testimony of the high standards achieved by Britain in her nineteenth century role as banker and money market of the world.

---

[1] HM/SM, 9 October 1861 : " . . . We enclose you 1st of Exchange (for £800 @ 90 days) drawn by us on Messrs. Maynard Brothers & Co. of 6 Pancras Lane, London which you will please have accepted and hold subject to our Bills upon you provided we should have to draw. They are first class and therefore you will have no difficulty in selling to meet our Bills. That is if we should draw which at present we do not think we shall, as by the next mail we expect money from the Cape . . . "   And on 19 November 1861 : " We enclose you our Bill No. 135 at Ninety days after sight on James Searight of London for Three hundred and Seventy five pounds which you will please have accepted and hold against ⅔ advance of Cargoes shipped to his house at Cape Town which we trust will be all correct . . . "

[2] HM/SM, 15 October 1861 : " If required you will please sell the Bills on Maynard Bros. & Co. after they have run 60 days to put you in funds and charge us with the interest and expenses . . . "

Chapter IX

STEPHEN MOULTON AND HIS FAMILY

IT is not intended to elaborate on the biographical aspects of this work, and those facts concerning Stephen Moulton and his family which are of historical interest will be set down as briefly as possible.

Stephen Moulton was born on 7 July 1794,[1] at Arlaw Banks, an estate at Whorlton, County Durham. His father, after whom Stephen was named, was born to Jonathan Moulton, " citizen and broker of London " and Rachael his wife on 30 July 1753, and is described in the London directories c. 1788-9 as a " stationer " and " law stationer " of 16 Chancery Lane. His mother, Catherine Moulton, (née Bellamy), was also a native of London, and at the time of Stephen's birth was staying with her sister, Mrs. Mabel Lonsdale[2] at Arlaw Banks. In addition to Stephen there were two other children of this marriage : his brothers Richard—who followed his father's profession in Chancery Lane— and George, about whom almost nothing is known.

Beyond the baptismal entry at Whorlton there is no further information about Stephen Moulton until his marriage on 26 December 1826, to Elizabeth Hales of South Willeton, County Somerset, at St. George's Church, Hanover Square, London. The fact that his wife hailed from the West country, coupled with the attempts made by Moulton to trace the burial records of his grandfather, Jonathan Moulton, to the parish church of Kilmington in the neighbouring county of Devon, suggests that Stephen's forbears came from those parts, and also helps to explain his return there in 1848. In fact it was Moulton's belief that he was descended from an armigerous West Country family, and that he was entitled to the use of arms and crest ; a right, although never established

---

[1] The entry of baptism in the Whorlton register (in the parish of Gainford) is as follows " . . . September 21 1794. Stephen, s. Mr. Stephen & Catherine Moulton, of the Liberty of the Rolls in the Parish of St. Dunstan in the West London. Born 7th July 1794. Baptised and christened at Whorlton Chapel. N.B. Mrs. Moulton is sister to Mrs. Mabel Lonsdale, Arlaw Banks . . . "

[2] Married to one Christopher Lonsdale, "gent," of a long-established family at Arlaw Banks.

THE MOULTON FAMILY TREE

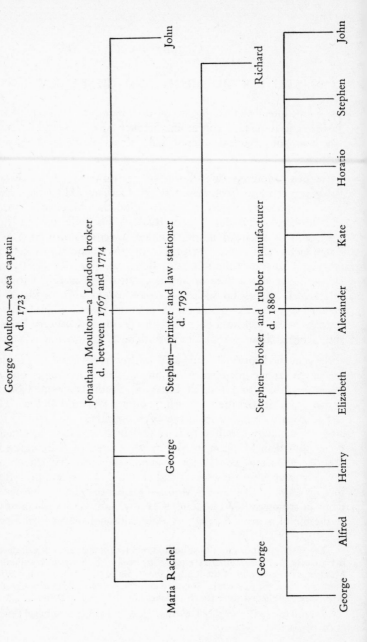

George Moulton—a sea captain
d. 1723

Jonathan Moulton—a London broker
d. between 1767 and 1774

| Maria Rachel | George | John |

Stephen—printer and law stationer
d. 1795

| George | Richard |

Stephen—broker and rubber manufacturer
d. 1880

| George | Alfred | Henry | Elizabeth | Alexander | Kate | Horatio | Stephen | John |

with the authorities, he exercised on his return to Britain from the United States in 1847 until his death in 1880.[1]

From Moulton's marriage with Elizabeth Hales—as the accompanying pedigree of the Moulton family shows—there were nine children: seven sons, Alexander, Alfred, Horatio, Henry, George, Stephen and John ; and two daughters, Elizabeth and Kate. Of these, all but Stephen, Alfred and Elizabeth returned with their mother to Britain in November, 1847 ;[2] and at one time or another four sons, Alexander, Horatio, Henry and George, assisted their father with his business. Until Henry returned to the United States in 1851 (where, as was recorded in an earlier chapter, he became a New York commission and shipping agent) he directed his father's London office. On his departure, this responsibility passed to George, who, in 1861, set up on his own behalf as a broker in Mincing Lane. Of the three sons who remained in the United Kingdom, Alexander and Horatio were associated with their father at Bradford. Alexander—a man of great business ability—was manager of the Kingston Mill from 1861 until his death in 1885, when the management passed into the hands of his brother Horatio, who outlived him by eight years. Thenceforth, although the youngest member of the Moulton family—John Moulton[3]— remained chairman of the combined Spencer-Moulton Company until his death in 1925, the impetus behind the Bradford concern

[1] On 10 May 1848 Moulton applied to the Heralds' College for a memorial for establishing arms and crest. He evidently did not proceed in this application and a search of the official records of the College of Arms shows that no such authority was ever assigned to him. A crest of identical design to the one used by Moulton until his death in 1880, but depicting the cuff argent, not ermine, was registered in 1620 for the Shapleigh family of Devon. In the same year a pedigree of five generations of the Moulton family of Plimpton and Cullompton, Co. Devon, was entered at the College of Arms, but with no mention of arms. Whilst the accompanying pedigree of the Moulton family is substantially the same as that registered in the visitation of Devon in 1620, except that Joan Snelling is noted as the first wife of William Moulton of Plimpton and this William had a daughter Jane, it has not proved possible to trace any connection between the known genealogy of Stephen Moulton's family and the registered pedigrees of sixteenth-and seventeenth-century Moultons.

[2] WR /SM, 26 October 1847 : " . . . your brother Richard thinks you are a fool and will bring the whole family down, but Mrs. M. and family will leave for Liverpool in the packet ship Victoria on 25th . . . "

[3] Only John remained to be educated when the Moultons came to Bradford. He was first sent to a private school outside Bath, then to St. Andrew's College, Reading. He read law at Pembroke College, Oxford, and eventually became a member of the Inns of Court.

was provided by the Spencers rather than the Moultons ; especially by Alexander Spencer, who for several years was managing director and, after John Moulton's death, chairman of the company.

Of the sons who remained in or returned to the United States, Stephen's lot can quickly be related. It is contained in two letters : one from the child himself—for despite his courage and enterprise his letters show him to have been little more than a child in years— the other from Moulton's American partner, William Rider. Stephen's letter was written from New York to his father at Bradford in May 1849. In his own words : ". . . knowledge of a business is worth more than a clerkship in a counting house . . . and I am going South this Winter for the purchase of tobacco . . ." Having informed his father : ". . . I am now a man and expect to be treated as such . . ." he evidently thought fit to conclude : ". . . I wish no allusions made to the writing of this letter for it was written without lines which I have given up using . . ." But his presumed manhood was fleeting. Hardly two months had gone by when news of his death from cholera was received at Bradford.

The other two sons in the United States, Henry and Alfred, became merchants ; one of them operating from northern and the other (Alfred) from southern ports. Perhaps one of the most illuminating chapters in the history of the Moulton family was the manner in which these two exiled Englishmen were prepared to do battle in the northern and southern armies :

> That we must have only one country [wrote Henry to his father in October 1861][1] is now nearly the whole voice of the North. Having cast my lot here I am willing to protect the Goverment I live under, and whenever it requires my aid I trust God will give me the courage and will to defend the same. To allow the

[1] HM/SM, 4 October 1861. Earlier on 17 August 1861, Henry Moulton had written to Bradford : ". . . I believe that New York will be under military law before long and there appears to be a very wide difference of opinion about this war, and a determination on the part of the Government to prevent it. What we are coming to God only knows. I trust that no foreign power will interfere. The President has issued a Proclamation forfeiting all Southern property belonging to citizens in the Southern States, which States have seceded from the Union. Poor Alfred will be a sufferer to a large extent as he is owner of vessels in port with parties here. Poor fellow I wish I could aid him in changing his property but of course it cannot be done . . . "
Stephen Moulton's views on the Civil War were expressed in a letter (SM/ Bashford & Moulton, 31 October 1861) written to his son at the end of that month : " . . . I cannot give you any political news that can be relied upon, but if sound sense, and good principles, were acted upon by the North, the War would not last another day . . . "

South to go would cause all foreign Powers to laugh at our once Great Country. I had a letter from Alfred about a month ago wherein he states that the South are determined to resist to the last the North, and that he is ready to give his life and all to effect that object. You, I no doubt, will laugh at this, but I have given it my most serious reflection and I am determined never mind what may be the result to do all in my [power] to perpetuate the United States . . .

Both these men survived the terrible conflict ; Henry to experience victory, and then to die of yellow fever ; Alfred to taste the bitterness of defeat.

As befitted the female members of a Victorian household the Moulton papers contain few references to Mrs. Moulton and her daughters. Yet there can be no doubt—as the Rider letters confirm —that Mrs. Moulton was acutely aware of the risks bound up with her husband's return to Britain ; and the task which awaited her arrival at Bradford in December 1847—in restoring and furnishing the Hall—must have made great demands upon her industry and frugality.[1] The glimpses obtained of Mrs. Moulton in her life at Bradford are of a pious lady reflecting the manners of her age. Outside the Hall, and the large garden which surrounded it, her chief interests lay in the religious and social activities of the parish ; and beyond the parish, in a wider sphere, in the education of the poor in the principles of the established Church.[2] Except for an occasional visit to the theatre in London, there is almost no evidence of what a later generation would call recreation ; and this is not because in the early years at Bradford private accounts were kept separate from those of the factory. Even when her husband made business trips to the Continent in the 'sixties she did not accompany him, and of regular annual holidays there is no mention. Of the daughters, Elizabeth and Kate, all that is known is that Elizabeth married a German and remained in New York after her parents' departure for England ; an arrangement not altogether to the liking of her father, who had no time for the " most happy and glorious " principles of the German revolution of 1848, and still less patience with his son-in-law's suggestion that The Times had " awfully misrepresented Germany's attack on Denmark." Kate Moulton became her

[1] For several years after her arrival in Britain she was allowed £5 per week to maintain her family at the Hall.

[2] In addition to supporting the National Society she also took an active interest in the Salisbury Diocesan Church activities.

mother's companion at the Hall ; later, she married the son of Sir Henry Denham, Admiral, of the Royal Navy, and died and was buried at Southsea in the spring of 1894.

It is not possible to speak of the private life of Stephen Moulton and his life as a manufacturer, for the simple reason that no such division existed or was intended. The two lives, at home and at work, the two establishments, the Hall and the Kingston Mill, were joined in one endeavour : the success of the Moulton Company. Physically, a narrow lane a few yards wide separated one from the other ; mentally, no such barrier existed. It was only when the Bradford company was established and famed for its products that the manufacturer came to think of his home and his counting-house as separate and distinct.

Perhaps the most notable feature to be discerned in this man was his spirit of enterprise and self-reliance—reflected in the pages of this volume as in his observations to William Rider in July 1848 :

1st I sail from America to England.

2nd Take out a patent with my own cash.

3rd Find a capitalist.

4th Investigate and get a just conclusion concerning the Law of the case.

5th Discover and put into practice a new and superior mode of manufacturing Rubber.

6th Actually make it myself in quantities and find a profitable sale for it.

7th Spend a whole year of time at my own cost and risk . . .

In his ability to deal with these problems lay the genius of his entrepreneurship. With unbounded energy and industry, a dogged determination to succeed, and a prodigous appetite for the big and the little things in his business life, nothing seems to have escaped him. An outstanding debt of a few shillings, a trade account which could be challenged, an incorrect inventory, a lad's application for a junior clerkship,[1] an ambiguously worded letter,[2] a worker's

[1] SM/Eaton, 17 September 1867 : " With respect to the new Clerk whose letter you enclosed, I think his letter shows carelessness which at 17 or 18 is not encouraging—and the handwriting and spelling not what they should be. Try and get another."

[2] When anyone wrote to Stephen Moulton that they were " thinking " of doing something (Young/SM, 5 May 1855 : " . . . I am thinking of selling India-rubber and etc . . . ") he underscored the " thinking " and marked " not answered ".

conduct, a slovenly dress—all were subject to his scrutiny. Nothing which impinged on his life was too small or unimportant for his attention. Wherever he detected inefficiency—particularly in himself[1] or his children—he roundly condemned it in terms unknown to a later generation. A hard master to be sure (though many men knew real kindness at his hands),[2] but one who set the same high standards of conduct for himself as for others. Moreover, he enjoyed no more self-indulgence than his family, unless it was in the restoration of his Elizabethan home.[3] Only the youngest child, John, matured in the University and the Inns of Court and spared the earlier trials of his house, knew the dignified leisure which his father's success had made possible. A good cigar, a bottle of wine, good food, good books,[4] and membership of a London club[5] and several societies[6] were the only extravagances Moulton allowed himself. The fruits of his labour were not to be dissipated at the hustings,[7] or in junketing, or apeing the aristocracy ; they were to pay off his debts, and to be ploughed back into his business, so that it might grow and prosper ; and his thrift was encouraged by the low

---

[1] SM/Scutt, 10 October 1851 : " . . . I am vexed beyond expression at all my irregularity and improper delay but it might take time to mature a concern like mine . . . the fact is I must have another head besides my own at the Desk . . . "

[2] As for instance with the carter Job Underwood in 1857. He gave 4 tons of coal to the poor at Christmas, and several men got a cape on the strength of a hard-luck story. Many of the so-called " loans "—for the principle of self-help was never sacrificed—were never repaid, and he never pressed for them.

[3] Undoubtedly one of his most praiseworthy acts. See Tunstall, *Extracts from Rambles about Bath* (1856), 274-5.

[4] Additions to his library in the 'fifties included Sir Wm. Jones' works, Tomlines' *Life of Pitt*, Locke on *Civil Government*, Du Bartes' *Divine Workes*, Kempis (*De Imitatione*), Duke's *Halle of Jno Halle, Old England*, 2 volumes. Among his purchases in 1861 was a Biblical Atlas, a large-type Testament, Macaulay's *England*, Alison's *Europe*, Encyclopaedia (21 vols.), Darwin's *Biblical Criticism*, and *Aids to Faith*. Other printed material received at the Hall included *The Times, The Field, The Saturday, Quarterly*, and *Edinburgh Reviews, Punch*, and *The Gentleman's Magazine*.

[5] The Gresham Club, which in 1843 took the place of the City of London Commercial Club.

[6] The British Archaeological Association, the Wilts. Archaeological Society, the Cavendish Society, and the Institute of Civil Engineers.

[7] Moulton, like his brother, was a Liberal. Doubtless—though a Liberal in politics—he would have been satisfied with a mercantile oligarchy.

rates of taxation[1] and by his unconquerable belief in the future. There was nothing of the sceptic or the cynic or the intellectual doubter in this man. What was good for him was good for Bradford, and what was good for England was good for the world.

Whilst Moulton does not appear to have had such a pious disposition as his wife, it would be true to say that the strongest traits in his character sprang from his religious convictions and impulses : " . . . I would do unto others that they should do unto me . . ." ; convictions formed by the principles of Thomas à Kempis as by the higher criticism of Darwin. For him, as for many other members of the mercantile class of the nineteenth century, salvation was to be achieved through hard work ; and there was nothing incongruous in providing the same horse-hair cushions for his counting-house and his pew in church at the same time[2]—both were a means of salvation.[3] The monetary reward[4] which his business yielded him, however, was as nothing compared with his sense of achievement at his success. Yet his success brought with it neither self-satisfaction, nor complaisance. Other men might have been prepared to watch their ship come home, and rest ; but Moulton was committed to a life of work and endeavour, and thus he continued until the end.

---

[1] For instance in 1854 he paid the incredibly small sum for a half-year's tax of £9.0s.6d.

[2] One of the first things he did (28 October 1848) was to have his church pew removed and a new one built. In the conveyance from Thomas Divett to S.M. in 1848 : " . . . There is an ancient pew or aisle in the Parish Church of Bradford which time immemorially has gone with Kingston House . . . "

[3] At times sought almost mechanically. Week after week in Moulton's petty cash book for Kingston House appears the entry " Charity 3 /6d."

[4] Moulton's salary until 1854 was £5 per week.

CONCLUSION

Whilst the nature of this study does not warrant any penetrating conclusions regarding the development of the entire rubber industry, there are several points about which a further word or two might profitably be said.

In the first place this work draws attention to the fact that the origins of the industry in the United Kingdom and throughout the continent of Europe, including European Russia, show a marked dependence of the Old World on the New ; and the branches of the American industry established in Europe not only resulted in a transference of technical knowledge as in Moulton's case, but also, as in the case of the North British Company, of Yankee marketing skill. It says a great deal for the progress made by the Americans that at the end of the century, when American rubber manufacturers turned their attention to the British market again (between the 'sixties and the 'eighties they had been preoccupied with the home trade), they were able to compete in finish and style as well as in price and utility. The presence of American-owned rubber factories in Britain today, coupled with the existence of agreements for the exchange of technical data between British and American rubber firms, emphasises the degree of interdependence as well as the increasingly scientific nature of present-day manufacture.

It is tempting to conclude from a study of early records that improvements in rubber manufacture in the nineteenth century were due more to the practical man with his hit-and-miss methods than to scientific design; whereas today (largely as a result of the tremendous expansion of the motor-car industry, which in two decades increased the annual production of rubber tenfold), much of the industrial art of rubber manufacture is being replaced by the science of rubber chemistry. To go beyond this and try to evaluate the individual contribution of the scientist and the industrialist is trying to separate the inseparable. The extent to which in the labours of Goodyear and Markham, for example, progress waited upon those who stood outside the industry altogether should not be overlooked.

The history of the rubber industry is a story of continuity and joint endeavour. Its earliest developments found root in the shadow of the older chemical and textile industries. While certain men such as the self-taught mechanic Nathaniel Hayward, the curiously dedicated genius Charles Goodyear, and the inventor and self-confident manufacturer Thomas Hancock, appear to have filled the most important roles, their dependence on other men (including those who failed as well as those who succeeded), was all-important. The degree of interdependence required to ensure the rise and progress of an industry is well illustrated in Moulton's relations with the inventors Goodyear and Thomas, the capitalist Palairet, the merchant Foster and the middleman Spencer. The list of mechanics, chemists, inventors, scientists, merchants, entrepreneurs and industrialists who contributed to the growth of this industry is endless ; their social origins too diverse to be classified. If the entrepreneurs led the way it was because they responded to the changing economic and social environment (to the growing needs of the rubber footwear and clothing industry, to the demands of steam and electricity, and of rail and road transportation), more promptly than the rest. It is also because they had a greater realisation of the ultimate utility of the industrial and scientific changes taking place around them. Yet having said this it is only right to draw attention to the peculiar unwillingness of those who led the early companies to seize the new opportunities bound up with the developments in road transportation at the end of the century.

The Moulton Company's reluctance to take up the manufacture of pneumatic tyres can be explained by its specialisation in rubber mechanicals. It is not surprising that they should have chosen to concentrate on these goods, for which they remain justly famed, rather than seek out new fields of endeavour. The intriguing question is why the other less specialised houses, including the American-led organisation in Edinburgh and the Manchester combine, should have done the same. With their entrenched positions and their accumulated knowledge and experience, the initiative in these matters rested with them. Yet against the more aggressive outlook of the new group of entrepreneurs who were eventually to dominate the tyre trade the advantages possessed by the pioneering companies were of little avail.

In trying to explain these events it is easy to lose historical perspective, crediting the early manufacturers with knowledge of subsequent developments that they could not have possessed, and overlooking their doubts, uncertainties and difficulties. Indeed, if there is one lesson that emerges from a study of the rise of the house of Moulton it is the unique character of a firm's history and the deceptive nature of historical simplifications. Whatever the reasons, the older companies were more concerned with expanding the sales of existing products rather than opening up markets for new ones. It required a new combination of inventive talent and commercial skill, new vision and imagination, to ensure the technical advance bound up with the development of the pneumatic tyre industry. Only thus was a new chapter added to the long history of the manufacturing arts.

This, however, is a story that must be told elsewhere. At the time of Moulton's death in 1880 control of the industry still rested with the pioneering companies of Lancashire, Wiltshire, London and the Scottish Lowlands. The industry's principal raw material, obtained from the uncultivated areas of South America, Central America and Africa, was as varied and as uncertain in quality as it had ever been. Not until the early years of the twentieth century did the more uniform plantation supplies of British Malaya, Ceylon and other parts of the Far East compete actively with wild rubber on the world market, and only in 1914 did they outstrip wild supplies. The chief products —rubber shoes, waterproof clothing and rubber mechanical goods— also remained unchanged. Likewise the manufacturing process rested on the foundation laid by Goodyear and Hancock a generation earlier, and the chief vulcanising agent, sulphur, was as vital at the end of the century as it had been in 1839. Decisive developments, such as the improvement in the internal combustion engine and the subsequent appearance of the new science of rubber chemistry, lay in the future.

That the story of the rise of an industry is not an arbitrary process but an intensely human affair, demanding the insight of the sociologist as well as the judgment of the historian, is well brought out in seeking an explanation of such matters as Moulton's departure from America for Britain in 1847. Was it because of the desire to return to his native land, in the hope of building a business that would live after him, as a means of improving his family's economic position, or because such a venture provided him with a greater outlet for his powers of leadership and innate commercial skill ? What was it that he eventually hoped to reap as a result of his exertions ? The explanation can hardly be that in the Kingston Mill Moulton sought the quickest avenue to wealth for its own sake. Events show that his aim was not so much the gathering of a large fortune upon which he could hope to retire, as the accumulation of industrial capital which would enable the Bradford business to prosper. Whilst it cannot be said of this man that he curried favour with anyone, his action in returning to Britain might also find explanation in his attempt to improve his family's social as well as its economic position.

The fact that his social status rose as his business grew reflects the esteem in which successful entrepreneurship was held in the Victorian era.

Moulton's spirit of enterprise—with the Riders and others he foresaw the industrial possibilities of vulcanised rubber—his willingness to take risks and his power to persuade others to do likewise, not only reflected the dynamic role of the class of entrepreneurs (if such a restrictive term may be used), to which he belonged, but also the " thunder-driven " age in which he lived. His belief that the Bradford venture would triumph never faltered, despite the fact that it was founded in circumstances of general industrial and political unrest. At the risk of over-simplifying a point about which very much more could be said it is suggested that the venture's ultimate success was due more to Moulton's commercial aptitude than to any other factor. Perhaps the finest tribute that can be paid him is to say that in the abandoned woollen mills of the West Country he introduced a new manufacture and a new livelihood. His life, and the history of the company he founded, serve to show the richness of the industrial past.

APPENDICES

APPENDIX I

Master Vulcanisation Patents of Goodyear, Hancock and Moulton

The Goodyear Vulcanisation Patent

No. 3461

THE UNITED STATES OF AMERICA

To all to whom these Letters Patent shall come :

Whereas Charles Goodyear, New York, has alleged that he has invented a new and useful improvement in India Rubber fabrics, which, he states, has not been known or used before his application ; has made oath that he is a citizen of the United States ; that he does verily believe that he is the original and first inventor or discoverer of the said improvement ; and that the same hath not, to the best of his knowledge and belief, been previously known or used ; has paid into the Treasury of the United States the sum of thirty dollars, and presented a petition to the Commissioner of Patents, signifying a desire of obtaining an exclusive property in the said improvement, and praying that a Patent may be granted for that purpose :

These are therefore to grant, according to law, to the said Charles Goodyear, his heirs, administrators, or assigns, for the term of fourteen years from the fifteenth day of June, one thousand eight hundred and forty-four, the full and exclusive right and liberty of making, constructing, using, and vending to others to be used, the said improvement, a description whereof is given in the words of the said Charles Goodyear, in the schedule hereunto annexed, and is made a part of these presents.

In testimony whereof, I have caused these Letters to be made Patent, and the seal of the Patent Office has been hereunto affixed.

Given under my hand, at the City of Washington, this fifteenth day of June, in the year of our Lord one thousand eight hundred and forty-four, and of the Independence of the United States of America the sixty-eighth.

J. C. CALHOUN,
Secretary of State.

Countersigned and Sealed with the
Seal of the Patent Office.

HENRY L. ELLSWORTH,
Commissioner of Patents

185

The Schedule Referred to in these Letters Patent,
and Making Part of the Same.

To all whom it may concern :

Be it known, That I, Charles Goodyear, of the City of New York, in the State of New York, have invented certain new and useful improvements in the manner of preparing fabrics of Caoutchouc, or India Rubber, and I do hereby declare that the following is a full and exact description thereof :

My principal improvement consists in the combining of sulphur and white lead with the India Rubber, and in the submitting of the compound thus formed to the action of heat at a regulated temperature ; by which combination and exposure to heat it will be so far altered in its qualities as not to become softened by the action of the solar ray, or of artificial heat, at a temperature below that to which it was submitted in its preparation, say to a heat of 270 degrees of Fahrenheit's scale ; nor will it be injuriously affected by exposure to cold ; it will also resist the action of the expressed oils, and that, likewise, of spirits of turpentine, or of the other essential oils, at common temperatures, which oils are its usual solvents.

The articles which I combine with the India Rubber, in forming my improved fabric, are sulphur and white lead, which materials may be employed in varying proportions ; but that which I have found to answer best, and to which it is desirable to approximate in forming the compound, is the following :

I take twenty-five parts of India Rubber, five parts of sulphur, and seven parts of white lead ; the India Rubber I usually dissolve in spirits of turpentine, or other essential oil ; and the white lead, and sulphur also, I grind in spirits of turpentine, in the ordinary way of grinding paint. These three articles, thus prepared, may, when it is intended to form a sheet by itself, be evenly spread upon any smooth surface, or upon glazed cloth, from which it may be readily separated ; but I prefer to use for this purpose the cloth made according to the present specification, as the compound spread upon this article separates therefrom more cleanly than from any other. Instead of dissolving the India Rubber in the manner above set forth, the sulphur and white lead, prepared by grinding, as above directed, may be incorporated with the substance of the India Rubber by the aid of heated cylinders, or callender rollers, by which it may be brought into sheets of any required thickness ; or it may be applied so as to adhere to the surface of cloth, or of leather of various kinds. This mode of producing and of applying the sheet Caoutchouc, by means of rollers, is well known to manufacturers. To destroy the odor of the sulphur in fabrics thus prepared, I wash the surface with a solution of potash, or with vinegar, or with a small portion of essential oil, or other solvent of sulphur.

When the India Rubber is spread upon the firmer kinds of cloth, or of leather, it is subject to peel therefrom by a moderate degree of force, the

gum letting go the fibre by which the two are held together ; I have, therefore, devised another improvement in this manufacture, by which this
tendency is, in a great measure, corrected, and by which, also, the sheet gum,
when not attached to cloth, or leather, is better adapted to a variety of
purposes than when not prepared by this improved mode, which is as follows:
After laying a coat of gum, compounded as above set forth, on any suitable
fabric, I cover it with a bat of cotton wool as it is delivered from the doffer
of a carding machine, and this bat I cover with another coat of the gum ;
a process which may be repeated two or three times, according to the
required thickness of the goods. A very thin and strong fabric may be thus
produced, which may be used in lieu of paper for the covering of boxes,
books, or other fabrics or articles.

When this compound of India Rubber, sulphur, and white lead, whether
to be used alone in the state of sheets, or applied to the surface of any other
fabric, has fully dried, either in a heated room, or by exposure to the sun
and air, the goods are to be subjected to the action of a high degree of
temperature, which will admit of considerable variation, say from 212 to
350 degrees of Fahrenheit's thermometer ; but for the best effect, approach-
ing as nearly as may be to 270 degrees. This heating may be affected by
running the fabrics over a heated cylinder ; but I prefer to expose them
to an atmosphere of the proper temperature, which may be best done by
the aid of an oven properly constructed, with openings through which sheets
or web may be passed by means of suitable rollers. When this process is
performed upon a fabric consisting of the above named compound, it must
be allowed to remain upon the cloth on which it is made, in order to sustain
it, as it is so far softened during the operation as not to be capable of supporting its own weight without such aid. If the exposure be to a temperature
exceeding 270 degrees, it must continue for a very brief period.

Having thus fully described the nature of the process by which I prepare
my improved India Rubber fabric, I do hereby declare that I do not now
claim the combining of sulphur with Caoutchouc, either in the proportion
named, or in any other, this combination having been the subject of a patent
granted to me on the 24th of February, 1839 ; but I do claim the combining
of the said gum with sulphur and with white lead, so as to form a triple
compound, either in the proportions herein named, or in any other within
such limits as will produce a like result. And I will here remark, that although
I have obtained the best results from the carbonate of lead, other salts of lead,
or the oxides of that metal, may be substituted therefor, and will produce
a good effect. I, therefore, under this head, claim the employment of either
of the oxides or salts of lead, in the place of the white lead, in the above
named compound.

I also claim the formation of a fabric of the India Rubber, by interposing
layers of cotton batting between those of the gum, in the manner and for
the purpose above described.

I likewise claim, in combination with the foregoing, the process of exposing the India Rubber fabric to the action of a high degree of heat, such as is herein specified ; by means of which my improved compound is effectually changed in its properties, so as to protect it from decomposition, or deterioration, by the action of those agents which have heretofore been found to produce that effect upon India Rubber goods.

CHARLES GOODYEAR.

Witnesses—$\left\{\begin{array}{l}\text{Thomas P. Jones,}\\\text{B.K. Morsell.}\end{array}\right.$

Specification of the Patent Granted to THOMAS HANCOCK, *of Goswell Mews, Goswell Road, in the County of Middlesex, Waterproof Cloth Manufacturer, for Improvements in the Preparation or Manufacture of Caoutchouc in Combination with other Substances, which Preparation or Manufacture is suitable for rendering Leather Cloth and other Fabrics Waterproof, and to various other purposes for which Caoutchouc is employed.*—Sealed November 21, 1843.

To all to whom these presents shall come, &c. &c.—The nature of my improvement or improvements in the preparation or manufacture of caoutchouc in combination with other substances, consists in diminishing or obviating their clammy adhesiveness, and also in diminishing or entirely preventing their tendency to stiffen and harden by cold, and to become softened or decomposed by heat, grease, and oil.

I will first describe the means by which I correct, obviate, or lessen, the clammy adhesiveness of caoutchouc, and caoutchouc in combination with other substances. And I would first premise, that as the essential oils employed in softening and dissolving caoutchouc are ultimately almost entirely evaporated, I wish to be understood when speaking of proportions, that the dry materials are meant, more or less solvent may be used, according as it may be convenient to employ the combination in a stiff and plastic state, or diluted in any degree down to the consistence of painters' varnish. I take ten pounds of caoutchouc, and pass it two or three times between iron rollers, until a roughly uniform sheet is obtained ; I then take twenty pounds of silicate of magnesia (sometimes called Venetian or French chalk and talc), and reduce it to a fine powder, and I continue rolling the sheet, sifting the silicate upon it as it passes through or between the rollers, and I carry on this operation until the whole is well mixed in. I then work up the mass into a state of uniform consistence by means of the machine or apparatus commonly employed in making what is called manufactured caoutchouc, which machine is fully described in the specification of a patent granted to me on the 18th day of April, 1837. If the mass is intended for cutting into sheets or other forms, I press it in moulds, and cut it up in the manner commonly practised, and well known to persons acquainted with such manufactures. When I require this combination in the form of large sheets, and they are not required of very fine quality, I pass it between rollers, beginning with them rather wide apart, and gradually closing them each time of passing through, until they produce the thickness I want. The rollers may be used cold, or heated to about 80° Fahrenheit. When it is required to spread the combination on cloth, either for the purpose of rendering a previous coating of caoutchouc unadhesive or upon the surface of the cloth itself, I proceed to soften the combination by the application of a small quantity of solvent, so as to make it of the consistence of dough or putty, in the manner set forth in the before-mentioned specification of a patent granted to me in 1837, in respect to caoutchouc ; and I spread it also in the manner and by a spreading machine similar to the one therein described. If very thin sheets or films are required, I spread the combination on cloth previously saturated with size, and proceed with this operation in the same manner as is set forth with respect to caoutchouc sheets, under a patent granted to me, bearing date the 23rd day of January, 1838. The combination in this state, if not of too soft a consistence, may be spread by means of iron rollers into sheets, either alone or upon cloth, so as to remain permanently attached to the same, or upon sized cloth, to be afterwards stripped off ; the surface of the iron in contact with the sheet should be kept wet, to lessen or prevent adhesion. Instead of a smooth even face, I sometimes obtain impressions on the surface by pressure between plates previously engraved of the desired pattern, or by means of rollers, by engraving one or both, so as to produce the required graining, or device ; these plates or rollers may be used cold, or if the consistence of the combination is hard and stiff, they may be heated to any required degree. If a dead or dull matted appearance is required, I pass woollen cloth or other suitable fabric through or between the rollers, in contact with the coated surface of the cloth or sheet, and afterwards strip off the fabric, which should be previously sized, as before stated. By these and similar means, I frequently give to sheets of the combination, or to fabrics coated with it, a very close resemblance to a variety of woven and other manufactures, some of which may be used as substitutes for the article imitated. For coarse and cheap articles a proportion of washed lime or fullers' earth, dried, and sifted very fine, may be mixed with the silicate, and the quantity of the latter proportionably reduced. I sometimes make the exterior of an article of a combination that will be inadhesive, and of fine materials, and the interior with a combination containing either more caoutchouc, or more of the lime or fullers' earth, as the case may require. The combinations hereinbefore described will be of a light drab colour, or of a darker shade, according to the proportion of the silicate ; but if required of other colours, I mix with the silicate any suitable pigment commonly used for such purposes. If patterns are required to be printed on these manufactures, I mix the colour with a thin solution of caoutchouc, as mentioned in the specification of my patent of the 23rd day of January, 1838. When a dark colour is not objectionable, I employ asphalte instead of, or combined with, the silicate. The combination of asphalte with caoutchouc may be effected in the dry state by reducing the asphalte to a fine powder, and treating it in the same manner as before stated in respect to the silicate. Plumbago may also be introduced when the colour is dark. I find that from six to seven pounds of asphalte, according to its quality, to eight pounds of caoutchouc answers the purpose ; if silicate also is used, the quantity of asphalte should be proportionably less. When this combination is required for spreading on cloth, or for thin sheets, I soften it, and treat it in the same manner as before described for the silicate ; if it is wished, more asphalte or silicate may be added during this operation. Nearly the same results are obtained by dissolving the asphalte in coal naptha, and employing such solution instead of naptha, or other solvent, in softening the caoutchouc, to bring it to a suitable consistence for the spreading machine ; and if silicate is employed with the asphalte, it may be sifted in, as directed in respect of colouring matters, in the specification before referred to, of 1837. Raised patterns may also be produced on the surface by the means before described. These combinations may be manufactured into sheets and various other articles, or applied generally to caoutchouc and caoutchouc manufactures, where it is desirable to obviate the clammy adhesiveness of the surface ; and I apply them for the purpose of rendering cloth more or less waterproof by means of the spreading machine before alluded to, and to other purposes, by means of a spatula, or other convenient instrument, and in a more diluted state, in the manner of painting, or varnishing with a common brush. Of course the different proportions may be varied according to the purposes to which the combinations are to be applied. It may be necessary here to observe that all the substances employed in the beforementioned combinations have a tendency to weaken, more or less, the elastic properties of caoutchouc, and in particular the proportion of silicate of magnesia may be increased until the caoutchouc is nearly deprived of these properties. Any person practically acquainted with caoutchouc manufactures will be able, from the descriptions already given, to obtain the proper consistence and quality, and to adapt the combinations to the various purposes for which they may be required.

It is well known that caoutchouc stiffens and becomes hard when exposed to a cold temperature ; and that it is liable to become soft and decomposed by heat and exposure to the atmosphere ; and by contact with oil or grease ; that it is easily acted upon by solvents, and its elastic properties weakened by the means usually employed for its manufacture. I diminish or obviate these effects by intimately blending sulphur with caoutchouc during the process of its manufacture or preparation, and then treating the combination in the manner hereafter described. Sulphur may be blended with caoutchouc in various ways, but the following I find to answer the desired purpose :— I melt in an iron vessel a quantity of sulphur, at a temperature ranging from about 240° to 250° Fahrenheit, and immerse it in the caoutchouc previously rolled into rough sheets, or cut to any convenient form or size, and allow it to remain until the sulphur has penetrated quite through the caoutchouc, which may be ascertained by cutting a portion of it asunder with a wet knife ; if the operation is complete, the colour of the caoutchouc will be changed throughout to a yellowish tint : if there is only a margin of yellow around the cut part the operation must be continued longer, until the colour of the whole is changed ; the sulphur adhering to the surface being scraped off, the caoutchouc will then have taken up a quantity of sulphur, from one-sixth to one-tenth of its weight. With caoutchouc thus prepared, I proceed with the further manufacture of it into the consistence of dough or putty, or making solutions of it, and spread it on cloth or into sheets in the manner already stated or referred to. Sulphur may also be blended with caoutchouc by reducing the former to a fine powder, and mixing it mechanically in the manner and by the means before mentioned for silicate of magnesia. Sulphur may also be blended with the surface of some articles, such as sheets of caoutchouc by heating the latter to about 200°, and sifting and rubbing flour of sulphur on it. Instead of the preceding, I sometimes blend sulphur with caoutchouc by means of a solvent. In that case I saturate the solvent I mean to employ with as much sulphur as it will take up by boiling, and employ as much of this saturated solvent as will, after evaporation, leave the requisite proportion of sulphur before indicated blended with the caoutchouc. When this saturated solvent is allowed to cool, any excess of sulphur will fall down in crystals ; if, therefore, for any purpose, it is wished to employ a larger proportion of sulphur, it must be kept hot. I prefer in this case to use oil of turpentine as the solvent. Either of the foregoing, or any other convenient mode, may be adopted for blending the sulphur and caoutchouc together, care being taken to ensure as much as possible a uniform mixture. The silicate of magnesia and the other substances mentioned in the first part of this specification may, if wished, be mixed with the combination of sulphur and caoutchouc in such proportions as may be necessary to obviate or correct the clammy adhesiveness before mentioned ; but I wish it to be clearly understood that the combination of the silicate of magnesia with caoutchouc has the effect in all cases of lessening its elastic properties in proportion to the quantity of silicate employed. This combination of sulphur and caoutchouc, and of sulphur and caoutchouc mixed with the silicate of magnesia and the other substances before mentioned, may be applied to various purposes in the manner hereinbefore stated or referred to, and introduced by similar or other convenient means into caoutchouc manufactures.

Having described the methods by which I blend sulphur with caoutchouc, and the manner in which I apply the same to various purposes, I would here observe that the combination is still as soluble as before, and has not yet undergone the change or modification by which the improvement or improvements contemplated in this portion of my invention are carried out. When caoutchouc alone is to be operated upon, I find that the desired effect, which for brevity's sake I will hereafter call the change, may be produced by immersing the caoutchouc in melted sulphur, as hereinbefore mentioned ; I then raise the temperature to 300°, from 300° to 370°, and continuing it

o

so immersed for a longer or a shorter period, according to the thickness or bulk of the caoutchouc or the extent to which the change is to be carried ; for instance, if sheet caoutchouc one-sixteenth of an inch thick is continued in sulphur at 350° to 370°, from ten to fifteen minutes, the change before alluded to is produced ; or, instead of so high a temperature, the sulphur is raised only from 310° to 320°, and the caoutchouc immersed in it from fifty to sixty minutes the result will be much the same ; and if continued for two hours at the same temperature, the effect will be proportionably increased : and if continued longer, the caoutchouc becomes a darker colour, and nearly loses its property of stretching ; and if carried still farther, turns nearly black, and has something the appearance of horn, and may be pared with a knife similarly to that substance. By the effect of this high temperature such a change in, or modification of, the properties of the caoutchouc and most of its combinations will be produced, that the elastic force or property of manufactured caoutchouc to recover its form after being extended is greatly increased, and it will, after being so treated, resist to a considerable extent the action of heat, oil and grease, as well as the effect of cold, and be more capable of resisting the menstrua by which caoutchouc is commonly dissolved. I would here observe that the temperature and the time which have been stated produced a degree of change suitable for many purposes, but may be varied discretionally. And I would here make this general remark, that the higher the temperature the shorter is the time required ; and, on the contrary, a lower temperature requires a longer time. And I would here observe that the proportion of sulphur is, to a certain extent, increased by continued immersion ; and the time and temperature just indicated is equally applicable to the combinations of caoutchouc and sulphur with the silicate of magnesia and other substances mentioned in the first part of this my specification. The sulphur which adheres to the surface may be easily removed by friction or scraping. I employ this mode of operating in preference generally where practicable, particularly for articles made of manufactured caoutchouc, such as sheets and thread for elastic manufactures, whether made from manufactured caoutchouc or of the raw material as imported. When the combination is spread upon cloth, or attached to other substances capable of enduring the necessary temperature, I pass such articles over plates or cylinders heated sufficiently to effect the change ; if the side on which the combination of caoutchouc and sulphur is spread is brought into contact with the heated surface of the plate or cylinder, the temperature and the time in contact formerly indicated in respect of metal sulphur will answer the purpose ; and this is the mode I prefer in cases where substances, such as leather, coated with the combination, will not so well endure a high temperature ; but when the combination is spread on cloth or other substance which is to be brought into contact with the heated surface, the temperature will required to be raised, or the article longer exposed to it, according to the extent to which the heat is impeded by the thickness or quality of the intervening substance, which may easily be ascertained by testing small pieces as a guide. In some cases,

such as for the strapping on the seams of garments, it may be useful to employ
hot irons to effect the change. Another mode of submitting the articles to
the necessary temperature, is by means of a stove heated to the required
degree, which degree, and the proper period for the article to remain in it,
must, as before stated, depend on the nature of the case : if it is sheet caoutchouc, or thread, or any similar article, the time and temperature before
indictated will answer, according to the extent to which the change is to be
carried, or the size or bulk of the articles to be operated on. If the article
is partly composed of cloth coated on one side, as, for instance, a single
texture of calico, rendered waterproof by a very thin coating of the combination, a temperature of from 290° to 300° will be sufficient, and the
period for remaining in or passing through the stove from one and a half
to two minutes. If a thicker coat of the combination is laid on the calico,
a somewhat longer time must be given ; and so in respect of a union of two
plies of cloth, the time and temperature must be regulated according to the
thickness of the textures and the interposed coating of the combination.
When a greater number of plies of cloth are required to be united, as in the
manufacture of artificial leather for straps, card-backs, hose-pipe, and the
like, I proceed as in the case just mentioned ; but if, from the thickness of
the cloth, or the number of plies required, I conceive the heat will not readily
or sufficiently penetrate the mass, I unite two folds of the cloth first, and pass
them through the stove until the change is effected ; I then unite another fold
to the former, and pass it again through the stove, and so proceed until the
required number of folds are united ; and, if required, I lastly coat the
surfaces in the above manner, and finish by again submitting the whole to
the stove. Another mode of obtaining the temperature for effecting the
change is by immersing the articles in water or steam, under pressure,
raised to the required temperature. I find that a very small quantity of
boiled linseed oil, stearine, or spermaceti, introduced with the sulphur,
communicates an agreeable smoothness to the surface. I would here also
remark, that when the surfaces are to be united, the union should be effected
before the change takes place. When the combination is required for purposes where it could not be conveniently used of the consistence of dough,
such as for saturating cloth, felt, or other similar purposes, or for coating
uneven surfaces, I dilute it with solvent to any required consistence, and
apply it with a brush, or other convenient means, and afterwards submit
the articles to the influence of heat, in the manner already described, or
by any other that may be convenient. The sulphur may, if required, be more
or less discharged from the caoutchouc, after it has undergone the change,
by submitting it to the known solvents of sulphur, of which I prefer a solution of the sulphite of soda in water, kept to a temperature of about 200°.
Other and similar modes may be devised for carrying these improvements
into effect. But enough has now been said to enable any person of common
skill, and practically acquainted with caoutchouc manufactures, to follow
out these operations with success. What I claim as my invention and
discovery is,

Firstly, The combination of caoutchouc with silicate of magnesia, where-by manufactured caoutchouc is rendered free from that clammy and adhesive character which it usually possesses.

Secondly, I claim the modes herein described of combining asphalte with caoutchouc ; and,

Thirdly, I claim the treating of caoutchouc (either alone or in combination with other substances) with sulphur when acted upon by heat, and thus changing the character of caoutchouc as herein described.—In witness, &c.

THOMAS HANCOCK.

Enrolled May 21, 1844.

A.D. 1847 . . . . . . No. 11,567

Treating Caoutchouc with other Materials, &c.

MOULTON'S SPECIFICATION

To All to Whom These Presents Shall Come, I Stephen Moulton, of Norfolk Street, Strand, in the County of Middlesex, Gentleman, send greeting.

Whereas Her present most Excellent Majesty Queen Victoria, by Her Royal Letters Patent under the Great Seal of the United Kingdom of Great Britain and Ireland, bearing date at Westminster, the Eighth day of February, in the tenth year of Her reign, did, for Herself, Her heirs and successors, give and grant unto me, the said Stephen Moulton, my exors, admors, and assigns, Her especial licence, full power, sole privilege and authority, that I, the said Stephen Moulton, my exors, admors, and assigns, or such others as I, the said Stephen Moulton, my exors, admors, and assigns, should at any time agree with, and no others, from time to time and at all times during the term of years therein expressed, should and lawfully might make, use, exercise and vend, within England, Wales, and the Town of Berwick-upon-Tweed, the Invention communicated to me by a certain Foreigner residing abroad, of " Improvements in Treating Caoutchouc with other Materials to Produce Elastic and Impermeable Compounds; " in which said Letters Patent is contained a proviso that I, the said Stephen Moulton, shall cause a particular description of the nature of the said Invention, and in what manner the same is to be performed, by an instrument in writing under my hand and seal, to be enrolled in Her said Majesty's High Court of Chancery within six calendar months next and immediately after the date of the said in part recited Letters Patent, as in and by the same, reference being thereunto had, will more fully and at large appear.

Now Know Ye, that in compliance with the said proviso, I, the said Stephen Moulton, do hereby declare that the nature of the said Invention, and the manner in which the same is to be performed, are particularly described and ascertained in and by the following statement thereof, that is to say :—

The Invention consists in treating caoutchouc by combining therewith calcined and carbonate of magnesia, and hypo-sulphite of lead, and the artificial sulphuret of lead, and submitting the combined compound to heat, as will be hereafter described, by which Invention I am enabled to dispense with the use of solvents, and to manufacture various goods free from the offensive smell occasioned by such solvents. But in order that the Invention may be fully understood I will proceed to describe the process pursued by me.

After the caoutchouc has been cut and cleansed, I put one or more pounds weight, as can be conveniently ground or mixed at a time, between two revolving iron cylinders or rollers, denominated the mixing rollers, heated internally by steam, when the caoutchouc, by the action of the rollers, soon presents the appearance of a rough uniform sheet, and is then ready for the mixing it with the following ingredients. If the goods that are to be made from the compound are intended to be elastic, and to be rendered unaffected by heat or cold, I mix in with one pound of caoutchouc, from one ounce to half a pound of the hypo-sulphite of lead, and the artificial sulphuret of lead, both or either, but I prefer them in equal proportions, but if they are used separate then the whole quantity mentioned will be used. If the goods are intended to be hard, of greater tenacity, and of less elasticity, I mix in from two ounces to half a pound of the calcined or carbonate of magnesia with one pound of caoutchouc, and then add both the hypo-sulphite of lead and the artificial sulphuret of lead, or either, in like manner and proportions as used for elastic goods. The materials above mentioned and the caoutchouc having passed repeatedly between the mixing rollers, so that the whole compound may be well combined, which will readily be seen by a workman accustomed to the working of caoutchouc, it is then removed to another similar pair of rollers, denominated the grinding rollers, and treated in like manner, which rollers are placed nearer to each other than the mixing rollers, in order that by these rollers a more perfect mixture of the compound may be effected. After this second process the compound is again removed to the third pair of rollers, also heated by steam, denominated the softening rollers, and again ground or mixed thereby, when it soon becomes fit for its final removal to the spreading machine. The spreading machine comprises two or more iron cylinders, which are heated internally by steam (the machine which I prefer consists of three rollers), one above the other, and of a smoother and finer surface that that of the rollers before mentioned. The compound is placed between the upper rollers, and passes to the lower one, upon which the cloth for its reception passes round, and thus receives on its surface the different coatings of the compound required. If sheet rubber is desired the compound is placed in like manner dispensing with the use of the cloth, and the sheet taken from the lower roller. Both the coated cloth and the sheet roller in passing off the lower roller are rolled up in dry cloth, to keep the surfaces apart, and is then fit for making up into such goods as may be required. In manufacturing goods from the compounds thus prepared, when manufactured they are dusted over with purified pipe or other clay of similar quality, finely powdered, to prevent the surfaces from adhering together, but they are as yet still liable to the action of all the solvents and other influences which act upon caoutchouc, and would accordingly become rigid in cold and soft and sticky in warm weather. To free the caoutchouc therefore from these its natural characteristics, it has been combined with the salts of lead above mentioned, and the goods manufactured from this compound have now to be subjected to heat in a suitable chamber or cylinder, and heated either by steam or dry heat (the former I prefer) of from two hundred and twenty to two hundred and eighty or three hundred degrees, according to the quantity of the goods heated at one time, and also as to the thickness of the compound put into the sheets or upon the cloth. The time required for heating goods will likewise vary according to circumstances last mentioned. Some heats may require three hours and some five hours, or thereabouts, and which is easily determined by any practical man acquainted with the business. After the goods have been heated as last-mentioned, they become elastic and impermeable, as set forth in the title above recited.

Having thus described the nature of the Invention, and the manner of performing the same, I would have it understood that I do not confine myself to the precise details herein given, so long as the peculiar character of the Invention be retained ; and I would remark that I do not claim as new the machinery described for reducing caoutchouc into a pulpy state ; but what I claim is, the treating caoutchouc with hypo-sulphite and artificial sulphuret of lead, and subjecting it to a high degree of temperature, as herein described. And,

Secondly, I claim the treating caoutchouc by combining therewith calcined and carbonate of magnesia, and hypo-sulphite of lead, and the artificial sulphuret of lead, and subjecting it to high degrees of temperature, as herein described.

In witness whereof, I, the said Stephen Moulton, have hereunto set my hand and seal, this Fourth day of August, in the year of our Lord One thousand eight hundred and forty-seven.

STEPHEN (L.S.) MOULTON.

AND BE IT REMEMBERED, that on the Fourth day of August, in the year of our Lord 1847, the aforesaid Stephen Moulton came before our said Lady the Queen in Her Chancery, and acknowledged the Specification aforesaid, and all and every thing therein contained and specified, in form above written. And also the Specification aforesaid was stamped according to the tenor of the Statute made for that purpose.

Enrolled the Seventh day of August, in the year of our Lord One thousand eight hundred and forty-seven.

LONDON :
Printed by George Edward Eyre and William Spottiswoode,
Printers to the Queen's Most Excellent Majesty.   1857.

APPENDIX II

Articles of Agreement between Stephen Moulton, James Thomas, William, Emory and John Rider
Dated 28 June 1847

THIS AGREEMENT made the twenty eighth day of June A.D. 1847 by and between Stephen Moulton of the City County and State of New York of the first part, and James Thomas of the City County and State aforesaid of the second part, and William Rider, Emory Rider and John Rider of the City County and State aforesaid, Copartners in business under the firm of W. Rider & Brothers of the third part.

Witnesseth whereas the said party of the first part obtained on the 8th. day of February last Letters Patent in England for Improvements in the treatment of Caoutchouc and in completing his experiments preparatory to filing his Specification to said Letters Patent has availed himself of the scientific knowledge and chemical information of the said party of the second part and whereas the parties of the third part are practical manufacturers of Caoutchouc and have rendered to the parties of the first and second part certain desirable facilities in the carrying on their experiments. Now therefore the following has been and is hereby agreed upon between the parties hereto :— First, The party of the first part in consideration of the premises and One dollar to him paid by each of the parties of the second and third part, the receipt whereof is hereby acknowledged, doth hereby agree to transfer and by these presents doth transfer and assign to the parties of the second and third parts an interest in said English patent. One third to the party of the second part and one third to the party of the third, subject to the payment of all reasonable expenses attending the taking out of the same such payment to be made only from the first monies realized from said patent. And it is distinctly understood and agreed upon by all the said parties that in case no profits shall be realized from said patent or that losses should occur by Law Suits or in any way whatsoever that such losses shall be borne by the parties of the first and third part and that no claim shall be made on the party of the second part either in Law or in Equity to compel him to make good such loss or any part thereof. The said party of the first part shall have the management of the patent in England but subject to the payment to the parties of the second and third parts respectively their Executors Administrators and Assigns their part of the nett proceeds arising from the said Patent either by Sale of Right, by License, or otherwise—

Second. The parties of the second and third parts hereby agree each for himself to render to the party of the first part all the assistance in their power with the view of enabling him to make the best possible Specification to his patent in England.

Third. It is mutually agreed between the parties hereto that should the experiments herein provided for, now making, or hereafter to be made result in the discovery of any improvements or alterations in the treatment of Caoutchouc the same shall become the joint property of the parties hereto and if the same shall be deemed of sufficient importance to patent in the United States then and in such case a Patent shall be applied for by the said party of the second or third part and if granted shall be managed by the party of the third part for the joint benefit of the parties hereto each sharing and receiving One third part of the nett proceeds thereof in the like manner as herein provided for in respect to said English Patent before mentioned.

Fourth. It is further understood and agreed by and between the parties hereto that the party of the first part shall be at liberty to make arrangements for and may take out patents for the improvements aforesaid under such European Goverments as he may deem advisable which shall be owned and divided as hereinbefore agreed upon with respect to said English patent and the expenses of obtaining such patents to be reimbursed from the profits of such patents respectively · without personal claims against the party of the second part.

Fifth. It is further mutually agreed by the parties hereto that each shall continue to experiment in caoutchouc with the view to improvements in its manufacture and all such improvments shall become the joint property of the parties hereto share and share alike.

Sixth. It is further mutually agreed between the parties hereto that neither the party of the first part nor the party of the third part shall be authorized to make any bargain or do any act whatsoever that shall create any debt or liability which the party of the second part shall be bound to pay nor do any act whereby the interests of the said party of the second part are or may be prejudiced in any way whatever.

Seventh. A true account of Receipts and disbursements shall be kept by the parties of the first and third parts subject at any time to the inspection of the party of the second part and the nett profits shall be divided as received from time to time at least quarterly and accounts to be closed between the parties hereto quarterly.

This Agreement to continue and be in force during the existence of the said patents respectively.

Signed and Sealed in the presence of F. W. G. Bellows	W. RIDER & BROTHERS, by William Rider. STEPH. MOULTON. JAMES THOMAS

APPENDIX III

An Analysis of Moulton's purchases of Raw Rubber
1850-1900

The following figures are largely self-explanatory but there are certain major points concerning their interpretation which ought to be mentioned :

1. The fact that the Moulton manufactory was able to subsist at times on Asiatic supplies.

2. The manner in which African rubber was substituted for Asiatic and Para during the 'eighties. This was due not only to the rise in price of the Eastern products but much more to the deterioration in its quality.

3. The further fact—also borne out by the North British records— that it was possible for a company to purchase its raw materials at a price considerably below general market quotations.

TOTAL PURCHASES OF PARA ASIATIC AND AFRICAN
RUBBER FOR THE KINGSTON MILL 1850-1900

Showing average price per lb.

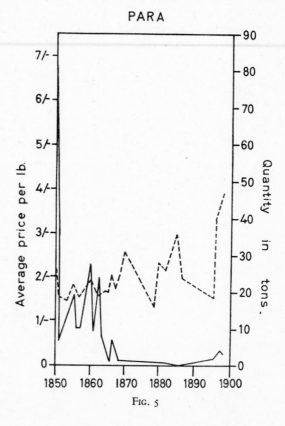

PARA

FIG. 5

Average price per lb.   ------

Quantity in tons   ———

Source :   Moulton's Invoices for these years

ASIATIC

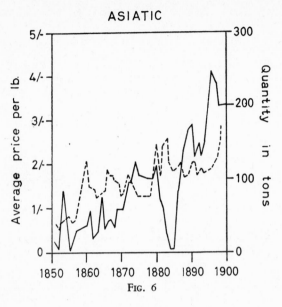

FIG. 6

AFRICAN

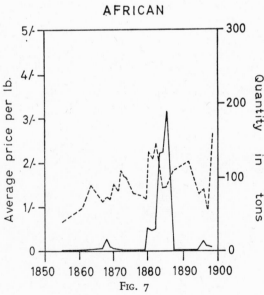

FIG. 7

APPENDIX IV

Statistics of the British Rubber Trade

IMPORTS OF CRUDE INDIA RUBBER (ALL KINDS) INTO THE UNITED KINGDOM 1850-1900*

	cwts.			cwts.	
1850	7,617	£21,355	1876	158,692	£1,536,660
1851	15,269	unenumerated	1877	159,723	£1,484,794
1852	19,607	unenumerated	1878	149,724	£1,313,209
1853	17,326	£48,513	1879	150,601	£1,626,290
1854	27,588	£250,362	1880	169,587	£2,387,947
1855	44,703	£261,352	1881	172,077	£2,254,618
1856	28,765	£163,421	1882	181,726	£2,754,692
1857	22,000	£128,458	1883	229,101	£3,652,817
1858	25,135	£132,877	1884	198,844	£2,272,499
1859	21,311	£212,602	1885	180,141	£1,981,735
1860	43,039	£470,518	1886	194,748	£2,222,156
1861	57,834	£435,923	1887	237,511	£2,704,568
1862	59,703	£483,934	1888	220,350	£2,555,341
1863	65,649	£512,399	1889	236,310	£3,617,369
1864	71,027	£502,645	1890	264,008	£3,265,088
1865	71,392	£530,538	1891	278,837	£3,351,938
1866	72,176	£728,416	1892	272,163	£2,982,412
1867	79,756	£696,377	1893	293,373	£3,330,418
1868	145,584	£1,195,226	1894	302,451	£3,272,104
1869	136,421	£1,134,585	1895	341,553	£3,760,178
1870	152,118	£1,597,628	1896	431,148	£4,991,122
1871	161,085	£1,597,628†	1897	396,929	£4,553,416
1872	157,436	£1,684,281	1898	489,581	£6,214,933
1873	157,436†	£1,746,095	1899	449,651	£5,923,897
1874	129,163	£1,326,605	1900	513,286	£6,986,133
1875	153,564	£1,570,558			

* Annual Statement of Trade.

† Thought to be an error in the Annual Statement.

EXPORTS OF CRUDE INDIA RUBBER (ALL KINDS) FROM THE UNITED KINGDOM 1850-1900*

	cwts.			cwts.	
1850	1,048	unenumerated	1876	69,661	£642,040
1851	3,098	,,	1877	79,510	£696,864
1852	5,335	,,	1878	87,379	£739,685
1853	5,987	,,	1879	90,730	£1,003,565
1854	10,872	,,	1880	76,732	£1,063,775
1855	8,350	,,	1881	94,913	£1,174,829
1856	9,709	£55,260	1882	101,655	£1,537,567
1857	7,661	£44,753	1883	102,570	£1,563,350
1858	14,607	£77,235	1884	109,856	£1,155,487
1859	10,770	£107,431	1885	89,810	£963,514
1860	12,895	£140,985	1886	111,437	£1,303,880
1861	19,110	£144,041	1887	116,572	£1,341,584
1862	24,199	£196,012	1888	126,587	£1,335,828
1863	20,610	£160,844	1889	130,506	£1,411,554
1864	29,107	£205,932	1890	142,524	£1,712,298
1865	26,050	£193,638	1891	156,259	£1,790,298
1866	24,990	£252,191	1892	150,601	£1,576,931
1867	27,930	£243,922	1893	159,203	£1,618,338
1868	40,859	£335,384	1894	171,217	£1,801,130
1869	34,586	£287,640	1895	202,485	£2,265,586
1870	50,737	£532,739	1896	235,454	£2,643,782
1871	65,443	£597,741	1897	237,671	£2,795,878
1872	60,451	£674,505	1898	294,853	£4,020,850
1873	54,395	£564,750	1899	306,110	£4,271,661
1874	53,405	£536,391	1900	293,624	£3,808,472
1875	69,757	£618,918			

* Annual Statement of Trade.

TOTAL ANNUAL EXPORTS OF CRUDE INDIA RUBBER OF
ALL KINDS FROM THE UNITED KINGDOM 1850-1900

By weight and value

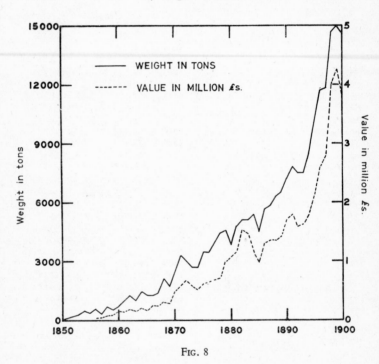

FIG. 8

Source : Annual Statement of Trade

UNITED KINGDOM IMPORTS AND EXPORTS OF
MANUFACTURED RUBBER PRODUCTS 1853-1900

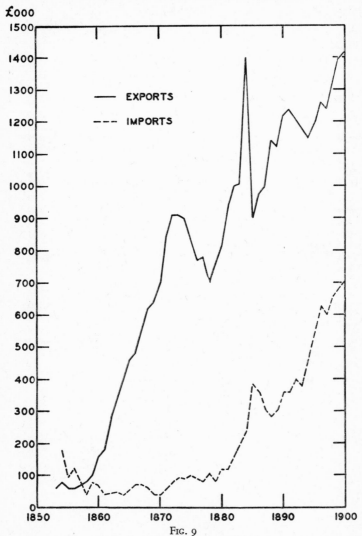

FIG. 9

Source : Annual Statement of Trade

Prior to 4th June 1853, Imports of Manufactured Caoutchouc goods were enumerated. The valuation of both imports and exports is the 'Declared Value' supplied by merchants in foreign trade. An article by A. Maizels, " The Overseas Trade Statistics of the United Kingdom ", *Journal of the Royal Statistical Society*, Vol. 112, pp. 211, gives details of valuation and some further references.

IMPORTS OF MANUFACTURED RUBBER COMMODITIES
INTO THE UNITED KINGDOM 1853-1900*

Year	Total Imports lbs.	Estimated Value	Year	Total Imports lbs.	Estimated Value
1853	629,499†	N.A.	1877	824,889	£86,676
1854	1,093,835	£191,421	1878	1,019,353	£110,156
1855	503,220	£88,063	1879	788,772	£87,591
1856	871,582	£130,738	1880	915,083	£122,522
1857	794,023	£82,240	1881	1,114,763	£125,759
1858	480,641	£41,150	1882	1,447,739	£154,924
1859	920,835	£79,581	1883	2,073,374	£211,408
1860	1,040,809	£74,952	1884	2,612,740	£262,336
1861	860,000	£41,311	1885	3,139,632	£397,730
1862	720,000	£44,682	1886	2,681,210	£353,729
1863	754,611	£48,080	1887	2,816,653	£317,489
1864	650,549	£45,398	1888	3,116,510	£290,573
1865	868,689	£46,616	1889	3,132,976	£318,439
1866	769,249	£72,467	1890	3,563,469	£360,123
1867	685,383	£73,772	1891	3,180,198	£362,384
1868	1,302,905	£66,199	1892	3,448,727	£408,150
1869	365,676	£45,617	1893	3,211,322	£375,487
1870	369,119	£39,200	1894	3,202,377	£445,327
1871	581,815	£51,631	1895	3,909,569	£550,103
1872	863,246	£80,677	1896	4,365,472	£634,868
1873	863,246	£95,601	1897	4,551,285	£611,110
1874	868,082	£93,036	1898	4,669,998	£659,445
1875	777,787	£99,073	1899	5,065,320	£691,611
1876	871,630	£95,212	1900	5,941,334	£712,081

ENTERED FOR HOME CONSUMPTION

	lbs.
1853	N.A.
1854	646,850
1855	630,711
1856	725,979
1857	685,579
1858	435,918
1859	858,849
1860	86,284‡

* Annual Statement of Trade.

† Included with "Goods Manufactured, Unenumerated" prior to 4 June 1853. Figure shown represents the period beginning 4th June to the end of year.

‡ For 3 months only. Figures after this date are not available. (N.A.).

EXPORTS OF MANUFACTURED RUBBER COMMODITIES
FROM THE UNITED KINGDOM 1853-1900*

	Weight	Declared Value		Weight	Declared Value
1853	N.A.	£62,012	1877	N.A.	£782,654
1854	84,813 lbs.	£79,580	1878	N.A.	£703,307
1855	67,185 lbs.	£66,008	1879	N.A.	£761,717
1856	112,256 lbs.	£66,488	1880	N.A.	£833,837
1857	110,486 lbs.	£70,421	1881	N.A.	£939,172
1858	51,426 lbs.	£76,995	1882	N.A.	£999,529
1859	99,063 lbs.	£99,438	1883	N.A.	£1,070,365
1860	119,037 lbs.	£173,614	1884	N.A.	£1,400,730
1861	62,623 lbs.†	£183,360	1885	N.A.	£910,763
1862	N.A.	£269,253	1886	N.A.	£971,108
1863	N.A.	£329,084	1887	N.A.	£1,070,311
1864	N.A.	£412,529	1888	N.A.	£1,143,271
1865	N.A.	£465,700	1889	N.A.	£1,125,555
1866	N.A.	£486,613	1890	N.A.	£1,222,400
1867	N.A.	£549,730	1891	N.A.	£1,242,794
1868	N.A.	£628,665	1892	N.A.	£1,215,307
1869	N.A.	£634,724	1893	N.A.	£1,185,597
1870	N.A.	£693,012	1894	N.A.	£1,152,854
1871	N.A.	£854,539	1895	N.A.	£1,190,885
1872	N.A.	£909,287	1896	N.A.	£1,261,774
1873	N.A.	£909,287‡	1897	N.A.	£1,230,445
1874	N.A.	£901,703	1898	N.A.	£1,328,702
1875	N.A.	£843,440	1899	N.A.	£1,388,805
1876	N.A.	£771,428	1900	N.A.	£1,423,464

* Annual Statement of Trade.

† After this date exports are listed by value only.

‡ Thought to be an error in the Annual Statement.

APPENDIX V

A Note and some Documents on
the American origins of the Scottish Rubber Industry
and that of Continental Europe

The American origins of the North British Rubber Co., of Scotland can be seen from the accompanying papers. Entirely American in leadership, equipment and ownership, it was established at Edinburgh in 1856 and remained under American direction until the closing years of the century. A more detailed account is contained in the author's article: "The American Origins of a Scottish Industry", *Scottish Journal of Political Economy*, Vol. II, No. 1, February, 1955, 17-32.

The oldest rubber factory in Europe was probably that founded by J. N. Reithofer in Vienna in 1821. See Johann Sloker, *Geschichte der österreichischen Industrie und ihrer Förderung unter Kaiser Franz I* (Vienna, 1914), 629 *et seq*. The earliest known factory in Germany was that established by François Fonrobert near Berlin in 1829, with whom Stephen Moulton had correspondence. Other early Berlin manufacturers were: Pflug, Jungblude, Elliot (an Englishman), Hutchinson (an American), Voigt, Winde, and Gebrüder Kessel. Factories were also established at Nuremberg, Harburg, Hamburg, Barmen, Hanover, Cologne, and Hildesheim. Americans (especially the pioneers Carl Maret and L. O. P. Meyer, who were both trained in the United States) were active in the establishment of the Gummi-waarenfabrik Hutchinson, founded in Hamburg in 1850, the New York-Hamburger Gummi-waaren, Co., also formed in Hamburg in 1856 to produce hard rubber goods, and the Harburger Gummi-Kamm Co., formed at Harburg in the same year. Although—until the 'sixties—the German industry lagged behind that of America, Great Britain and France, its rapid growth in the last quarter of the nineteenth century can be seen from the fact that the number of factories grew from 14 (mostly in Prussia) in 1852 to 111 in 1875, and 339 in 1895. Likewise the number of workers had grown from 300 to approximately 30,000 in the same period. See F. Diestelmeier, "Über die Entwicklung der Gummi Industrie, insbesondere der deutschen, in den ersten fünfzig Jahren", *Kautschuk*, Vol. IV, No. 5 (May 1928), 92-6. Also H. Schmidt, *Kautschuk und Guttapercha-Waren* (Weimar, 1856).

The first French rubber factory was founded by Rattier and Guibal at Saint-Denis near Paris, in 1928. (Claims made for an earlier Saint-Denis establishment have not been substantiated). Other early companies include Hutchinson et Cie, Langlee, founded by Hiram M. Hutchinson (American holder of Goodyear footwear rights in Europe) in 1849 ; the Compagnie Nationale of Paris, founded by J. H. Canfield, friend of Charles Goodyear, in 1850 ; and Lejeune, Chapel et Cie, of Belleville in 1851. An important waterproof clothing manufactory was founded by J. B. Torrilhon at

Clermont-Ferrand in 1852. Whilst the number of French factories increased from 1 to 160 between 1828 and 1875 the subsequent rate of growth was slower than that of the other Great Powers after 1870. The beginnings of the French industry are dealt with by J. M. D. Aigueperse in the *Revue Générale du Caoutchouc* for 1949, 26 *et seq.* Also *Mechanics' Magazine,* Vol. 27, 109-11 (20 May 1937).

The development of the industry in Eastern Europe and Russia was also assisted by American skilled artisans and managers, especially the Russian-American India Rubber Manufacturing Co., established at St. Petersburg in 1830. "We would remark" wrote a London house to Bradford in June 1861, "that the Americans have established a large manufactory at St. Petersburg, and we have to compete with them as regards price." See Arvid Neintz, *Hundert Jahre russische, und Osteuropäische Gummi-Industrie,* Riga, 1933. Also *IRW*, 15 October 1894 : "The India Rubber Factories of Russia ".

Memorandum of Association of "The North British Rubber Company, Limited", with Articles of Association annexed

1st, The name of the Company is " The North British Rubber Company, Limited."

2nd, The registered Office of the Company is to be established in Scotland.

3rd, The objects for which the Company are established are : " The manufacture of articles and goods of every description, either solely in Caoutchouc, or India Rubber, Gutta Percha, and other Gums in all their varieties, or in the manufacture of which the above mentioned or other Gums are used or employed to any extent ; and also the dressing and preparation of the said Gums for these purposes, and the manufacture or preparation of any or all of the various textile fabrics which may be combined with the above mentioned or other Gums, in the production of the said articles or goods, and generally the doing all such other things as are incidental or or conducive to the attainment of the above objects—the said manufacture or manufactures being carried on in such way and manner as the said Company may legally and competently do, and specially without in any way prejudicing the said generality under patent methods now in use, and which the Company are entitled to exercise, or which may hereafter be granted to them, or they may otherwise become entitled to use and exercise."

4th, The liability of the Shareholders is " limited ".

5th, The capital of the Company is £100,000 Sterling, divided into 1000 shares of £100 each.

We, the several persons whose names are subscribed, are desirous of being formed into a Company in pursuance of this Memorandum of Association, and we respectively agree to take the number of shares in the Company set opposite our respective names. In witness whereof, We, the said several persons, have set and subscribed our names to these presents, written by William Paterson, clerk to Messrs. Murdoch and Boyd, Solicitors before the Supreme Courts of Scotland, in manner following ; that is to say, we, Henry Lee Norris, Spencer Thomas Parmelee, William Judson, Benjamin Franklin Breeden, and John Ross Ford, for ourselves, by me the said John Ross Ford, for and on behalf of Christopher Meyer, and by me the said Henry Lee Norris, for and on behalf of James Bishop and James A. Williamson. All at Edinburgh, upon the twenty-six day of September in the year of our Lord one thousand eight hundred and fifty-six, before this witness, the said William Paterson.

[The names of subscribers under this Memorandum of Association and the number of shares taken by each subscriber are given on the following page.]

The list of machinery, fixtures and fittings purchased by the North British Company in the United States is too detailed (14 pages) to appear here. It provides an example of the movement of a complete rubber manufactory (with the exception of power supply) across the Atlantic Ocean.

The following documents may be consulted at the North British Rubber Company, Edinburgh.

13 October 1855. Statement of Machinery and Fixtures bought by Norris & Co., from the Ford Rubber Co., New Jersey.

24 October 1855. Statement of machinery etc., on board sloop " Fox ", shipped per New Jersey Railroad for the ship " Harmonia ", sailing to Glasgow.

30 October 1855. Shipping Note re Machinery and Fixtures shipped by James Bishop & Co., on board the ship " Harmonia " lying at the Port of New York and bound for Glasgow.

Names and Addresses of Subscribers*			Number of Shares taken by each Subscriber	
Henry Lee Norris, Redford, near Edinburgh, County of Edinburgh	...	...	Fifty-five shares...	55
Spencer T. Parmelee, Pembroke Lodge, near Edinburgh, County of Edinburgh	...	...	One hundred shares	100
William Judson, New York, United States	...	...	Three hundred and thirty-three shares	333
B. F. Breeden, New York, United States	...	...	Seventy-four shares	74
John R. Ford, New Brunswick, N. Jersey, United States	...	...	One hundred and sixty-four shares ...	164
For Christopher Meyer, of New Brunswick, N. Jersey, United States. John R. Ford	...	...	One hundred and sixty-four shares ...	164
For James Bishop, of New Brunswick, New Jersey, United States, Henry Lee Norris	...	...	Fifty-five shares...	55
For James A. Williamson, of Jersey City, New Jersey, United States, Henry Lee Norris	...	...	Fifty-five shares...	55
			Total Shares taken ...	1,000

Witness to the above Signatures,
Wm. Paterson, residing in Leith,
    Clerk to the said Messrs. Murdoch & Boyd.

* All of whom were American citizens closely connected with the industry in the United States.

Financial Relations of The North British Company with a New York Shipping & Commission Agent, 1855-7

THE NORTH BRITISH RUBBER COMPANY IN ACCOUNT (WITH INTEREST CHARGED AT 7% TO JANUARY 1ST 1857) WITH JAMES BISHOP & CO.

Dr.

Date		$	$	Due date	Mos.	Days	Interest due $
1855				**1855**			
Oct. 22	To Cash Paid H. L. Norris £100 ...	488·00	1192·45	Oct. 22	14	9	99·44
,, 22	,, S. P. Parmelee a/c Salary	600·00					
,, 22	,, Louise Dixon ,, ,,	7·00					
,, 22	,, Sophia Terry ,, ,,	10·00					
,, 22	,, Walter P. Dunn ,, ,,	5·00					
,, 22	,, Chas. Edwards, Counsel Fees	82·45					
,, 23	,, Passage Norris & Co. to Europe		400·00	,, 23	14	8	33·29
,, 26	,, 6¼ hands to Liverpool ...		195·00				
,, 26	,, Expense of baggage to Ship ...		2·00	,, 26	14	5	16·28
,, 29	,, to date of J. P. Morrison...		8·37				
,, 29	,, ,, ,, W. P. Dunn ...		13·42	,, 29	14	2	1·81
,, 31	,, Insurance on Machinery $15,000 @ 1¼% and 3 Policies		191·25	**1856** March 4	9	27	11·04
1855				**1855**			
Nov.24	,, Cash Pd. A. Terry a/c S. Terry Wages ...		8·00	Nov. 24	13	6	·62
,, 30	,, Postage and Freight this month ...		5·17	,, 30	13	0	·38
Dec. 4	,, Dft. remitted Norris & Co. £350 @ 8¼%		1687·78	Dec. 4	12	27	127·02
,, 7	,, Cash Pd. for Books of a/c.		18·75	,, 7	12	24	1·41
,, 31	,, ,, Postage to date		9·64	,, 31	12	0	·68
1856				**1856**			
Jan. 19	,, ,, Journal Commerce to Jan. 1/57		6·08	Jan. 19	11	12	·40
,, 30	,, 2 Bags Rubber as for Bill rend. 6 Mos....		26·24	Aug. 3	4	28	·75
,, 30	,, Dft. (H. L. Norris) on J. & M. Nov. 15/55 £150.9.0		728·33	**1855** Nov. 15	13	15	57·32
Apr. 30	,, Invoice pr. Africa due Sept. 20/56		1177·92	**1856** Sept. 20	3	10	22·91
			$5670·40				$373·35

The North British Rubber Company In Account (With Interest to January 1/57) With James Bishop & Co.

Dr.

Date	Particulars	$	Due Date	Mos.	Days	$
1856	Brought forward :	5670·40				373·35
May 14	To Cash Pd. passage Mary O'Donnell & G. Henry Wife & 2 children	120·00	1856 May 14	7	17	5·30
" 30	" Invoice for Edinburgh May 17/56	1356·66	1857 Jan. 4 1856	0	4	1·05
July 12	" " " Cash	23·41	July 12	5	19	·76
" 23	" " " Lebanon July 7/4 Mos.	198·42	Nov. 10	1	20	1·92
" 23	" Freight and Ctage on Goods for Baltic	1·78	July 23	5	8	·06
Aug. 2	" Invoice for Niagara, July 12/4 Mos.	311·19	Nov. 15	1	15	2·73
" 15	" " Glasgow " 28/4	168·36	Dec. 1	1	0	·98
Nov.15	" Freight and Crge on Roller fm Edinburgh	2·00	Nov. 15	1	15	0·02
" 30	" Invoice fm Tempest Cash	1501·65	" 30	1	0	87·51
Dec. 5	" " Glasgow Nov. 24/8 Mos.	489·20	July 27	6	27	19·68
" 31	" The following items fm B. Shipley & Cos. a/c.					
	" May 24/56 Dft £750 @ 10%	3666·67	May 24	7	7	154·72
	" July 7/56 " £500 " 10%	2444·44	July 7	5	24	82·70
	" Oct. 4 " £500 " 9⅞%	2441·67	Oct. 4	2	27	41·31
	" Dec. 22 " £1000 " 9%	4844·44	Dec. 22	0	9	8·48
	" Interest to Dec. 31/56 as fm their a/c £23. 4. 1					
	" Stamp duty on Bills 17. 6					
	" Postages 1. 2. 2					
	" Frght on Pkge to Newton & Son 5. 0					
	" Comm. on £2750 @ 1% 27.10. 0					
	" " 9¾% 52.18. 9					
	" Postage fm Dec. 31/55 to Feb. 1/57	258·22	Dec. 31	0	0	0·00
	" Balance of Interest a/c	62·26	Dec. 31	0	0	0·00
	" " to New a/c	413·33				
		585·44				
		$38059·54				$759·84

214

R

		$		$	1855	Mos.	Days	$
1855								
Oct. 23	By Cash fm John R. Ford	1250·00		3250·00	Oct. 23	14	8	270·47
,, 23	,, ,, C. Meyer	1250·00			1856			
,, 23	,, ,, B. F. Breeden	750·00						
1856								
Dec. 2	,, ,, Ford Breeden Meyer & Parmelee as fm statement rend. Dec. 56			9809·54	Dec. 2	0	29	55·31
,, 31	,, Our ¼ of N.B.R. Cos Stock			25000·00	,, 31	0	0	0·00
	,, Interest fm Dr (in red)							20·73
	,, Balance of Interest to Dr.							413·33
				38059·54				759·84
				$38059·54				$759·84
	By Balance							$585·44

North British MSS.

APPENDIX VI

Specimen labour contract for the American rubber workers brought to Scotland in 1855

Articles of Agreement, made, concluded, and agreed upon the 22nd day of October A.D. 1855, between Louise Dixon of the City of New Brunswick, County of Middlesex, State of New Jersey, U.S., on the one part, and the North British Rubber Co., Norris & Co., of the other part, as follows :—
The said Louise Dixon, for the consideration hereinafter mentioned, doth hereby covenant and agree, that she will sail by the next passage of the ship Harmony for Glasgow, Scotland in the Kingdom of Great Britain, and there render such lawful and reasonable service, or labor, as may be required by said Company, until they shall have made such preparations as are necessary for the manufacture of Rubber Boots & Shoes, and that she will, after they commence the manufacture of Boots and Shoes, labor for the said Company, for the term of one year, and make herself generally useful to the Company in making Boots and shoes learning, and instructing others in that art ; And the said North British Rubber Co., Norris & Co., doth covenant and agree that they will pay to said Louise Dixon, the sum of one dollar for each day from the time she arrives at Glasgow, Scotland, until such time as they are ready to commence the manufacture of Boots and Shoes, in Scotland, and after such commencement, the sum of one dollar for each day's services, or labor, rendered to said Company, and said Company further agree to pay the passage of said Louise Dixon on board ship Harmony to Glasgow, Scotland, and all other necessary traveling expenses, from New Brunswick to Glasgow and at expiration of above time and labor, if said Louise Dixon desires to return to America, the said Company do agree to pay her passage and necessary traveling expenses from Scotland to New Brunswick, New Jersey, U.S.

To the true performance of the several covenants and agreements aforesaid, the parties bind themselves individually, by these presents, in witness whereof we have hereto set out hands and seals, on the day and year above mentioned.

LOUISE DIXON.

Witness
A. Hannah.   Norris & Co.

APPENDIX VII

Some early Bradford accounts
and notes on the profitability of the pioneering Firms

STEPHEN MOULTON & CO. BALANCE SHEET 1ST SEPTEMBER 1851.

Dr.	£	s.	d.	Cr.	£	s.	d.
Trade a/c.	5167	18	0	Stephen Moulton, Stock a/c.	700	0	0
Cash a/c.	75	9	5	Rider Bros.	24	0	0
Salary a/c.	159	17	0	Holmes & Whittle	6	0	8
E. Rider	81	9	2	Routram & Co.	447	17	3
W. Frost	413	7	11	L. Berger & Son	11	9	10
Alford & Chapman, Bradford	6	12	0	Geo. Rolfe...	20	12	5
W. Coles, Bradford	1	4	5	Kirkman Brown	16523	18	1
G. & T. Fuller, Bath	25	16	9	W. Gregory	4	4	0
I. V. Deane, L'pool	26	4	1	Phipson & Co.	0	11	0
E. P. & S. A. Cooper, Bradford	1637	11	3	Chas. Price & Co.	9	8	6
R. & E. Vesey, Bath	58	6	3	Bowyer & Son	24	10	0
C. R. Thompson, London	450	8	6	Edmunds & Rourke	38	8	5
W. S. Cooper, London	98	9	6	Sam Taylor	33	9	3
T. & E. Taylor, Bradford	67	10	0	V. Everett ...	25	2	9
Braithwaite Bros., London	966	4	8	R. G. Reeves	22	4	6
Harding & Son, Manchester	190	10	9	R. Tarr ...	6	1	0
Fred. Huth & Co., London	355	6	1	Edw. Cooper	3	19	2
W. & W. H. Taylor, London	3	15	0	John Williams		16	6
Chas. Gray & Son, Bristol	2	5	0				
D. Gooch, London...	1	4	0				
C. Stanley & Co., London	30	8	2				
W. R. Withers, Bath	7	11	0				
John Stratton, Bradford	2	0	0				
J. S. Furgusson, London	9	9	0				
Wilson & Son, Bath	1	18	0				
Chas. Roach, Devizes	11	6	6				
c.f.	£9852	2	5	c.f.	£17902	13	4

	£	s.	d.
Continued—Bt. forward ...	9852	2	5
P. Llewellyn, Bristol ...	4	6	2
Weaving Machine... ...	70	8	0
S. E. Norris, London ...	24	8	6
G. Western Railway ...	145	6	6
L. Simpson, Melksham ...	3	11	8
Silver & Co., London ...	2	16	6
Edw. Davy, Critterton ...	2	9	0
D. Joshua, London... ...	3	9	0
J. Berry, Plymouth ...	50	6	8
S. L. Miers, London ...	4	16	6
Swayne & Adeney, London ...	9	12	3
F. James, Stroud ...	4	8	6
Sladen, Trowbridge ...	3	8	4
John Kingston, Trowbridge ...	1	17	6
Wages ...	1592	8	11
W. W. Glass & Co., Bath ...	5	19	8
Stephen Moulton ...	2389	0	8
Petty Sales ...	292	6	7
I. I. Evans, Monmouthshire ...	194	13	1
Bremel, London ...	52	15	3
R. Brotherhood, Chippenham ...	75	10	0
S. Devon Railway... ...	25	1	9
Consignment a/c. ...	2844	15	2
Gough & Bowen, Birm. ...	9	11	3
Greenhill Fry & Co., London ...	19	1	6
Gishford, Bradford... ...	20	18	0
Staverton Mill & Bridge a/c. ...	197	12	6
	£17902	13	4

	£	s.	d.
Bt. forward	17902	13	4
	£17902	13	4

Liabilities	£	s.	d.
To Rider Bros, New York ...	24	0	0
,, R. Outram & Co., London ...	335	6	0
,, Bergers & Sons, London ...	11	0	10
,, Geo. Rolfe ...	167	1	5
,, Kirkman Brown & Co. ...	15225	9	7
,, W. Gregory ...	4	4	0
,, Phipson & Co. ...		11	0
,, Price & Co. ...	9	8	6
,, Bowyer & Son ...	24	10	0
,, Edmunds & Rourke ...	8	3	5
,, R. G. Reeves ...	36	12	6
,, John Stratton ...	124	0	0
,, R. Tarr ...	6	1	0
,, G. J. & G. N. Haden ...	107	0	0
,, W. Coles ...	132	17	4
,, Norris & Co. ...	40	0	0
,, C. Devaux & Co. ...	12	0	0
,, Cook Sons & Co. ...	7	1	4
,, Edward Cooper ...	393	2	6
	£16668	9	5

Assets	£	s.	d.
By Stocks in Bradford Mills ...	6645	0	0
,, ,, ,, at 2 St. Dunstans Hill ...	1005	0	0
,, ,, ,, Exhibition ...	70	0	0
,, ,, ,, Braithwaite Bros. ...	576	0	0
,, ,, ,, with sundry other persons ...	231	0	0
,, Stock of Para and Java Rubber in London ...	2346	0	0
,, Money owing this 7th Oct. for goods sold from Bradford ...	2075	0	0
,, Money owing this 7th Oct. for goods sold from London...	540	0	0
	£13488	0	0

	£	s.	d.
Gutta Percha and India Rubber Patents cost ...	270	0	0
Expended on Staverton Mill... ...	261	0	0

STEPHEN MOULTON, PRIVATE ACCOUNT, 1851

Dr.	£	s.	d.	Cr.	£	s.	d.
To J. Long (Builder)	397	0	0	By Kingston Mills & House prime cost	7500	0	0
" "	39	0	0	" Expended in improvements in House paid for	1750	0	0
" " (Plasterer) about	200	0	0	" Small Mill, cost	325	0	0
" " (Painter & Glazier) about ...	100	0	0	" Improvements, not yet pd for, as p. Contra	872	0	0
" Sundry Petty Personal a/cs.	70	0	0	" Machinery and Improvements on Mills	4250	0	0
" Jas. Lester for Timber...	175	0	0				
" Richard Moulton for a loan... ...	300	0	0				
" Geo. H. Foster, loan on Mortgage...	6000	0	0				
" " " for interest on 2 loans	275	0	0				
" " " for Loan in small Mill	325	0	0				
	£7881	0	0		£14697	0	0

The following is an extract from a report prepared by Stephen Moulton in an attempt to forecast the annual costs and profits of the London India-Rubber Company—of which he was the Managing Director—formed in 1860 :

Plan No. 1

Assume that, though we can make much more, we sell for some time only 6 tons per week, and that the " No. 3." rubber on which we get least profit and which is in demand at 9¼d. per lb.

To make 6* Tons—120 cwts.

	£	s	d
60 cwt. Old Rubber @ 20/-	£60	0	0
7½ „ Caoutchouc, say @ 150/-	56	5	0
52½ „ Composition averaging 12/6d.	32	16	3
6 Tons Coals @ 13/od.	3	18	0
Cartage up and down	2	8	0
Incidental expenses of all kinds	4	12	9
Wages, say (including bookkeeper)	28	0	0
	£188	0	0
Add 1 weeks Standing Expenses	120	0	0
	£308	0	0

Standing Expenses

	£
Rent of Factory	500
Rent of Warehouse	300
Rates, Taxes and Insurances	200
Directors	500
Managing Director	800
Manufacturing Manager	500
Secretary, Clerks, Warehouseman & Porters	800
Percentages to Travellers & Agents	600
Stationery, Incidents & Bad debts	500
Solicitors, Law, and Patent Charges	300
Depreciation in Value of Plant & bldgs.	1,000
	£6,000

* There is considerable waste on manufacture of foreign matter to an amount at present unascertained, but which may be considered well covered by assuming that the Ton of Raw Material of 2240 lbs. is reduced to one of 2000 lbs. manufactured rubber, to sell at 9¼d. per lb. By the above calculation every pound of such a Ton costs nearly 6¼d. (out of which 3¼d. cost of material and manufacture) and at 9¼d. gives 3d. profit.

Say £120 per week, £20 per day, or on a weekly production of 6 tons : 2½d. per lb.

6 Tons " No. 3 " @ 9¼d. nett sell for	£463	10	0
Deduct Cost	308	0	0
	£155	10	0
On a year of 50 wks. that makes clear profit	£7,725	0	0
Deduct 12½ per cent on Sinking Fund	965	12	6
	£6,759	7	6

At the rate of dividend this will give

Directors take another £250 0 0			
and Manager £500 0 0			
	£750	0	0
Leaving available for dividend ..	£6,009	7	6

which gives nearly 12½%

Plan No. 2.

To make 6 Tons (120 cwt.) " No. 2 " Selling price 1/3d. nett.

65½ cwt. Old Rubber @ 20/- ..	£65	10	0
11 „ Caoutchouc @ 150/- ..	82	10	0
43½ „ Composition @ 12/- ..	26	2	0
6 Tons Coals @ 13/-	3	18	0
Cartage up and down	2	8	0
Incidentals, say	4	12	0
Wages, including bookkeeper, say ..	25	0	0
	£210	0	0
Add weeks Standing Expenses ..	120	0	0
	£330	0	0

By this calculation a pound costs a fraction over 6½d. of which 4d. material, power and labour, and gives 8½d. profit.

6 Tons " No. 2 " at 1/3d. nett sell for	£750	0	0
Deduct Cost	330	0	0
	£420	0	0

On a year of 50 weeks that makes clear profit £21,000.

Plan No. 3.

Assume that we can sell 6 Tons a week and not more in equal quantities of Nos. 2 & 3. The year's profit will be :

Half of £7,725 :	£3,862 10 0	
& of £21,000 :	£10,500 0 0	
		£14,362 10 0
Deduct 12½ per cent as Sinking Fund	1,795 6 3	
		£12,567 3 9
At the rate of dividend this will give Directors and Manager will take another £500		1,000 0 0
Leaving available for dividend ..		£11,567 3 9

Which gives nearly 24 per cent.

Plan No. 4.

If we assume that we sell but 6 Tons a week, one third No. 2, one third No. 3, one third floor cloth about same cost as No. 3, and not yielding a larger profit—one year's profit will be :

2/3rds of £7,725 :	£5,150	
1/3rd of £21,000 :	7,000	
		£12,150 0 0
Deduct 12½ per cent Sinking Fund ..		1,518 15 0
		£10,631 5 0
At the rate of dividend this will give, Directors and Manager each take another £500		1,000 0 0
		£9,631 5 0

Which gives nearly 20%

Many interesting points arise from a study of this document. For instance, the manner in which the manufacturer made his calculations on the basis of existing prices ; the emphasis placed on output ; the allowance for more reserve capacity ; the addition of standing expenses ; and the plan to produce either the whole of one or parts of two or more kinds of rubber according to the needs of the market.

Yet whilst the practice of adding a costing margin for indirect expenses (as these papers illustrate) was common to these early companies, neither the adding of a costing margin nor the intention to secure a certain profit on sales was independent of market activity.

Finally, it is worth mentioning that Moulton did not measure the progress of his business according to the return on capital but as a profit margin on sales ; as did the larger companies, for instance :

" The Directors in submitting the Balance Sheet of the Coy. for the past year, with the auditors report thereon have to express their disappointment at the result of the year's trade. The Net Profit of £12,285 upon Sales amounting to £180,000 is a return less than might have been reasonably expected . . ." (Extract from the minute of meeting of Directors, the North British Rubber Company, 29 January 1867).

And again : " The Manager submitted the question of advance in prices of manufactured goods, stating that we were, owing to the present enhanced cost of materials entering into our manufactures, working at a reduced rate of profit. After full discussion it was decided that the Company should issue new price lists for all goods, based on present cost of materials and labour, treating the prices therein to such discounts as should leave a profit on sales not less than 18% ." (Extract from the minute of meeting of Directors, the North British Rubber Company, 4 July 1872).

It should be noted however that when Moulton was estimating the future profitability of the London India Rubber Company he was concerned with the return on capital.

It is an interesting fact that the North British Company, on occasions, could prosper while other rubber Companies were languishing. Announcing the excellent results for the trading year 1865 the Directors pressed upon the shareholders : " . . . the firm belief that their future prospects depend largely upon the results of the Company's business not being made public. Within the past few weeks one of the Rubber Companies in London has determined to wind up, another Company on the Continent is in a weak state, and a third company who promised a most troublesome competition, has lately had trouble among its disappointed and dissatisfied shareholders. The latter company, might, however, take heart and prosecute with new energy their undertaking if they learn of our prosperity." Extract from the minutes of the meeting of shareholders. 29 January 1866. Speculative disaster (a constant threat to those purchasing large crude rubber stocks) overtook the Company in the following year and in large part accounts for the poor trading results. (North British MSS.)

The only available figures for the Manchester Company, (Chas. Macintosh & Co.) are as follows :

	Net Profits		Sales
1831	£17,690	1846	£ 60,000
1832	£19,964	1852	£180,000
1835	£40,828	1860	£300,000
1836	£70,708		
1839	£94,619		

	Net Profits	Sales
1847	£46,154	
1853	£40,053	
1854	£23,949	
1856	£42,681	
1857	£37,968	
1860	*	

According to a note written by Cecil Birley (grandchild of T. H. Birley, founder-member of Chas. Macintosh & Co.) dated 8 August 1915, the pioneering firm in the U.K. had a very thin time in the first twelve years of its life : " . . . I know that the result of the first 12 years (i.e. from the early 'twenties to the early 'thirties) was *nothing*. The profits for some years were offset by losses in other years . . ." (Macintosh MSS.)

* On 2 June 1860 C. Daft (who for eight years had been employed as the consulting engineer at the Macintosh Company), wrote to Moulton : " . . . I have it as a fact that Mac. & Co. make over £50,000 profit in one year . . . "

S. MOULTON & CO. 1854-60

In his letter to Jennings (29 July 1861) Moulton stated that for the period 1849-60 "The whole business had made £20 p.c."

	Sales	Net Profits	Capital	Profits expressed as % of*	
				Capital	Sales
1854	£19,807.19. 5	£6,369.19. 3	£12,041.17. 9	53	32
	(1 May 1854 to 30 Dec. 1854)				
1855	£29,859. 5.10	£8,383. 9.10	£20,173. 4.11	42	28
1856	£18,922. 4. 0	£4,678. 6. 3	£23,535.12. 9	20	25
1857	£17,739.18. 9	£3,353.18. 9	£22,678. 5. 9	15	19
1858	£16,407.16. 5	£4,309. 2. 5	£20,891.15. 3	21	26
1859	£23,969. 1. 1	£4,839.18.11	£23,404. 9.10	21	20
1860	£29,525.15. 7	£3,869.15. 8	£22,490.17. 4	17	13

NORTH BRITISH RUBBER CO. LTD. 1857-71

	Sales	Net Profits	Dividends Declared	Capital Stock*	Profits Expressed as % of	
					Capital	Sales
1857	NA	£28,049.15. 9‡	10%	£50,000	56	
1858	NA	£48,977. 3. 7	25%	£68,000	72	
1859	NA	£64,439. 8.11	20%	£92,000	70	
1860	NA	£39,624. 9. 5	30%	£100,000	40	
1861	NA	£40,733.14. 0	35%	£100,000	41	
1862	NA	£26,496.13. 9	40%	£100,000	26	
1863	NA	£28,701.19. 7	25%	£100,000	29	
1864	NA	£27,647. 8. 9	10%	£120,000	23	
1865	NA	£37,790. 6.10	15%	£130,000	29	
1866	£180,000	£12,592.18. 5	28%	£130,000	10	7
1867	NA	£32,782.16. 5	9%	£143,000	23	
1868	NA	£40,000. 0. 0	25%	£143,000	28	
1869	£217,100	£34,478. 0. 0	25%	£143,000	24	16
1870	£219,300	£42,609. 0. 0	25%	£143,000	30	19
1871	£223,000	£43,237.12. 0	28%	£143,000	30	19

*Excluding bank overdrafts and trade credits.

APPENDIX VIII

On Original Sources

The chief sources on which this study is based are :

1. *The Moulton Papers.* These consist of :

   A. 30 cases chiefly of incoming letters and accounts numbering many thousands dating from the founding of the Company in 1848 until 1900. Some of these papers have been damaged by rot and damp but the majority are intact.

   B. *Special collections of letters.*

      i. The Rider/Moulton correspondence (approx. 200 letters) dating from 23 July 1847 until 16 September 1852 from New York to Bradford, together with copies of some of Moulton's replies.

      ii. The Goodyear/Moulton correspondence (approx. 100 letters) dating from 22 January 1850 to 29 December 1858 from the inventor Charles Goodyear in Britain and the United States.

   C. *Account books.*

      There are rough account books, day books, estimate and costing books, stock accounts and ledgers, etc. to cover most of the period from 1848-1900. The following records are complete and undamaged :

i.	Sales Books (18 vols.)	1857-1900
ii.	Ledger Accounts	1854-1860
iii.	Cash Books (2 vols.)	1850-1885
iv.	Wages Books (14 vols.)	1848-1900

      incomplete for 1858, 1887-90, 1894-7.

2. *The Moulton Papers.* These are the private records of A. E. Moulton, Esq., The Hall, Bradford-on-Avon. It is impossible to understand the early negotiations between the American and the British branches of the industry without their use. Apart from the notes made by Stephen Moulton during his visits to Britain there is an exceedingly valuable letter-book into which the manufacturer copied all his most important communications to British and American houses.

3. *The North British Papers.*

   All the important correspondence, documents, agreements, etc., dealing with the establishment of this Company in Edinburgh have been preserved, and it is possible to trace the American origins of this firm and study its growth in detail during its first 25 years.

   These papers are adequately supplemented by a record of the minutes of the Company since 1857.

4. *The Birley Papers.*

These are scattered and imperfect compared with the other two collections. Nevertheless anyone who has studied the Moulton and North British Papers finds many items of information in the assortment of papers and account books in the possession of the Birley family.

There is firstly a collection of various family letters, etc., dealing with the early Macintosh Company, some of which have been used in this book. In addition there are various other letters written between the 'fifties and the 'eighties dealing with company matters, such as the letters of H. C. Birley to Macintosh & Co., from New York and parts of New England in the winter of 1882.

In addition to jotting books which carry copy letters and cost estimates for new processes in the rubber plant there are the following volumes dealing with the Birley-Macintosh-Hancock combination :

 i. Private Letters Copies book, Birley & Co., Chorlton, Manchester, from 24 August 1841 to 17 April 1846.

 ii. Chas. Macintosh & Co's Ledger, 1827-58.

 iii. Birley & Co's Ledgers : 1810-1820
           1821-1842
           1843-1877

 iv. The private ledger of Henry Birley (partner of Chas. Macintosh & Co.) 1842-77.

INDEX

Electric Telegraph Co., 156n
Electrical applications, 72, 144, 154
Elliot, 209
Ellsworth, Henry L., 185
Elston, 121n
Emory, 112
Empire trade, 106
Employment, in rubber industry, 71,
    74, 112-32 ; statistics 1850-1900,
    116-7
Empreza Industrial du Gran Para, 66
Engineer, consulting, 226n
Englefield, James, 60n, 110n ; J. &
    Co., 161n
' Entrefine ', grade, 51n
Esch, W., 8n
Ether, 2
Europe, branch factories in, 106
Evans, 165n ; I. I., 219
Everett, V., 218
Exchange, medium of, 158-72 ; see
    also Bank Notes, Bills, Cheques,
    Overdrafts and Promissory Notes
Exchequer, Chancellor of, 19n
Exelby, H. R., 20n
Exhibition of 1851, 13 ; Brussels,
    90n
Expenses, 222
Export, manufactured rubber from
    U.K., 207, 205 ; raw rubber from
    U.K., 46-9, 203, 204 ; trade,
    106-7
Eyre, George Edward, 196

Fabrique de Produits Chimiques, 61n
Factories, built in Britain by
    Americans, 180 ; number of, 71 ;
    working conditions in, 129
Fanshawe, 141
Faraday, Michael, 2n
Fearns, J., 163n
Ficus elastica, 38, 42
Fillers, 60, 188-9 ; misuse of, 78
Finance, easier in England, 18
' Fine ' grade of rubber, 51n
Fisher, H. L., 41n

Flax, 60
Fletcher, Charles, 160n
Flint, Charles R., 73n
Flour mill, 21n
Fonrobert, François, 209
Fonrobert & Reimann, 149n
Fontainmoreau, de, 147
Footwear, 10, 72, 87, 144, 182 ;
    contract for manufacture of, 217 ;
    costs, 83, 85-6 ; early, 6 ; French
    manufacture of, 99 ; growing
    need for, 182 ; imports from U.S.,
    106, 133, 134n, 140n ; ingredients,
    86n ; lower grade, 60 ; patents,
    153-4 ; U.S. dealers in, 34
Ford, John Ross, 211, 212, 215
Ford & Co., 61n
Ford Rubber Co., 211
Fordred & Atkin, 100n
Forth, Firth of, 44
Foster, George Holgate, 29, 30n, 31n,
    33n, 181, 221 ; G. H. & Co., 30n ;
    Henry, 164n, 166, 168
Foster & Williams, 102n
Fox, H. G., 146n
Foxwell, 113n
France, Goodyear's rights in, 142 ;
    Government, 91n ; growth of
    factories in, 210 ; imports, 49 ;
    market in, 107 ; rubber factory,
    209
Fresneau, François, 2
Frost, Mr., 16n, 25, 28 ; W., 218
Fuller, G. & T., 218 ; W. C., 69n
Fuller's earth, 189
Funeral club, 131n
Furgusson, J. S., 218
Futures market, 53

Gainford, Co. Durham, 173n
Garments, waterproof, British
    methods used in U.S., 76 ; cost,
    83 ; female labour, 119n ; French
    factory for, 209 ; Glasgow trade
    in, 128n ; growing demand for,

Netherlands Trading Co., 50
New Brunswick, 212, 217
New England Car Spring Co., 149n
New Jersey, 211
New Saron, 166
New York, citizens of, 212 ; commission agent, 171-2, 175 ; Goodyear of, 9, 185, 186 ; Moulton's sojourn in, 11 ; Rider Brothers of, 197, 220 ; rubber business in, 63 ; rubber factory in, 15
New York-Hamburger Gummiwaaren Co., 209
New York Packing & Belting Co., 171n
Newark, Viscount, 21n
Newark Co., 141n
Newcastle-on-Tyne, 88n; 170
Newmann, G. L. & Co., 49n
Newport, 79n
Newton, Alfred Vincent, 141n, 143n, 154
Newton & Son, 214
Nitric acid, 8
Norris, Henry Lee, 90n, 143n, 211, 212, 213 ; Mr., 50 ; S. E., 219
Norris & Co., 211, 213, 216, 220
North British Rubber Co., 44, 63n, 73n, 77n, 92, 181, 182 ; agents of, 102 ; benevolent fund, 131n ; calender man, 112n ; capital of, 210, 212 ; cost system, 85 ; French prices undercut by, 98-9; founded at Edinburgh, 143, 154, 209-15 ; machinery for, 211 ; memorandum of association of, 210-11 ; payroll, 71n ; prices, 96n, 98-9 ; production, 80n, 82 ; profits, 105n, 225 ; raw material prices, 199 ; records of, 228 ; relations with U.S., 170, 171 ; retail shop in London, 89n ; sales in 1860, 93 ; subscribers, 211-2 ; wage rates, 126n ; workers, 130n, 216
Norwich, printers in, 166n
Nüremberg, factory, 209

Octogenarians, 121n
O'Donnell, Mary, 214
Oenslager, 75n
Oils, deleterious effect of, 78-9 ; linseed, 193
Organic substances, 75
Outram, R. & Co., 60n, 220
Ovens, for vulcanising, 186
Overdraft, 32, 160, 171
Overheads, 222 ; see Standing expenses
Overtime, 119-21 ; beer allowance for, 128 ; desired by employees, 126
Oxford, Pembroke College, 175n

Packing, production of, 83
Paget, 109n
Palairet, Septimus, 18n, 19, 29, 30, 181
Para, Brazil, 36
Para rubber, 45, 51, 55n
Paris, St. Denis, 209 ; samples sent to, 107
Parkes, Alexander, 12, 13n, 62n, 75, 76, 136, 144
Parmelee, Spencer Thomas, 90n, 171n, 211, 212, 213, 215
Patent agent, 147-8, 153n
Patent agent, Institute of, 148
Patent Law Amendment Act, 146
Patents, bought, not contested, 156 ; coal tar oil as solvent, 4 ; cold vulcanisation, 12-3 ; Commissioner of 185 ; cost of obtaining, 150-1 ; disadvantages of, 153 ; effect on prices, 156-7 ; elastic thread, 4 ; examination introduced, 155 ; Fanshawe's, 141 ; frivolous and fraudulent, 155 ; Goodyear's, 8, 11n, 143n, 185-8 ; Hancock's, 4, 5, 188-94 ; Hayward's, 8-9 ; licences, 153n ; litigation, 135ff ; Moulton's, 148, 193-5, 194-6 ; numbers of, 144n,

Date Due

MAY 8 1959			
MAY 2 9 1959			
DEPARTMENT			
	PRINTED IN U. S. A.		